Ultimate Weekends Australia

Emma Shaw

Hardie Grant

EXPLORE

Contents

Come & Explore Australia   IV
Map of Australia   VI
Travelling Australia in a Vintage Caravan   VIII
Tips for Sustainable Travel   X
Travelling Aus App Guide   XII
The Ultimate Aussie Wildlife Guide   XIV

New South Wales & ACT	**1**
Victoria	**35**
South Australia	**71**
Western Australia	**109**
Northern Territory	**143**
Queensland	**175**
Tasmania	**219**
Index	**240**
Acknowledgements	**254**
About the Author	**255**

COME & EXPLORE AUSTRALIA

Welcome to our travels. I'm Emma, and along with my husband Thom you might have seen us online @exploreshaw. We're a couple from Melbourne who fell in love with travelling Australia, discovering incredible destinations, remote beaches, hidden waterholes and magical landscapes all over the country. Over the years, we've travelled around Australia in lots of different ways – from caravanning and camping, to flying to a destination for a quick luxe weekend getaway, relocating campervans on one-way road trips and travelling for a year in our vintage caravan. There are an endless number of ways to explore this great country.

Our love of exploring Australia started with weekend trips. Whenever we had a free weekend we would hit the road and head somewhere new, to explore more of our own great backyard. Our long weekends were always full, especially during the winter months, when we would fly north to experience a new place, in search of sunshine and warmer weather.

It was on our first visit to Uluṟu and Australia's Red Centre that we started seriously talking about the 'Big Lap'. There's just something inspiring and life-changing about the desert for us. It's where we can see things more clearly, have our best ideas and often make big life-changing decisions. We had been in Alice Springs for only a few hours when I called my mum and said, 'So, we've decided, we're going to travel all around Australia for a year'.

Not everything went to plan on our Big Lap of Australia. Mainly because a certain global pandemic sent us home only three months into our trip for a short hiatus, and continued to wreak havoc over the tourism industry for the months that followed. But we persisted when we could, gratefully picking up our trip and continuing on after the first national lockdown came to an end, on an adventure that saw us criss-crossing across this great land, in all different directions, often backtracking and re-routing, to explore as many corners of Australia as we could.

This book was written to help you find a destination for your next weekend getaway. Whether you have time for just a daytrip, a long weekend or an extended period of time to plan for, we've put together some of the best places to visit around Australia to give you some great ideas. These are some of our favourite spots, hidden secrets and can't-miss experiences that you can use to plan your next getaway, however long you might have to spend.

Weekend getaways and short trips have been found to be extremely beneficial for your mental health and wellbeing. In many cases they often do a lot more for you than going on an extended trip. There are many different reasons behind this: they're easier to plan, less of a financial commitment and often people are more able to disconnect on a short getaway, knowing they'll only be away for a few days. Short trips also boost creativity, bring relationships closer together, help you worry less and maximise the time you have to get out and do as much as you can.

Australia is made for weekend trips and short getaways. You're only a few hours away from anywhere in the country by plane and for those who like to hit the road, there are endless highlights and places to visit along the way. Embark on them one at a time, or string a few of them together to create a longer itinerary. No matter what you're looking for, Australia literally has endless ultimate weekends away. From tropical islands to desert plains, epic snowfields and more than 10,000 beaches. The only question is, where are you going to explore next?

Emma Shaw

@exploreshaw | exploreshaw.com

Acknowledgement of Country

We acknowledge the Traditional Owners of Country throughout Australia, and recognise their continuing connection to land, waters and culture. We pay our respects to Elders past and present, and are thankful for the opportunity to travel through so many Aboriginal lands during our travels. As you embark on your travels across Australia we encourage you to always be mindful and respectful of the land and it's traditional custodians, and ensure you respect places of spiritual significance you visit along the way.

Opposite Nitmiluk (Katherine) Gorge, NT
Previous Locks Well Beach, Eyre Peninsula, SA

Map of Australia

New South Wales & ACT pp.XIV–33
Sydney
Blue Mountains
Byron Bay
North Coast
Lord Howe Island
Broken Hill & Outback NSW
South Coast
Canberra & ACT

Victoria pp.34–69
Melbourne
Yarra Valley & Dandenong Ranges
Great Ocean Road
Gariwerd (Grampians)
Murray River
Mt Hotham & The Snowfields
*Unique weekend: Alpine Nature
    Experience*
Mornington Peninsula
Phillip Island
Gippsland

South Australia pp.70–107
Adelaide
Barossa Valley
Fleurieu Peninsula & McLaren Vale
Kangaroo Island
Eyre Peninsula
Unique weekend: Travelling on The Ghan
Flinders Ranges
Yorke Peninsula
Coober Pedy
Limestone Coast
Riverland
Oodnadatta Track

Western Australia pp.108–141
Perth
Rottnest Island
Exmouth & Ningaloo Reef
Unique weekend: Sal Salis Ningaloo Reef
Esperance
Coral Coast
Margaret River region
South-west
Broome
Kalgoorlie & the Golden Outback

Northern Territory pp.142–173
Darwin
Uluru
Alice Springs
Red Centre Way
Katherine
*Unique weekend: Top End
    Safari Camp*
Kakadu
Tiwi Islands
East Arnhem Land

Queensland pp.174–217
Brisbane
Minjerribah (North Stradbroke
    Island)
The Gold Coast
K'gari (Fraser Island)
Yunbenun (Magnetic Island)
Bundaberg region
Tropical North Queensland
The Great Barrier Reef
The Whitsundays
*Unique weekend: Bareboating
    in the Whitsundays*
Hamilton Island
Torres Strait Islands
Outback Queensland

Tasmania pp.218–239
Hobart
Bruny Island
East Coast
Launceston
Unique weekend: Captain's Rest
Western Tasmania

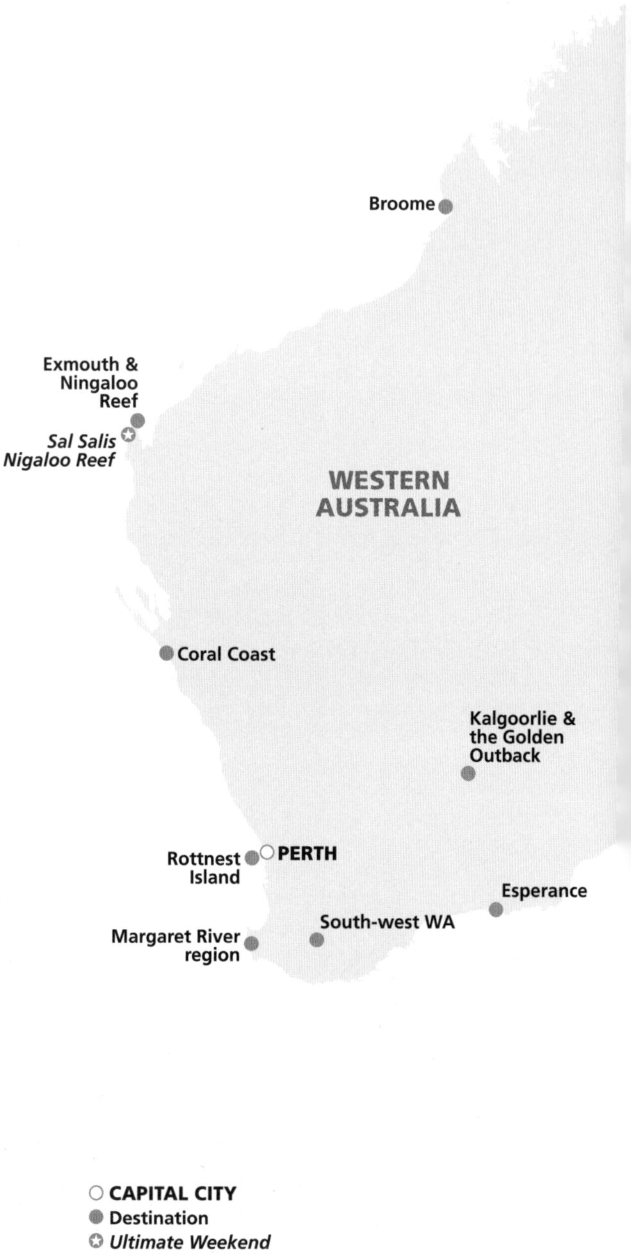

Broome

Exmouth &
Ningaloo
Reef

*Sal Salis
Nigaloo Reef*

**WESTERN
AUSTRALIA**

Coral Coast

Kalgoorlie &
the Golden
Outback

Rottnest
Island **PERTH**

Esperance

Margaret River
region

South-west WA

○ **CAPITAL CITY**
● **Destination**
✪ *Ultimate Weekend*

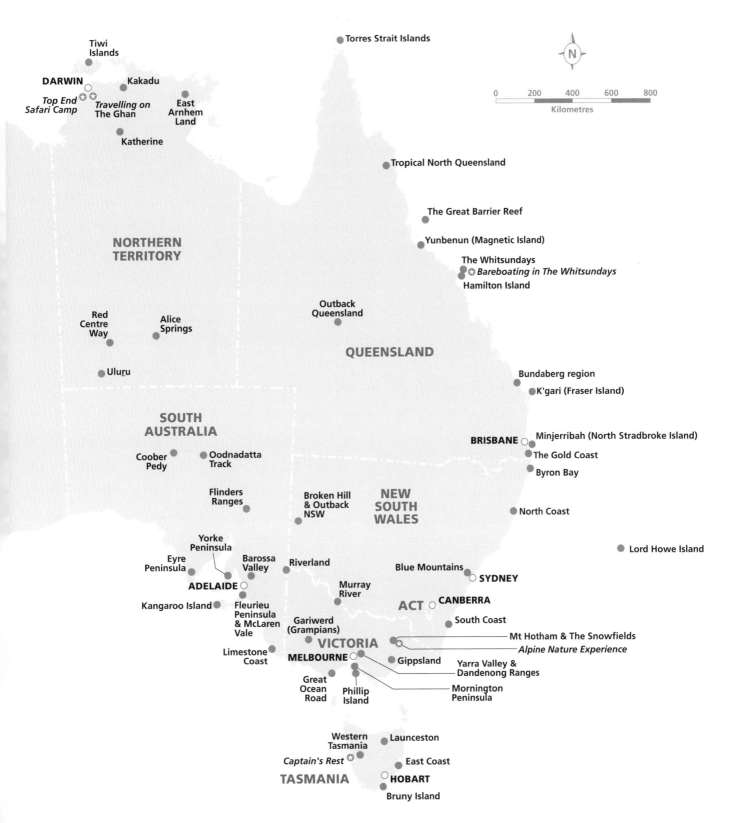

Tiwi Islands

Torres Strait Islands

DARWIN

Top End Safari Camp

Kakadu

Travelling on The Ghan

East Arnhem Land

Katherine

NORTHERN TERRITORY

Tropical North Queensland

The Great Barrier Reef

Yunbenun (Magnetic Island)

The Whitsundays

Bareboating in The Whitsundays

Hamilton Island

Red Centre Way

Alice Springs

Outback Queensland

QUEENSLAND

Uluru

SOUTH AUSTRALIA

Coober Pedy

Oodnadatta Track

Bundaberg region

K'gari (Fraser Island)

BRISBANE

Minjerribah (North Stradbroke Island)

The Gold Coast

Byron Bay

Flinders Ranges

Broken Hill & Outback NSW

NEW SOUTH WALES

North Coast

Yorke Peninsula

Lord Howe Island

Eyre Peninsula

Barossa Valley

Riverland

Blue Mountains

SYDNEY

ADELAIDE

Murray River

ACT **CANBERRA**

Kangaroo Island

Fleurieu Peninsula & McLaren Vale

South Coast

Gariwerd (Grampians)

Mt Hotham & The Snowfields

Alpine Nature Experience

Limestone Coast

VICTORIA

MELBOURNE

Gippsland

Yarra Valley & Dandenong Ranges

Great Ocean Road

Phillip Island

Mornington Peninsula

Western Tasmania

Launceston

Captain's Rest

East Coast

TASMANIA

HOBART

Bruny Island

TRAVELLING AUSTRALIA IN A VINTAGE CARAVAN

We couldn't even really tell you where the idea came from. We always had a vision of our van being a very unique one. But somehow we ended up with a very extreme renovation, much bigger and harder than we originally thought, although it was definitely worth it in the end. We found ourselves working through the bitterly cold Melbourne winter nights of 2019, to transform a vintage Viscount caravan into our dream beach house on wheels, with the intention of living in it for at least a year as we lapped Australia. We stripped it back to almost a complete skeleton with no walls or roof before we started putting it back together. It even had a new chassis built underneath, making it bigger and tougher than ever, ready to tackle all those unsealed remote outback roads we couldn't wait to explore.

We chose our van because of all the windows. The light that poured into it made it feel big and airy, not like we were living in a caravan at all. And of course, because it was cute. I loved the curved roof, the wrap-around windows, and the shape of the van. We changed the whole inside layout, installed a toilet and a shower, included lots of modern amenities like solar power, a slide-out outdoor kitchen, an air-conditioner that doubles as a heater, an internet booster, and painted a bright pink stripe along the outside. We're impossible to miss on the road.

Although a pesky little pandemic tried to make it quite difficult for us, we did actually get to spend almost a year living in our little van and we absolutely loved it. It quickly felt like home to us. She's been to so many places – from the remote dirt roads and long intense drives, to camping in some of the most beautiful places, on beaches, riverbanks, mountain ranges and gorges.

If you're planning a long trip to explore Australia and thinking about your set-up for the journey, some of the things that made our trip a lot more comfortable and stress-free were:

A Cel-Fi Go: This handy device takes one bar of phone or internet service and boosts it right up to full bars. It meant we had phone/internet service whenever we needed it, and we could always find somewhere that had at least a little bit to boost up to full service.

A toilet: An absolute game-changer, lots of people attempt a trip around Australia without a toilet but it makes life so much easier. We could literally pull up wherever we wanted and didn't have to worry about searching for a bathroom or a place to go at the end of the day. We were grateful more times than we could count that we added it to our van.

Solar power: Invest in a good solar set up that works for 12V and 240V power and you'll never have to worry about power again. Our solar system could run everything we needed in our van, including the kettle and toaster, chargers for all our cameras and devices, and even a hairdryer in an emergency! We could go for weeks at a time without needing to plug in to power and we rarely dipped below 80 per cent.

Dust reduction system: If you're planning on taking your van on a lot of unsealed roads like we did, the Dust Reduction System (DRS) from Dometic will change your life. It literally pressurises your van to stop any dust getting in, keeping the surfaces in your van dust free. It was incredible, especially working with our dodgy windows that often popped open mid-drive. Way less cleaning than we expected and our bed never got dust in it. Definitely more of a consideration for those of you with older or renovated vans, as many of the newer vans are beginning to include the DRS.

Although it might have seemed like a crazy idea in the beginning, we are so glad that we chose a vintage caravan for our travels. We were able to give an old van a new life, really design and create it to be everything we wanted for our journey, and created the perfect light beach house on wheels that we had been dreaming of.

To see more of our van renovation, including all our tips and tricks for rebuilding a vintage caravan and our first failed attempt at vanlife where we bought an absolute dud van, check out our blog at exploreshaw.com/vanlife.

TIPS FOR SUSTAINABLE TRAVEL

With more people travelling around Australia than ever before, it's never been more important to consider the footprint you're leaving behind when you travel. There are lots of different ways that you can make just a little bit of effort that can have a super big impact if we all work together.

Sustainable travel helps to minimise the negative impacts of tourism, helping you to travel a little more eco-friendly, without harming the environment or the communities that you're visiting. Here are some easy ways that you can make a positive impact whenever you travel.

Pack reusable items and reduce your one-use plastic consumption: A super-easy way to make an impact is to take your own shopping bags, water bottles, keep cups, face masks, straws and a little cutlery set wherever you go, so you don't need to use one-time-use options while you're out. Try to avoid using plastic water bottles, take-away coffee cups, or plastic bags from the supermarket.

Carbon offsetting: When you book a flight these days there is an option to offset your carbon footprint. It's normally only a few dollars, generally less than a cup of coffee at the airport, especially for domestic flights. Carbon offsetting helps to combat global climate change, funding solutions to reducing carbon emissions with every flight. Booking a direct flight is also more fuel efficient than taking connecting flights, and produces less carbon emissions per passenger.

Choose eco-certified tours and experiences: Many touring companies will advertise if they are eco-certified and what they are doing to help the environment that they do tours in. This can include anything from keeping safe, respectful distances from wildlife, to going above and beyond with recycling, waste management, avoiding excess plastic use on tours and minimising fuel consumption and emissions.

Choose eco-friendly accommodation: Similarly, where you can, try and choose eco-friendly and sustainable accommodation for your stay, with hotels and resorts that are focused on energy- and water-saving techniques to reduce their environmental impact. Opt not to have your sheets washed every day, keep your towels until they need to be changed, and bring your own toiletries to avoid waste. And of course, camping is the most eco-friendly way to have a weekend getaway, provided you leave your camping spot exactly as you found it, you're virtually leaving no footprint at all.

Take public transport where you can: An extra easy one if you're getting around a city. Many cities in Australia have free transport in their CBD, which often makes it easier to get around than driving, or you can jump on e-scooters or bikes to freely zip around a city in a fun way.

Support local communities: Shopping for local produce at farmers markets, buying from independent shops and choosing tours and cultural experiences run by locals, helps to keep money in the community you're visiting – where it's truly beneficial and gives back in a meaningful way.

Choose reef-safe sunscreen: An important one if you're planning on doing a lot of swimming, particularly in reef areas or where there is marine wildlife. Always choose a sunscreen that is considered reef-safe to protect the ocean and its creatures from harmful toxins and chemicals.

Respect the environment around you: If you're hiking or visiting cultural sites, stay on the marked pathways to avoid damage to fragile environments. Respect the customs and cultures of the communities you're visiting, and don't take photos without permission or where it's clearly marked not to. And make sure you don't touch wildlife or feed it (*see* p. XIV for more about wildlife).

Use solar energy: If you're caravanning or camping make sure you have a good solar system, giving yourself the ability to use solar energy to power your set-up so you're not needing to rely on being plugged into power all the time. If you're travelling in a caravan you can easily create a permanent set-up with a solar panel on your roof, or if you are camping you can pick up a portable solar blanket that you can take anywhere you go and that's super easy to pull out and set up whenever you need a little boost.

Clean up after yourself: No matter where you go in the world, always make sure that you never leave anything behind. Whether you're camping, hiking, road-tripping or stopping for a picnic, always double check to make sure that you've taken all your rubbish with you, and never leave toilet paper behind a tree when you're camping – it's just disgusting.

Opposite Pinnacles Beach, Ben Boyd National Park, NSW

TRAVELLING AUS APP GUIDE

There are plenty of helpful apps to have on your phone, with quick, up-to-date, information wherever you are. Plus, most of them are free!

MAPS

WikiCamps Australia ($7.99) is the best value app you'll ever pay for. WikiCamps shows you where you can find caravan parks, free camps, rest stops, water, toilets, dump points, points of interest, phone reception and more. Most of the content is also available offline, making it super easy to find a campsite or somewhere to stop for the night, no matter where you are or how far away from internet reception you find yourself.

Fuel Map (free) is a map of all your closest petrol stations, as well as current up-to-date petrol prices so you never get ripped off when there's a cheaper option down the road. The app also includes a handy fuel log, so you can keep track of your fuel consumption and costs as you travel.

Google Maps (free) is obviously a great app for directions and getting from one point to the next, but if you put Google Maps on Earth view it's also a great way to explore the coastline and land wherever you're going.

Toilet Finder (free) is one that I'm sure we've all needed once or twice when we're on the road! Toilet Finder will tell you where the nearest public toilets are and even give you directions to get there. See all your options on a map of the area so you can make the easiest stop.

WiFi Finder + Map (free) can quickly and easily find all the wi-fi hotspots around you, including free, paid and public wi-fi spots. It works online and offline and is available in more than 144 countries, which means you'll never be crazily searching for wi-fi on your travels again.

BOOKINGS

Hopper (free) is a great app for finding the cheapest flights all around Australia and the world, which not only shows you the best deals and discounts at the time, but also predicts when exactly you're likely to get the best rates for flights and hotels, within a 12-month period. You never need to worry about missing out on the best deals for your travels again.

HotelsCombined (free) compares the price of hotels for your destination from every booking website on the internet to make sure you're always getting the best price and don't miss any deals. Another great app is **HotelsTonight** which shows you the best last-minute deals on hotels for tonight.

HEALTH & FIRST AID

Emergency Plus (free) is the emergency app that gives you your exact address and coordinates so you can tell 000 in an emergency, plus you can call 000, the SES and the police straight from the app.

Sunsmart (free) is a great app to make sure you're protected from the sun at all times. Each day Sunsmart will let you know the hours of the day that you need sun protection as well as the UV rating, and it can also send you notifications specific to your location so you don't forget.

First Aid (free) is an easy to use app with step-by-step instructions to help you in any situation where you might need some first aid. Created by the Australian Red Cross, the app will tell you what to do to treat breaks, bites, stings, burns, allergies and more, as well as info about resuscitation and CPR for any emergency. **Australian Bites and Stings** is another handy app to have for these kinds of situations.

HELPFUL

AusPost (free) is perfect for people who are travelling for longer, as AusPost allows you to create your own unique addresses to have parcels delivered to any post office around the country, giving you the freedom for online shopping and care packages to be delivered no matter where you are in Australia.

The Happiest Hour (free) is the perfect app to find all the drink, food and cocktail specials near you, no matter where you are in Australia. A great way to find the local secrets, daily specials and bars offering happy hour around the country.

TripIt (free) keeps everything for your trip in one place, where you can forward your confirmation emails for flights, hotels, car rentals and activities. TripIt puts together a perfect itinerary of your whole trip. It's a great way to stay organised, easily access booking and reservation numbers and see what you've planned, especially if you're booking in advance.

BOM (free) has the most accurate weather forecasts you can find. The BOM app updates regularly, has a rain radar so you can see if you're going to find yourself in a shower, and gives you information about sunrises, sunsets and the moon phases so you can time your photoshoots perfectly.

SkyView ($2.99) means that you can spend your evenings star gazing and learning more about the night sky, with SkyView sharing the constellations, planets and stars you can see wherever you point your phone.

Left The Great Australian Bight, SA
Right The famous Nullarbor Road House, SA

THE ULTIMATE AUSSIE WILDLIFE GUIDE

There's nothing more thrilling than spotting your favourite animal in the wild. Just going about their daily life, completely uncaring that you are watching them starstruck. Australia is home to so many incredible wildlife experiences. There are opportunities to spot your favourite native animals in the wild in every state of Australia, with crocodiles roaming the NT, koalas eating through the gum trees of Victoria and NSW, turtles swimming along the reefs of Queensland and Western Australia, wombats wandering around Tassie, and emus running free across the land in SA. You can even plan your next weekend getaway to experience some of Australia's incredible wildlife, with some once-in-a-lifetime encounters.

As tempting as it might be to reach out and pat a turtle as you snorkel above it, it can be extremely distressing for the animal. Always keep a respectful distance from wildlife to ensure that it feels safe and calm with you around.

Koalas
Scattered from Brisbane down to Victoria and all the way across to Kangaroo Island in South Australia, there are lots of great places to spot koalas in their natural habitat all year round. Some of the best places to see them in the wild include the Koala Walk in Kennett River (see p.44) in Victoria, Hanson Bay on Kangaroo Island (see p.80) in SA, and on Minjerriba (North Stradbroke Island, see p.178) in Queensland.

Kangaroos
Spotted all over the country at all times of the year, kangaroos are without a doubt the most easily seen animal in the wild, often found only a short distance from major cities and jumping anywhere there's an open paddock. Some of the most reliable places to find kangaroos include the Anglesea Golf Club (see p.43) in Victoria, and Eyre Peninsula (see p.84) in SA.

Crocodiles
Northern Australia is absolutely croc-territory, with these snappy predators taking over all kinds of waterways, from beaches to rivers, gorges and swimming holes. The Yellow Water Cruise in Kakadu (see p.164) in the NT is a great place to see them in the wild, or to get up close take a cruise of the Adelaide River (see p.144) just outside Darwin or visit Hartley's Crocodile Adventure (see p.196) in Tropical North Queensland.

Sea Turtles
Both the Southern Great Barrier Reef (see p.198) in the east and Ningaloo Reef (see p.115) in the west are great places to spot sea turtles in the wild, with green turtles and loggerhead turtles sighted all year round. Some of the best spots for guaranteed sightings are Fitzroy Island (see p.200) and Lady Musgrave Island (see p.200), both in Queensland. You can see nesting happening from November to February and baby hatchlings emerging from January to March in the Southern Great Barrier Reef and along the Ningaloo Coast.

Quokkas
Found only on Rottnest Island (see p.112) in WA, Quokkas are the worlds' happiest animals, never shying away from a selfie and always smiling up at the camera. They can be spotted all over Rotto, often the most active in the mid to late afternoon, although you can see them napping in the shade during the day as well.

Emus
Found all over the country, emus are absolutely wild, and can often be found running frantically along the side of the road or wandering lazily across beaches. South Australia is a great place to find them in the wild, in particular along the Eyre Peninsula (see p.84), Coffin Bay National Park (see p.86) and Innes National Park (see p.93) on the Yorke Peninsula. In January and February you can often spot male emus wandering with their babies.

Wombats
Perhaps the most elusive of animals to find in Australia, wombats are super difficult to spot in the wild, especially because they're mostly nocturnal and hide away during the day. However, Ronny Creek in Cradle Mountain (see p.236) and Maria Island (see p.228), both in Tasmania, have wombat sightings all year round and are a great place to see baby wombats grazing along the grass.

Australian Sea Lions
Appropriately named the puppies of the ocean, sea lions are some of the best animals to interact with in the wild. They want to play, chase you, and literally swim circles around you, and it's so much fun. You can hop on a tour to swim with sea lions with Adventure Bay Charters (see p.84) from Port Lincoln

in SA for a morning in the ocean you will never forget. Port Lincoln is also the great white shark capital of Australia, another bucket-list swim to tick off your list.

Echidnas

Even cuter in real life than you might expect, echidnas can be found around much of south-eastern Australia, although it's mainly good luck that lets you see one in the wild. Some of the places we've come across a few include Kangaroo Island (*see* p.80) in SA, Cradle Mountain (*see* p.236) in Tassie, and Murramarang National Park (*see* p.27) near Batemans Bay in NSW.

Platypuses

Difficult to spot and often hiding amongst lilypads and water reeds, platypuses are is extremely difficult to spot. Plus, they're super small. Much smaller than we thought they'd be when we finally found one in the wild. The only place we've managed to find them is Platypus Park in the Atherton Tablelands (*see* p.196) in Tropical North Queensland, where they're sure to show themselves if you are very calm and quiet.

Camels

It's thought that there are a million feral camels running around the outback in Australia, and having crossed the country in many different ways, I can safely say that if there are, they are super difficult to find!

Whales

As whales migrate up and down the coastlines of Australia, they can almost be spotted all year round from different places. Head to Exmouth (*see* p.115) in WA from April to July to swim with whale sharks and watch orca whales swimming in pods on a cruise from Bremer Bay (*see* p.134), also in WA. Spot humpback whales swimming along the southern coastlines during the winter months from June to November, regularly spotted in every state except the NT.

Tasmanian Devils

Almost impossible to spot in the wild due to their critically endangered status and the fact that they are nocturnal, Tassie Devils are best visited in the zoos and sanctuaries around Tasmania. Head to Bonorong Wildlife Sanctuary (*see* p.220) or East Coast Nature World (*see* p.227).

Red Crab Migration

Each year for about 18 days in December, starting when the first rains of summer begin to fall, Christmas Island is covered in more than 50 million red crabs, coming out from the rainforest and making their way down to the ocean, where they mate for the season. Whole roads look completely red, with almost every surface of the island covered in these bright red crabs, and it really needs to be seen to be believed.

Top Sea lion at Seal Bay, Kangaroo Island, SA
Bottom Koala mum and baby at Hanson Bay, Kangaroo Island, SA

Can't-miss place
Lord Howe Island (*see* p.16)

Top experience
Climbing the Sydney Harbour Bridge
(*see* p.2)

National Parks Pass
Of NSW's 870 national parks and
reserves, park entry fees only apply at
45 of them. You can buy a digital pass
(nationalparks.nsw.gov.au/passes-and-
fees) or via the NSW National Parks
app, with a single pass costing $8 to
$12 per day or $22 per vehicle for one
year and a multi-park pass costing
$65 per vehicle for a year, excluding
Kosciuszko National Park. Before you
visit, check the website for a full list of
which parks have entry fees.

Important dates
Plan your visit to NSW around some of
these key dates:

- New Year Celebration
- Tamworth Country Music Festival (Jan)
- Mardi Gras Festival & Parade (March)
- Vivid Sydney (May)

Time zone
NSW follows the Australian Eastern
Time Zone (GMT +10), with daylight
savings time (GMT +11) in effect
between October and April.

Stay connected & get featured
Follow @visitnsw for all the inspiration
and best places to visit in NSW, and
have your NSW photos featured by
using hashtags #newsouthwales or
#visitnsw.

Helpful websites
- Caravanning and camping
  caravancampingnsw.com
- Bushfires and warnings
  rfs.nsw.gov.au/fire-information
- National parks
  nationalparks.nsw.gov.au

New South Wales & ACT

There's so much to love and even more to explore in New South Wales (NSW). This epic state sitting along the East Coast of Australia really has it all. From the big city buzz of Sydney (*see* p.2), to the quiet beach towns of the South Coast (*see* p.26), and the vastness of the NSW outback (*see* p.22), the landscapes change dramatically across the state, offering a myriad of wonderful weekends away.

The busiest state in Australia is also home to some of the country's most-loved iconic attractions, including the Sydney Harbour Bridge, Sydney Opera House, and the world-famous Bondi Beach. With 892 beaches and 870 national parks across the state, great snowfields and bushland, you'll be kept busy exploring a different destination every weekend.

Within NSW you can also find the Australian Capital Territory (ACT), which is the smallest territory in the country, while also being home to Australia's largest inland city and the nation's capital, Canberra (*see* p.30). It's a great weekend away to explore museums and galleries, to learn more about Australia's history and government, as well as to sample its booming foodie scene.

SYDNEY

The Traditional Owners of the Sydney area are the Gadigal people of the Eora Nation

CULTURE BUFFS

There is a long ongoing feud, or debate shall we say, about whether Sydney or Melbourne is the best city in Australia. While Sydney has iconic landmarks, beautiful beaches and a distinct chilled-out vibe, Melbourne has been crowned as one of the most liveable cities in the world numerous times, so it's definitely a stiff competition. Everyone has a different opinion about which city is their favourite, but no matter which way you cast your vote, there's no denying that Sydney is an amazing place.

Sydney is unique, where big city life lies right next to some of the best surf beaches on the East Coast. It's a wonderful mix of business and pleasure all in one place. There is so much to do in Sydney, so much to see and explore and you just can't go past the good weather all year round and the extraordinary Harbour views, beaches and national parks within the city.

Whether you want to spend your days shopping and dining, walking in bushland or lazing at the beach, you won't want to leave after your weekend away. Sydney is so laid-back and cool, and it's easy to feel instantly at home here.

BEST PHOTO SPOTS

Head to Mrs Macquarie's Chair for one of the best photo spots in the city, where you can capture the Sydney Harbour Bridge and the Opera House sitting side by side. Sunset here is particularly pretty and photogenic.

Sydney

CAN'T MISS

Climb the **Sydney Harbour Bridge** for some of the best views over the Harbour, or if you're not keen on heights, you can walk alongside the road in the pedestrian lane.

Spend the day at **Bondi Beach**, Australia's most famous beach and home to the iconic Bondi Surf Bathers' Life Saving Club.

Catch an iconic ferry across the Harbour to **Manly Beach** for a laid-back beach only an hour from the city itself.

Pop into **The Grounds of Alexandria** for a weekend brunch, with archways covered in greenery and fairy lights, market stands on the weekends and rustic sheds that are set up as unique dining areas.

Check out the views from the **Olympic Pool**, one of the most picturesque public pools you'll come across - which is saying something, given how many iconic ocean pools Sydney has.

Walk the **Bondi to Coogee Coastal Walk** to explore some of Sydney's best beaches. Or for something a bit longer, try the **Bondi to Manly** track.

Jump on a free walking tour around **The Rocks** historical district to see some of Sydney's oldest buildings and their stunning architecture.

Catch a show at the iconic **Sydney Opera House**, or just take your best pics out the front.

Take a dip in some of Sydney's favourite **ocean pools**; **Bronte Beach** and **Bondi Beach** have some of the best.

Explore **Circular Quay** and **Darling Harbour** entertainment and dining precincts.

Take the ferry to **Taronga Zoo** to make friends with some of their cheeky animals, who live on some of the best real estate overlooking the Harbour.

Grab a delicious colourful drink at one of Sydney's many **rooftop cocktail bars**.

The view from Mrs Macquarie's Chair
Opposite Overlooking the Opera House and city from the Sydney Harbour Bridge
Previous Sunrise at Ned's Beach, Lord Howe Island

DAYTRIPS

Spend a day exploring **Royal National Park**, about 45 minutes south of Sydney, and home to incredible coastal walks, secluded beaches, whale sightings and Insta-famous spots like the Wedding Cake Rock and Figure Eight Pools.

Take a road trip north to the **Hunter Valley** to Australia's oldest wine region, with great vineyards and cellar doors offering wine tastings and menus filled with local produce and incredible views over the valley.

PLAN YOUR TRIP FOR

Visit during the incredible **Vivid Sydney** festival to watch the city come to life during this epic festival of creativity with countless light displays, artworks, performances, street markets, parties and more. Usually running for around three weeks during winter, it's a great way to explore more of Sydney.

Where

Sydney is located on the East Coast of Australia, about halfway along the coast of New South Wales.

Getting here

Sydney Kingsford Smith Airport (SYD) is the only airport here and is located about a 25-minute drive away from the city, depending on the traffic conditions. The airport is conveniently connected to the city by the local train system, taking just 13 minutes to reach the city centre. The Airport Link train runs every 10 minutes or so between 4.30am and 11.30pm daily. If you're planning to explore a bit beyond Sydney, you can rent a car from the airport terminal, giving you the ultimate freedom as soon as you land.

Getting around

Sydney is well connected by public transport, with trains, buses, ferries and the light rail getting you around the city. Grab yourself an Opal card from convenience stores, supermarkets, post offices or newsagencies, that you can top up whenever you need to, and simply tap and go on any public transport you want.

When to go

Between October and April, when the sun is shining and the weather is warmer is generally the best time to visit Sydney. For the best experience, avoid the Easter and Christmas holidays and public holidays if you can, as crowds surge during these times, with people from all over Australia coming to experience Sydney's summery vibe.

Where to stay

To stay right in the heart of Sydney, book accommodation around **The Rocks** district, a great place to base yourself and within walking distance of Sydney Harbour and Circular Quay, train stations and the ferry terminals. There are heaps of great restaurants and cafes here, and with cobblestone streets and historical buildings, it's definitely one of the nicest areas in Sydney.

For more of a beach vibe, head out to **Bondi** and base yourself right on the famous beach. The biggest of all beaches in the area, Bondi has the most options for restaurants, shopping and cafes, as well as the biggest supermarket right on the main street.

If you're not too fussed about the location and are looking for more of a budget stay, try options around **Kings Cross**. Here you'll find heaps of hostels and budget hotels, while still being super close to the city's main train station, connecting you to everywhere you need to go. Kings Cross is a bit more of a youth area, so expect lots of bars and pubs and more parties in the streets.

Get planning

Start your planning at sydney.com. Check out @sydney and @visitnsw for all the inspiration you need to plan your visit to Sydney, and tag #ilovesydney and #newsouthwales in your photos to be featured.

BLUE MOUNTAINS

World Heritage wilderness

NATURE LOVERS

Sprawling across one million hectares of forest, with a blue horizon of eucalypt trees that stretches further than the eye can see, the Blue Mountains is a very special region. Home to canyons, waterfalls, native bushland, underground caves and more than 140 kilometres of walking tracks, there's a huge amount to explore here.

A visit to the Blue Mountains will take you back more than 340 million years, where you can experience some of the world's oldest caves, float high above the mountains in a glass cable car, or travel through the tightest parts of the forest on the Scenic World Railway.

Only 90 minutes from Sydney, the Blue Mountains is an ideal destination for a weekend getaway, where you can spend your days in nature, disconnected from the real world, with incredible views to immerse yourself in. Listed as a UNESCO World Heritage Site, there are plenty of ways to get off-the-beaten track, to find your own space and a piece of the bush completely to yourself.

BEST PHOTO SPOTS

Take a drive out to **Hanging Rock** for some of the best photos in the region. Follow the hiking trail to Baltzer Lookout and continue along the path to actually stand on what feels like the end of the world. It's a good idea to take a friend with you to take a photo of you from the lookout, otherwise it could be quite tricky to get the shot. It's definitely one of the hardest hikes in the park, so do plenty of research before you go, take lots of water and sunscreen and wear appropriate footwear.

CAN'T MISS
In the morning:
Start at the iconic **Three Sisters**, three giant limestone pilings rising up out of the mountains and perched perfectly on their own little ledge. You can see them from the lookout at Echo Point or follow the **Prince Henry Clifftop Walk**, which has lots of different panoramic views over the Southern Blue Mountains, taking you from Scenic World to Leura.

Allow yourself some time to explore **Scenic World** to get the full Blue Mountains experience. With panoramic views of the wilderness, waterfalls, valleys and rugged sandstone tablelands, Scenic World has the best views in the region from either the glass-floored Skyway cable car, which floats 270 metres in the air before dropping into the Jamison Valley, or by riding the world's steepest incline railway. At the bottom of the Jamison Valley you can walk along the Southern Hemisphere's longest boardwalk that snakes around the floor of the Jurassic Rainforest.

If you're brave enough, take a walk down the **Giant Stairway**, made of 980 steps that will take you through the Three Sisters and right down to the valley floor. From the bottom, catch the **Scenic Railway** back to the top, the steepest passenger railway in the world that climbs the mountain at an incline of 52 degrees.

Take a morning dip in some of the secluded **swimming holes** that are dotted around the Blue Mountains. Some are at the bottom of waterfalls while others are completely surrounded by bushland, and just unexpected in the mountains! Our favourites include **Glenbrook Gorge**, **Jellybean Pool**, **Minnehaha Falls**, **Blue Pool** and **Crayfish Pool**.

Enjoy the views from **Govetts Leap Lookout**, where you can see one of the tallest, thinnest waterfalls in the national park. It's a great spot to visit after the rain, when the waterfall is flowing a little harder.

In the afternoon:
Have lunch in **Leura**, the cutest little town in the Blue Mountains. With vines winding through the whole street and historic building fronts, Leura is a lovely place to come for a snack between hikes and visiting lookouts. There are lots of cute cafes and takeaway stores to choose from.

Blue Mountains

Govetts Leap Lookout

Explore the **Jenolan Caves**, one of the most ancient open caves in the world, full of underground rivers, stunning limestone formations and guided walking paths. There are a few different caves to explore, some of the best include River Cave and Lucas Cave. Take a moment to watch the blue pools near the entrance of Lucas Cave too, as platypus are sometimes spotted there.

Wander into some of the hidden spots around the mountains to see the **bright glow worms** that inhabit them. There are lots of different spots to see glow worms, often hanging from cave ceilings or under cliff edges, creating a bright turquoise colour. Some of the best spots to find them are Cataract Falls, Horseshoe Falls, and The Grand Canyon. Just remember if you do visit a glow worm spot, don't use any flashes or lights (including lighting up your phone), instead just experience this incredible sight for yourself.

In the evening:
After a day of hiking and exploring, stop by **Mountain Culture Beer Company** to try some of their craft beers. There's a great deck outside to enjoy a beer on a balmy summer's night.

See the Blue Mountains by moonlight with a stroll along the **Katoomba Night Walk** (open until 10.20pm nightly). The whole walking trail is only 2.4 kilometres, so it's an easy walk to some of the best Blue Mountains attractions, which have all been lit up for a completely unique night-time view. Choose a clear night and you'll also be strolling under a bed of stars.

Where
The Blue Mountains are about 50 kilometres west of Sydney.

Getting here
The closest airport to the Blue Mountains is Sydney Kingsford Smith Airport (SYD). From the airport, there are several different ways to get out to the Blue Mountains. You can either pick up a rental car from the airport and hit the road for an easy 90-minute drive into the heart of Katoomba, or jump on a train from Sydney's Central railway station for one of the most scenic ways to get to the Blue Mountains.

Getting around
The easiest way to explore the Blue Mountains is by car. Bring your own, or rent one at the airport for the freedom to go wherever you like. Otherwise, grab a ticket for the **Blue Mountains Explorer Bus**, which will give you a hop-on, hop-off ticket and gets you to 29 stops around the mountains, including Katoomba, Leura and Wentworth Falls.

When to go
Significantly cooler than Sydney and the coast of New South Wales, it's never very warm in the Blue Mountains. In fact, the average temperature in the Upper Blue Mountains in summer is only 18°C, while in winter it doesn't often top 5°C. Plan your visit around the weather, with the best time to visit often being on a clear weekend (hot or cold doesn't really matter, you just want to avoid those low-hanging clouds), just after a decent rainfall to see the many waterfalls in full force. The shoulder seasons during autumn and spring are often a good time to find this kind of weather, although that might mean a last-minute weekend getaway.

Main towns
Katoomba and Leura are the main towns in the Blue Mountains, where you can find all kinds of accommodation, cafes and restaurants, supermarkets, petrol stations, shops and boutiques.

There are plenty of hotels, hostels and caravan parks to choose from super close to town, or for something a little more unique, book in with **Love Cabins** in Wollemi, where you can stay in a private treehouse surrounded by bushland.

Get planning
For everything you need to know to plan your visit, head to visitbluemountains.com.au and bluemts.com.au and check out @bluemtns_explore for an insight into some of the best places to go and insider details.

View of the Three Sisters from Echo Point

BYRON BAY

The ultimate coastal and boho town

NATURE LOVERS

'Cheer up, slow down, chillout'. The sign on Ewingsdale road leading into Byron Bay sums up the vibe here perfectly. The famous beach town, right in the northern pocket of New South Wales, holds a reputation completely unique to any other in Australia.

Whilst it's well known for its beautiful coastline, great weather, surf breaks and close proximity to the pretty hinterland hills, it's the distinctive barefooted, colourful gypsy vibe that makes it quite a special place. The centre of town is only a block away from the beach, with plenty of cafes and restaurants offering superfoods healthy smoothies and dishes that include every colour of the rainbow. It's a place where a hula-hooper would fit right in, painted kombi vans fill the carparks, and shoes are definitely optional. But it's also become a place where boutique shops abound, real estate prices have boomed and you're as likely to be surfing next to a backpacker as you are a Hollywood celebrity.

Australia's easternmost town, you'll be the first in the country to see the sun rise on your Byron weekend, before a day filled with beach hopping, swimming in waterfalls and cold-pressed juices. Keep your eyes peeled for a celebrity sighting, with Chris Hemsworth and Zac Efron often being spotted around town.

PLAN YOUR TRIP FOR

Head to Byron Bay during winter to experience **Splendour In The Grass**, the three-day music extravaganza that seems to get bigger each year. With plenty of Aussie talent, as well as huge names from around the world, Splendour is an experience for the senses with outdoor dance stages, crazy light shows, circus acts, silent discos, healing sanctuaries, craft markets, cabaret performances, glitter body paint and more.

Surfers at Little Wategos Beach

Byron Bay

CAN'T MISS

In the morning:

Spend your morning hopping around the **beaches of Byron Bay**. With crystal-clear waters, consistent surf breaks, and dolphins and whales often spotted in the distance, the beaches here make it super easy to fall in love with Byron. Main Beach and Clarkes Beach are the go-to for water sports like snorkelling, bodyboarding, windsurfing and paragliding, or head around to Wategos for surfing and Little Wategos for great swimming and sunbathing conditions.

Explore **Cape Byron Marine Park** on a guided kayak tour with **Go Sea Kayak** for the chance to get super up-close and personal to wild dolphins.

Jump on a sea turtle snorkel tour with **Byron Bay Dive Centre** to explore **Julian Rocks Nguthungulli Nature Reserve**.

Head to the **Byron Community Market** held on the first Sunday of every month (8am to 3pm) at Main Beach for an interesting collection of stalls that just scream Byron Bay. It's a super lively market, with local musicians, great food, authentic products and the best of Byron Bay.

Indulge in wellness experiences, with Byron Bay offering some of the best acupuncture, reflexology, reiki, healing, detox therapies, yoga and massages to absolutely relax you. Book treatments at **Gaia Retreat and Spa** in the hinterland, or **Byron Wellbeing Retreats** for some of the best experiences.

Take a walk to the most easterly point in Australia, where the **Cape Byron Lighthouse** has been watching over the oceans of Byron Bay since 1899. The lighthouse is still a working masterpiece and the brightest light of its kind in the Southern Hemisphere. It's a great place for whale watching in winter, or to just see the spectacular views.

Shop up a storm at many of the unique boutiques and bohemian stores that call Byron Bay their home. A top favourite is always **Spell & The Gypsy Collective**, who have created a cult following with their limited-edition drops and beautifully designed pieces. Head to their boutique on Browning Street for all the Byron Bay vibes. Bay Street, Fletcher Street and Marvell Street also offer beautiful boutiques.

BEST PHOTO SPOTS

For some of the prettiest beach and surf photos around, head down to Wategos and Little Wategos, lined with tropical pandanus palms.

In the afternoon:

Take an afternoon dip in **Killen Falls**, just 20 minutes out of Byron Bay towards Ballina. When you get to the lookout over the falls, follow the smaller walking trail right down the river to the little pool that the falls run into for a great secluded spot for an afternoon swim. Visit after some rain to see the falls at their best, but be careful of submerged rocks underwater and unexpected drop-offs in the pool.

Head to **The Farm @ Byron Bay** to see how a real working farm has created a beautiful experience for visitors to learn about farm life, how their food is locally grown and produced and how they work to inspire their visitors to make tiny changes that lead to a healthier lifestyle. They also have a herd of gorgeous Scottish Highland Cattle that you definitely don't want to miss. Stay for lunch at their onsite restaurant **Three Blue Ducks** who source as many ingredients as possible from the farm.

Grab an ice-cream from **Beaches and Cream**, the super-cute store on Bay Street that's sure to leave you in a sugar coma. With homemade ice-cream and Instagram-worthy donuts topped with all sorts of sweet treats, it's a great 3pm pick-me-up to keep you going through the afternoon.

Explore the **Crystal Castle & Shambhala Gardens**, home to the biggest and most beautiful crystals in the world. You can stand between the two tallest crystals on earth, or sit in an ancient amethyst cave, wander through the tropical rainforests or just grab yourself a few special crystals to take home from the gift shop.

In the evening:

Grab dinner at the **Beach Hotel**, Byron's most famous pub that offers live entertainment, a huge beer garden overlooking the ocean and classic pub meals. It's where you can unwind, kick back and enjoy the balmy nights with a tropical cocktail and a group of mates.

Top Dolphins swimming along the Byron coastline
Middle Sunset walks on Byron's Main Beach
Bottom Welcome to Byron Bay sign
Opposite Lazy afternoons at Killen Falls

Byron Bay

Where

Byron Bay is in the very north-east corner of New South Wales, about an hour from the Queensland border.

Getting here

Ballina Airport (BNK) is the closest airport to Byron Bay, around half an hour drive from the beach town. There are daily direct flights from Sydney and Melbourne with a handful of airlines, as well as regular direct services to Ballina from Newcastle, Dubbo and Canberra. Alternatively, you can choose to fly into Gold Coast Airport (OOL), about a 50-minute drive just over the Queensland border, which has frequent direct flights from many airports around Australia, as well as a few from New Zealand.

Getting around

Byron Bay is quite small and is easy to get around by bicycle. Head to **Byron Bay Surf and Bike Hire** or **Sunshine Cycles** to grab some wheels, and if you're planning to explore a little further choose an electric bike - you'll love it!

When to go

Despite its sunny beachside reputation, you'll actually find that there's quite a lot of rain throughout the year in Byron. Visit between September and November for warm sunny days and the lowest average rainfall. And try to avoid NSW school holidays if you can, when crowds absolutely flock to Byron.

Where to stay

There is accommodation for every type of budget in Byron, from backpacker hostels to insanely luxurious beach houses. If you're coming with a caravan, head to **Clarkes Beach Holiday Park**, full of palm trees and greenery and right across the road from the beach, this is the perfect base for your visit. Check out **Airbnb** and **Byron Bay Luxury Homes** for some of the most incredible beach houses for your stay. For a little boutique luxe, stay at **The Atlantic**, with its coastal chic cottages, communal kitchens and fire-pits. Or for a budget option stay at the **Arts Factory Lodge**, the famous hostel nestled in the hinterland that will absolutely give you the alternative Byron vibe you might be looking for.

Get planning

For everything you need to plan your visit to Byron Bay, head to visitbyronbay.com and for all the best spots from the locals @byron.bay.nsw on Insta.

NORTH COAST

Beach hop your way along the coastline

NATURE LOVERS

Stretching all the way along the northern coastline of New South Wales, from Newcastle up to Byron Bay is a region filled with stunning beaches, sweeping sand dunes, small coastal towns, and plenty of great food and wine. It's the kind of place where you can do nothing at all and just have the best time.

It's also a great destination for wildlife spotting, from koalas and kangaroos on the land to wild dolphins, seals and whales in the sea. The North Coast is teeming with native wildlife and natural beauty.

If you're looking for a weekend to really unwind and relax, beach hop your way along the coastline, stopping into as many little beaches and bays as you can find. One of our favourite ways to explore this region is to just pull off the road down any dirt or sand track that looks big enough to fit a car and see what we find at the other end. We've found some of the best secluded little beaches and rockpools all to ourselves this way - it's definitely the most exciting way to explore. The beaches along the North Coast are some of the most beautiful in the state, and with warm sunny weather most of the year, there's never a bad time to have a weekend here for some R&R.

PLAN YOUR TRIP FOR

Head to Port Macquarie in December to the **Festival of the Sun**, its annual outdoor music festival held at the Sundowner Breakwall Tourist Park. With an epic line-up of live music, food trucks serving every kind of cuisine, silent discos, silent comedy and more, it's a great place to have some fun in the sun.

Just one of NSW's many beautiful beach regions

North Coast

CAN'T MISS

In the morning:

Hike the **Tomaree Head Summit Walk** for some of the best views over Port Stephens, Fingal Bay and Shark Island. The hike is only a 2.2 kilometre round-trip, but it is quite steep the whole way up. The summit stands 161 metres above Port Stephens and provides outstanding views of the whole coastline. Another great lookout over Port Stephens is the **Gan Gan Hill Lookout** with views out to Myall Lakes in the north and Newcastle in the south.

Stock up on fresh produce and local goodies at the **Newcastle City Farmers Market**. On every Sunday (7am to 1pm) at the Newcastle Showgrounds, you can meet the local farmers and buy products straight from the source. It's a great way to support local growers and to find out a little more about where your food is coming from.

Learn about the local culture on the **Gaagal Wanggaan National Park Tour** with **Unkya LALC Cultural Eco Tours**, where you get to explore the beautiful national park, taste and feel traditional foods, participate in Gumbaynggirr ceremonies, learn about native plant species, medicines and their holistic uses and also discover a little of the Gumbaynggirr language.

Jump in the water for a swim with wild dolphins with the team at **Dolphin Swim Australia** in Port Stephens. The first wild dolphin swim of its kind in the world, you'll be taken offshore to a special location where you can swim with these magical creatures as part of their pod.

See more of this unique region by embarking on a **coastal walk**. There are different walking trails all along the coast to choose from, some of our favourites include **Bathers Way** in Newcastle, **Port Macquarie Coastal Walk** in Port Macquarie, **Aboriginal Cultural Ways** in Ballina and **Yuraygir Coastal Walk** between Yamba and Wooli.

Head a little inland to explore **Dorrigo National Park**, part of the Gondwana Rainforests UNESCO World Heritage Area, where you'll find plenty of waterfalls (don't miss Dangar Falls and Crystal Shower Falls), bushwalking trails, and the Skywalk Lookout, a 70-metre-high boardwalk that puts you directly above the rainforest.

In the afternoon:

Explore the incredible **Stockton Bight Sand Dunes**. Sitting within the Worimi Conservation Lands, between Anna Bay and Port Stephens, the sand dunes here are always changing, in fact they are the largest moving sand dunes in the Southern Hemisphere. Spend your afternoon sand-boarding, quad-biking or driving around the dunes, or hop on a camel for a leisurely stroll along the beach.

Stop into the **Koala Hospital** in Port Macquarie, which takes in about 200 koalas a year who need medical attention, commonly for issues such as chlamydia, or injured by cars or in dog attacks. There's a guided tour at 3pm each day where you can watch the koalas being fed and learn more about the koalas that are currently living at the hospital.

Look for the koala sculptures that are dotted around Port Macquarie, making up the **Hello Koalas Sculpture Trail**. There are sculptures all over the town, which have all been individually designed and handpainted by local artists and sponsored by local businesses. New sculptures are added every year, so there's always a new koala to find.

Take a swim in **Newcastle Ocean Baths**, built alongside an Art Deco pavilion that has been standing since the early 1900s and sitting on the rocky cliffs of the ocean, It's a great place for a swim, sunbathe or quick photo opportunity as you're passing through.

BEST PHOTO SPOTS

Stop for an iconic photo at the **Big Banana** in Coffs Harbour. Arguably Australia's most popular *big thing*, the Big Banana is a favourite photo stop for anyone road tripping along the Pacific Highway. Call in for one of their famous banana treats - our favourite is banana dipped in chocolate and sprinkles.

Where

The North Coast sprawls across the top half of NSW, from Newcastle up to Byron Bay.

Getting here

There are quite a few airports along the North Coast, so depending on where you'd like to stay, there's always somewhere to fly to close by. Options include Newcastle Airport (NTL) with regular direct flights from Brisbane, Melbourne, Canberra, the Gold Coast and Sydney, as well as a handful of regional airports along the East Coast: Port Macquarie (PQQ) has direct flights from Sydney and Brisbane, or Coffs Harbour (CFS) has direct flights from Sydney, Melbourne and Brisbane.

When to go

Head to the North Coast during the summer months to take advantage of the long hot days and sunny weather. This coastal region really comes to life in the sunshine, with the reflections glittering off the water and the sand burning hot underneath your feet. Come between May and November for whale-watching season, where large pods of humpback whales migrate south, only metres from the shore.

Views from the Tomaree Head Summit Walk, Port Stephens
Opposite Try a chocolate and 100s and 1000s dipped banana at the Big Banana

Main towns

Newcastle, Port Stephens, Port Macquarie and Coffs Harbour are the main towns along the North Coast of NSW. Base yourself in any of these spots to be right in the heart of the action. If you're looking for more of a quiet break, there are also plenty of tiny coastal towns along the way to check out.

Where to stay

You can literally find every kind of accommodation you could be looking for along the northern coastline of NSW. From beachside camping to luxury resorts, unique holiday homes and secluded properties in the hinterland, there's all kinds of great places to choose from. **Reflections Holiday Parks** has lots of locations along the coastline if you're looking for caravan parks. They have a great rewards program where you can earn discounts and rewards and their parks are always in great locations, super clean and modern with friendly, helpful staff.

Get planning

For everything you need to plan your visit to the North Coast, head to visitnsw.com/destinations/north-coast, portstephens.org.au and coffscoast.com.au and check out the regional profiles on Insta, including @portstephens, @portmacquarie, @coffscoastnsw and @cityofnewcastle.au.

LORD HOWE ISLAND

Just paradise

OFF-THE-BEATEN TRACK | NATURE LOVERS

One of the most unique and untouched of any Australian islands, Lord Howe Island has been called 'the last paradise' as it was the last island 'discovered' in the world in 1788. Overflowing with incredible nature hikes, stunning beaches, tall palm trees and the world's southernmost coral reef, the island boasts UNESCO World Heritage status. Everywhere you turn you're greeted with beautiful landscapes and idyllic scenes, making you wonder why you hadn't visited earlier.

The remains of a now-extinct volcano, which dates back more than 7 million years and has eroded to 5 per cent of its original size, Lord Howe Island is an extremely special environment. Quite a small island, only 11 kilometres long and about 2 kilometres wide, it is believed that Lord Howe Island was uninhabited for millions of years, with no record of Indigenous Australians having ever lived on the island.

Only allowing 400 visitors onto the island at any one time, and with not a scrap of phone reception to be found, Lord Howe Island is never crowded and really gives you the ultimate island vibes. The only thing to do is disconnect, hit the beach and enjoy your time swimming and exploring every corner of this tropical paradise. Regular flights from Sydney mean that you can easily head here for a weekend of relaxation, but book your accommodation before your flights to make sure you don't miss out.

BEST PHOTO SPOTS
For the most iconic views over Lagoon Beach and the famous twin peaks of Mount Gower and Mount Lidgbird that stand tall over the water, head to **Signal Point**, only a few metres from the main beach.

One of our favourite views
on Lord Howe Island

Lord Howe Island

CAN'T MISS

In the morning:

Get to know the island better by hiking around it. There are plenty of **walking and hiking trails** that offer unique viewpoints and perspectives of this magical little oasis. Some of the top choices include Malabar Hill, Kim's Lookout, Valley of the Shadows and Goat House Cave.

Mount Gower, one of the main two peaks overlooking the lagoon, is rated as one of the best day hikes in Australia. Covered in rainforest, with a cloud forest near the top and epic views across the island from the summit, it's a highlight for anyone who tackles it. You'll need a guide for this one, so find local Jack Shick who has been a mountain guide for more than 30 years and knows everything there is to know about this epic hike.

Hop across the best beaches on the island. From the calm bays of **Old Settlement Beach** and **Lagoon Beach** that are lovely for snorkelling, to the epic **Blinky Beach** with huge surf breaks, there are so many great little spots if you really get out and explore.

Feed the fish at **Ned's Beach**, one of the prettiest little beaches on the island. You can buy a cup of fish food at the little information hut on the shore, and there are always fish swimming around there just waiting for a snack. You can also go snorkelling right off the beach - there are often turtles spotted out here.

Jump on a bus tour with **Chase 'n' Thyme Island Tours**, proudly the first tour on the island to be inducted into TripAdvisor's Hall of Fame. Locals Peter and Janine take you on a tour of Lord Howe, sharing some of the island's history, favourite landmarks and stories from growing up on the island.

Kayak to Rabbit Island (also known as Blackburn Island), a small island right in the middle of the lagoon. You can rent a kayak from many of the boat shops on the shore, hike to the top of the island, and view a different perspective of the island and the lagoon, right from the middle of it.

In the afternoon:

Jump on a glass-bottom boat tour with **Lord Howe Environmental Tours** to explore some of the epic reefs that lie in the lagoon. Stopping at a couple of different spots, including Erscotts Hole, you're sure to see some of the most beautiful marine life, including turtles and reef sharks. The tour goes for two hours and is a great way to see the best spots in the lagoon.

Another great spot for sea turtle sightings is **Upper Settlement Beach**, especially around an hour before high tide. There's plenty of seagrass here for them to feed on, so you can often spot them nibbling on a snack in the afternoon.

Pop into **The Crooked Post** for an afternoon cocktail on a swing. In the mornings this place doubles as the local physio, transforming into the local cocktail bar in the afternoons. Try one of their signature cocktails, often made with Lord Howe Island gin or come down for lunch on Taco Tuesday to grab a quick taco - they're absolutely delicious.

Enjoy a **game of golf** at one of the prettiest golf courses in the world. Dotted with palm trees and with the twin peaks standing tall in the background, it's definitely a picture-perfect place for nine holes of golf. Reserve a table for dinner at the golf club before you leave - it's definitely one of the best meals on the island.

Where
Floating in the Tasman Sea, Lord Howe Island is about 600 kilometres off the coast of Australia, almost directly in line with Port Macquarie.

Getting here
Fly directly to Lord Howe Island Airport (LDH) from Sydney with QantasLink. Flight schedules change throughout the year, although there are normally at least a couple of flights each day. There are extremely strict luggage restrictions when flying to Lord Howe Island, due to the smaller light aircraft. Make sure your checked luggage doesn't weigh more than 14kg per bag to avoid it being off-loaded, and only bring a small handbag or backpack with you on the flight, as there's nowhere to store carry-on suitcases. Most, if not all, accommodation around the island will pick you up from the airport, so let them know your flight details before you arrive.

Getting around
Bicycles are the main form of transport around the island, which can be rented from **Wilson's Hire Service** for $10 a day. The island is quite hilly in places though, so consider where you're staying if you're planning to rent a bike. There are about six automatic rental cars that can also be organised through Wilson's, although you will definitely need to book in advance for these. In the evening, your accommodation courtesy bus will drop you off for dinner and the restaurant's courtesy bus will take you back when you're done.

When to go
January to March are considered the best months to travel to Lord Howe Island, when the weather is a little bit warmer, there is little rainfall and you can take advantage of all the water sports and activities on offer. Due to its location in the sea, it never gets very hot on the island (although it can get extremely humid at times), with temperatures normally averaging about 25°C in the summer months.

Where to stay
To avoid having to ride up a steep hill every time you need to go back to your room, choose accommodation as close to the main corner (Ned's Beach Road and Lagoon Road) as you can. **The Blue Lagoon**, **Somerset Apartments**, **Pine Trees** and **Beachcomber Lodge** are all in a great spot, making it easy for you to go back and forth from your room to the beach whenever you want.

If you're celebrating something special and looking for some luxury options, check out **Cappella Lodge** and **Arajilla Retreat**.

Need to know
There is absolutely no phone reception on the island, in fact the locals don't even use mobile phones. Double check with your accommodation that wi-fi is available if you need it during your stay, or completely immerse yourself in island life with a few days off the grid. There is public wi-fi in the main street of town that costs $10 per GB, and it can also be dependent on good clear weather, so it's best not to rely on it. Your accommodation should have a landline telephone to make bookings and reservations, or there is a free phone near the information board in town.

Get planning
For everything you need to plan your ultimate island getaway to Lord Howe, head to lordhoweisland.info and check out @visitlordhoweisland on socials for all the best secret spots around the island.

Snorkelling the reef with Lord Howe Environmental Tours
Opposite Rent a bike from Wilson's Hire Service to explore the island

Stay in a tiny home

If you want to immerse yourself in nature, go off-the-grid and into the wild with a weekend away in a tiny home. Dotted all around New South Wales (as well as in Victoria, Queensland and South Australia), In2thewild has been popping up tiny homes all over the place. Finding the best locations, often on huge properties with nothing but bushland around, they have created the ultimate weekend getaways and places to recharge in nature.

With most tiny homes located within one to three hours from cities or major towns, there's not a lot of travel time involved, which means you can spend longer enjoying your weekend. The tiny homes have everything you could need, including toilets, hot showers, barbecues, fire-pits, book, games and amenities. All you'll need to bring is your food and drinks and get ready to relax.

The tiny homes change location all the time, with the exact location staying a secret until just before your stay. When you book your stay, you'll choose your house, and the general area you're going to, and then your secret address will be emailed to you with details, directions and an information pack just two days before you arrive. How exciting! Each tiny house also offers its own unique experiences for your stay, with anything from horseriding, wineries to visit, waterfalls or pretty lookouts nearby, to really take advantage of the region.

A tiny home will give you a much-needed recharge!

IMPORTANT INFO

In2thewild offers lots of different tiny homes around New South Wales. They have lots of pet-friendly choices too, so you can bring your fur babies with you to designated homes, and they offer discounts throughout the year when you book directly via their website.

Mobile phone reception isn't guaranteed at all of their properties (the prettiest places often don't have service). The tiny homes are also solar powered, so you're able to charge your phone via USB, but don't expect to charge a laptop or camera during your stay. Come with everything fully charged and ready to go!

Head to in2thewild.co to choose from all the different tiny houses, and sign up to their mailing list for $25 off your first stay.

BROKEN HILL & OUTBACK NSW

Australia's Silver City

OFF-THE-BEATEN TRACK

The unofficial capital of Outback NSW, Broken Hill is an extremely unique place. In the middle of the desert, miles from any major city in Australia, and famous for its presence in cult classic film, *The Adventures of Priscilla, Queen of the Desert*, Broken Hill is a melting pot of miners, artists, great food and colourful characters.

Crowned as Australia's first Heritage Listed City in 2005, Broken Hill is recognised as an exceptional place that contributes to the country's national identity. What an honour for a town in the middle of nowhere! It's also the home to Australia's union movement and the eight-hour workday – Something all of us take for granted most of the time, but are enormously thankful for.

There's so much to explore in Broken Hill, a city bursting with impressive galleries, mining history, great cafes, and surrounded by national parks with incredible flora and fauna, desert sculptures and outback lookouts. You'll be cramming a lot into your weekend as you adventure into the vast outback of NSW.

PLAN YOUR TRIP FOR

Throw yourself into Broken Hill's colourful culture, and get the full *Priscilla, Queen of the Desert* experience by visiting during the annual **Broken Heel Festivals** (normally in Sept each year), where Drag Queens and Drag Kings head to the outback to perform all kinds of entertainment, comedy and cabaret shows, live music and activities to pay tribute to the iconic movie. There's a huge street parade called the Main Drag In Drag that gets the whole community involved!

CAN'T MISS

In the morning:

Take a guided tour of the **Royal Flying Doctor's Visitors Centre**. Operating from Broken Hill since 1936, providing medical support and care to the many tiny outback towns and stations that are remotely located around the NSW outback, the Royal Flying Doctors is an incredibly special service. Looking after an area of more than 640 million square kilometres, the Broken Hill base is the largest in the country.

You can find the world's largest canvas painting within the caves of the **Silver City Art Centre & Mint**. *The Big Picture* ticks another box on your 'big things' list, and is an incredible canvas painting of Broken Hill and the surrounding country landscape. Hanging in a circular room, the painting is 100 metres long, 12 metres high and required more than nine tons of paint to complete. On your way out you can also grab all kinds of chocolatey treats from the local **chocolate factory**.

Set off on a self-guided walking tour to see some of the **street art** around the city. On many of the streets in the city centre you will find stunning murals, keeping the streets beautiful and colourful. There are lots of incredible Aboriginal art pieces around the city, as well as full walls sharing the history of the outback through art.

Hop your way through the cafes and pubs of Broken Hill, with some great food and dining choices around the city. For a beautiful breakfast, with a menu that includes smoothie bowls and avo on toast, stop by the **Silly Goat Cafe**, or for a sugar fix grab a milkshake from 1950s inspired **Bell's Milk Bar**.

In the afternoon:

Take an afternoon to explore Silverton and pop into the famous **Silverton Hotel** for a beer, one of the most iconic outback pubs, seemingly in the middle of nowhere. But take the time to see some of the other attractions around the tiny town, including the **Mad Max Museum**. You can also take a tour of the **Silverton Gaol**, check out artwork by local John Dynon and make friends with the local donkeys that roam up and down the main street.

Just past Silverton you will find the Mundi Mundi Plains. It's definitely worth making a stop at the **Mundi Mundi Lookout** to appreciate just how wide and expansive this country is, how remote and completely removed some of these outback towns are from the built-up areas along the coastlines. There is just so much *nothing* out here, it's incredible.

Opposite The iconic Silverton Hotel

For the best views over the city, head up to the **Line of Lode Lookout** at the **Miner's Memorial**. Sitting on the edge of the mine that is literally positioned right in the middle of the city, the memorial holds the names of more than 800 miners who have lost their lives working in the Broken Hill mines since the late 1800s. From the lookout you can see right across the city, all the way out to the ranges in the distance.

Broken Hill has a thriving arts and cultural scene, so give yourself some time to visit the **local art galleries**. In fact, there are twice as many galleries than pubs in the city - who would have guessed that! Some of the best galleries include **Pro Hart Gallery**, **Broken Hill Regional Art Gallery** and the **Silver City Art Centre & Mint**.

In the evening:
Explore the **Living Desert Sculpture Park**, sitting amongst the Barrier Ranges about 12 kilometres out of Broken Hill. Visit at sunset for stunning views over the ranges, as well as to see the sculptures light up as the sun dips slowly behind them. At the bottom of the hill you can also check out the **John Simons Flora & Fauna Sanctuary**, where a 2.2 kilometre cultural walking trail will lead you through native wildflowers, scenic lookouts, a prospector's mine site and past many local red kangaroos.

Have dinner at the **Palace Hotel**, which was famously featured in the iconic movie *The Adventures of Priscilla, Queen of the Desert*. Known for its heavily decorated walls, featuring all kinds of murals and paintings, the hotel hasn't changed much since the days of the movie, and is a great place to grab a drink and a meal, and experience the uniqueness of the city. For a night you'll never forget, drop by on the third Tuesday of every month for a night of Drag Bingo, one of the most entertaining and outrageous bingo games you've ever seen.

BEST PHOTO SPOTS
Silverton really seems to have all the best photo spots out here. Head to the **Mundi Mundi Lookout** to appreciate the vast nothingness of the outback, and stop by the Silverton Pub for a photo at one of Australia's most iconic outback pubs. Visit early in the morning for the best photos, before the street is lined with cars.

DAYTRIPS
Take a daytrip to another outback town to really hit the outback road and get a deeper understanding of just how huge and incredible Australia really is. Head to **Menindee** (1 hour, 15 minutes from Broken Hill) to see the epic Menindee Lakes, with some of the best fishing and camping spots around, stop at the Darling River and explore some of the town's most historical sites along the Heritage Trail. Find yourself something special in **White Cliffs** (2 hours, 30 minutes from Broken Hill), a popular area for opal mining in NSW where the 200 permanent residents live underground to escape the heat. Or head to **Cameron Corner**, actually in Queensland (4 hours, 30 minutes from Broken Hill), to see more of the outback before hitting the point where three states come together.

Where
Located in the outback of NSW, Broken Hill is about halfway between the Queensland border in the north and the Victorian border in the south, only 25 kilometres from the South Australian border in the west.

Getting here
You can fly directly into Broken Hill Airport (BHQ) with Rex Airlines, with direct flights into the outback town from Adelaide, Dubbo and Mildura, and with connections to other major cities around the country. From Adelaide, it's a 5-hour, 45-minute drive by road along the Barrier Highway. If you're travelling from Melbourne, the drive takes 9 hours along the Calder Highway through Mildura. Sydney is actually the furthest city away, despite being in the same state, with the road trip taking 13 hours through the Blue Mountains, Mudgee and Dubbo and then onto the Barrier Highway.

When to go
Head to Broken Hill during the summer and shoulder months, from roughly September until April, when you are likely to find hot summer weather and limited rainfall. Despite being in the outback, it doesn't seem to get too hot out here, with the highest average temperature around 34°C in January. Winters can be cold, especially in the morning, so always take a jacket with you if you're visiting during this time.

Get planning
Head to destinationbrokenhill.com.au for everything you need to plan your visit to Broken Hill.

Opposite top Sunsets in Menindee
Opposite bottom Life on the farm in Outback NSW

SOUTH COAST

Coastal wilderness

NATURE LOVERS

This special coastal region of NSW might be one of the most underrated in the whole country. Stretching from Wollongong in the north, all the way to the Victorian border in the south, and encompassing the regions of Shoalhaven and the Sapphire Coast, the South Coast of NSW encompasses beautiful quiet beaches, impressive national parks, delicious food and drinks, and up-close whale-watching sightings.

Fighting back since the devastating bushfires in the summer of 2020, with some of the most harrowing days in bushfire history, decimating towns, homes, wildlife and natural environments, the NSW South Coast has been rebuilding and reopening, showing the rest of the country that they are open for business.

Spend your weekend hopping your way through the many sleepy beach towns – some of our favourites are Kiama, Merimbula, Eden and Batemans Bay. You can try some of the freshest locally caught seafood you can find, swim in the turquoise ocean and explore the wilderness of the surrounding bushland that's right on your doorstep. It's just an incredible place, with so much more to see and do than you might expect.

PLAN YOUR TRIP FOR

Head to Jervis Bay (*see* p.32) in October for the **South Coast Food & Wine Festival**, a weekend of cooking masterclasses with award-winning chefs sharing secret recipes, indulgent food and wine celebrations, including the can't-miss Jervis Bay Beach Party, plenty of live music and beautiful beachfront locations.

Top Limestone cliffs on the beach in Ben Boyd National Park, Eden
Bottom Kangaroos on the beach at Merry Beach Caravan Park

CAN'T MISS

In the morning:

Jump on a **fishing charter** from Bermagui, where you can try your luck at catching big game or reef fish, with plenty of different charter options. While you're in Bermagui, make sure you stop at the **Blue Pool** for a swim, a pretty little rockpool with plenty of marine life.

Embark on the epic **Kiama Coast Walk**, a 22 kilometre one-way walk that normally takes about 6 to 7 hours. It's also broken up into three sections if you only want to walk a short section of it. The walking trail will take you past some of the top highlights in the area, including Kiama Blowhole, Cathedral Rocks, Bombo Headland, Minnamurra River and Werri Beach. Head inland to Berry from Kiama to wander through its famous antique stores and stop for a coffee at one of its many cafes.

Head to **Eden** for some of the best whale-watching locations in Australia, with the third-deepest harbour in the Southern Hemisphere. Whale-watching tours are available between September and November, with more than 25,000 humpback whales expected to pass along the coastline each season, or head to the **Killer Whale Museum** to learn about Australia's early whaling history.

Give yourself some time to explore **Macquarie Pass National Park**, home to waterfalls, ancient trees, steep ridges and deep gullies, as well as koalas, wombats, platypuses, wallabies and goannas. It's a beautiful place to bring a picnic lunch to enjoy after a bushwalk.

In the afternoon:

Spend an afternoon hopping your way across beaches as part of **Shoalhaven's 100 Beach Challenge**. With a list of 100 beaches that are all within a 2-hour drive from Sydney and Canberra, these are some of the best secret locations in the state, which you'll often find you have all to yourself.

Hit up some of the local restaurants along the coastline to feast on some of the freshest **seafood** around. With freshly shucked oysters and fish caught that same morning, you won't find anything fresher. **Bermagui** is a great place to find fresh seafood, where you can pair your meal with a crisp local wine to feast on a local delicacy.

Pop into **Bega** in the hinterland, known for its award-winning cheeses. Head straight to the **Bega Cheese Heritage Centre** where you can taste test your way through local cheeses and delicious milkshakes, or create your own cheese platter and set up a picnic alongside the Bega River.

Don't miss the wildlife at **Jervis Bay Marine Park**, where the crystal-clear blue waters are home to dolphins, fur seals, little penguins and even whales at different times of the year.

Head out on a tour on the water with **Jervis Bay Wild** to get even closer to the action, with day and twilight tours on offer.

Hop your way across many of the **national parks** along the South Coast to find some of the best hidden gems - rockpools full of starfish, hiking trails with beautiful lookouts, secluded little coves that you have all to yourself, and an abundance of native wildlife. Some of the best spots can be found in **Booderee National Park**, **Murramarang National Park** and **Mimosa Rocks National Park**.

Stop to view the impressive design of the **Sea Cliff Bridge** in Wollongong. It's a highlight along the Grand Pacific Drive, swinging the road out wide around the rock faces, right over the ocean, twisting with the natural curve of the cliffs. There's a viewing platform here to admire the impressive design, which is also a great spot for whale-watching in the right season.

In the evening:

Head to **Merry Beach** in the evening to see kangaroos hopping right along the beach. The Merry Beach Caravan Park offers campsites right on the water, and is full of resident kangaroos who like to hop between the beach and the bushland behind the campsites. There are even a few albino kangaroos who call this patch of land home! They're not shy though, so make sure to pack away all your food and rubbish after you've had dinner to avoid them rifling through your bags looking for snacks. While you're in the area, **Pretty Beach** and **Pebbly Beach** are two of our other favourites, such pretty spots - so well-named!

BEST PHOTO SPOTS

You can't go past **The Pinnacles** in Ben Boyd National Park for an absolutely incredible backdrop to your photos from the South Coast. With rock formations that change from white at the bottom to bright red at the top, this landscape will have you feeling like you're in another world. Head down to the beach to explore a little further, there are endless great places for photos down here. Keep an eye out for the resident wombats while you're in Ben Boyd National Park - they often like a cheeky photobomb along the walking trails.

Where
The South Coast of NSW stretches from Wollongong all the way down the coastline to the Victorian border.

Getting here
There are a few different options for getting to the South Coast. You can either catch a flight to Sydney Kingsford Smith Airport (SYD) and then rent a car and head south for a road trip along the coastline, or you can fly directly into Merimbula Airport (MIM), with direct flights from Melbourne and Sydney on Qantas and REX. Merimbula is about halfway between Sydney and Melbourne (about a 1-hour flight or 6-hour drive), landing you right in the bottom corner of New South Wales and the South Coast.

When to go
Head to the South Coast in summer to take advantage of the long warm days and with the best conditions to spend plenty of time in the ocean. If you're coming for whale-watching season, spring is the best time to visit, when Humpback, Baleen, Southern Right and Toothed Whales migrate south with their calves. September to November is the peak time to spot whales from this part of the coastline.

Main towns
Wollongong is the largest town along the southern coastline, as well as being the third-largest town in NSW. However, most of the small towns along the coastline have everything you need for a weekend stay, including fuel, supermarkets, accommodation choices and great places to eat and drink. Check out Kiama, Merimbula, Eden and Batemans Bay.

Get planning
Head to visitnsw.com/destinations/south-coast, sapphirecoast.com.au and shoalhaven.com, and check out @sapphirecoastnsw, @visitshoalhaven and @visitwollongong for all the best spots.

Aerial view of the Gantry at Bawley Beach

CANBERRA & ACT

The capital of Australia

CULTURE BUFFS

Affectionately known as the 'bush capital', due to its remote location surrounded by bushland, Canberra is the land of the Ngunnawal and Ngambri people, and takes over most of the very small Australian Capital Territory (ACT). Despite being the capital of Australia, Canberra is often overlooked. The city is home to some of the most important buildings in the country, including Parliament House.

However, there's lots more to Canberra and the ACT than politicians. With some of the best museums, memorials, zoos and galleries in the country, Canberra is the place to enlighten you on the history of Australia, the legacy of our wartime experiences, space exploration, science and technology and more. There's enough to capture your attention for days.

With suburbs that are named after ex-prime ministers, streets named after cities around the country, and more roundabouts than straight roads, secret tunnels and underground highways, Canberra is certainly a unique city, and one that is definitely worthy of a weekend visit.

PLAN YOUR TRIP FOR

Head to Canberra during the **Enlighten Festival** for 17 days of exciting activities in March annually. An epic celebration to commemorate Canberra Day, there are symphonies in the park, hot-air balloons taking over the city, colourful light installations, outdoor movies, live music and lots of great food and drinks.

Opposite The Australian War Memorial, Canberra

CAN'T MISS

Wake up before the sun for a beautiful **hot-air balloon** ride over the city. With the city surrounded by so much bushland, the views from the sky are incredible and Canberra looks so pretty from above. Plus, it's one of the only places in the world where you can fly directly over a Parliament House.

Learn all about Australia's past, present and future at the **National Museum of Australia**. Home to interactive displays, a huge array of artefacts, and the beautiful Garden of Australian Dreams, it's a special place to find out more about the history of Australia.

There's heaps to do in Canberra with kids. Step back to the Jurassic era and visit the **National Dinosaur Museum**, with all kinds of skeletons, fossils and models. Spend a morning at **Questacon** to learn all about science and tech, with lots of interactive and hands-on experiments and activities.

The award-winning **National Zoo and Aquarium** is home to animals from all over the world and offers incredible interactive tours where you can hand-feed a lion, pat a shark, meet a cheetah or come nose-to-nose with a giraffe. For the full safari experience, stay the night at the zoo's **Jamala Wildlife Lodge**, where you can literally sleep alongside the animals in the lodge's incredibly luxurious rooms.

Head to the **Old Bus Depot Markets** on a Sunday morning to browse an eclectic collection of vintage collectables, fashion, homewares, jewellery, crafts and food. A unique collection of stalls, the market is a favourite in the local community.

Wander through the exhibits at the **National Gallery of Australia** to see some of the unique permanent and temporary displays, with big exhibits coming in from all around the world. Be sure not to miss Yayoi Kusama's permanent exhibit - Spirits of the Pumpkins Descended into the Heavens - for some incredible rooms filled with bright colours and optical illusions.

Pay your respects at the **Australian War Memorial**, commemorating the men and women who have lost their lives fighting for Australia, as well as recognising those who continue to serve today. In the courtyard you'll find the beautiful Pool of Reflection and Eternal Flame that's surrounded by the Roll of Honour walls with the names of every person who has died serving, decorated with bright red

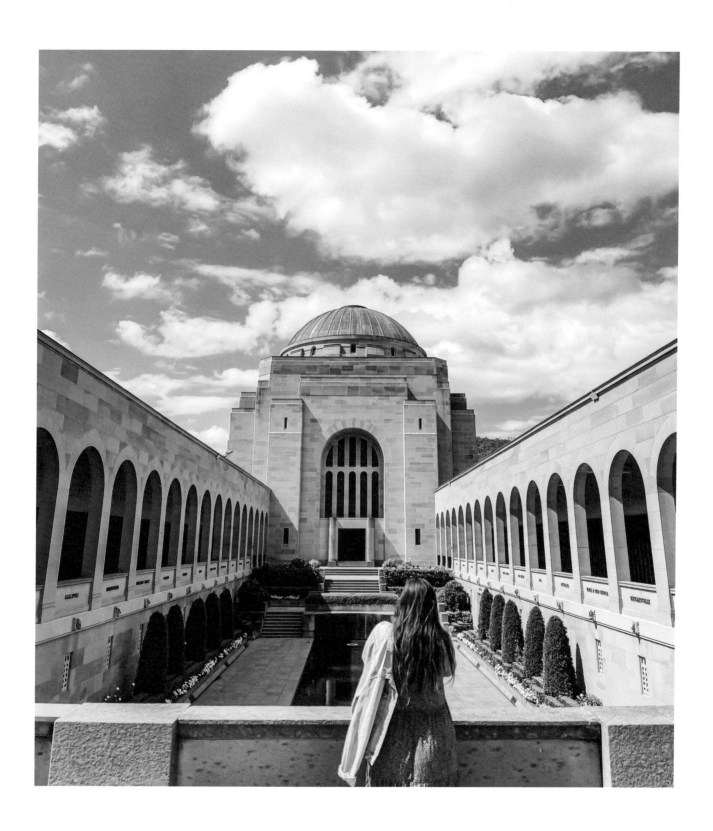

poppies. Visit the Commemorative Courtyard at 4.55pm for their daily Last Post Ceremony, a special place to experience this silence.

Rent a kayak or a paddleboard from **The Paddle Hub** and slowly make your way across the water of **Lake Burley Griffin**. Open for rentals from October to April, it's a great way to spend a leisurely afternoon and see Canberra from a different angle.

Canberra has become a hub for **boutique distilleries and breweries**, with more and more popping up each year. Creating unique flavours for beer, spirits, and even moonshine, there's always a new tasting paddle to try. Some of the best include **Capital Brewing Co.**, **Underground Spirits**, **BentSpoke Brewing Company** and **Baldwin Distilling Co.**

Capture an iconic Canberra photo out the front of **Parliament House**, one of the most recognisable buildings in the country. Take a guided tour to get an in-depth overview of the building or book a seat at question time to watch politicians in action.

Take a drive around the streets of the **National Circuit** where you can see the embassy buildings for countries from all around the world. Such a unique part of Canberra, many of the embassies are designed to reflect the style of their home country, with every building on the block looking completely different to the next.

DAYTRIPS

Head out to the Australian Capital Territory's coastal town, **Jervis Bay**, a 2-hour and 45-minute drive from the city. In 1915, Jervis Bay became part of the ACT when it was decided that the capital city needed a port. As it was the closest body of water to Canberra, Jervis Bay became part of the ACT. Home to beautiful deserted beaches, plenty of bushland and lots of wildlife, it's a great place to visit for a daytrip. You'll need a National Parks Pass to visit Jervis Bay and Booderee National Park, which you can buy from the ticket booth at the entrance. A 2-day pass costs $13 per vehicle, with additional fees if you plan to camp.

Top The National Parliament of Australia
Bottom Red poppies on the War Memorial's Roll of Honor

BEST PHOTO SPOTS

Head to the top of the **Telstra Tower** at Black Mountain for stunning 360-degree views over the whole of Canberra. The tower itself is quite dated, but the views are spectacular, especially on a clear sunny day. It costs $7.50 per adult to get to the top, but it's definitely one of the best lookouts in the ACT.

Where

Canberra sits a little inland from the coast, within the Australian Capital Territory.

Getting here

Jump on a flight to Canberra Airport (CBR), with direct services from every state in Australia except the NT, including many regional services from the East Coast. You can take the Rapid 3 bus route from the airport, which operates every 15 minutes and gets you into the city in less than 20 minutes with stops at the City interchange, Belconnen interchange, Cohen Street interchange and Spence Terminus. Alternatively, Canberra is a 3-hour drive from Sydney and a 7-hour drive from Melbourne.

Getting around

Pick up an e-scooter for a super quick and easy way to get around the city, or you can hire a bike to get around the self-proclaimed cycling capital of Australia, with plenty of bike paths and off-road mountain-biking trails that are great for sightseeing.

When to go

Autumn is a particularly pretty time to visit Canberra, when the weather is still quite warm and the whole city seems to be lined with picturesque red, gold, orange and ochre leaves. With four distinct seasons in Canberra, this is the city in Australia that's the closest to snow in the winter, with the Snowy Mountains only a short drive out of town, while still having hot sunny weather in summer.

Where to stay

To soak up everything Canberra has to offer, book your accommodation right in the heart of the city. You'll be within walking distance of great bars and restaurants, plenty of shopping, and never far away from the top sights. Big name boutique hotels have recently moved into the city, with **QT Canberra** and **Ovolo Nishi** offering great places for your stay.

Get planning

Head to visitcanberra.com.au for everything you need to plan your visit to Canberra, and check out @visitcanberra on socials for all the best spots to pop into during your visit.

Can't-miss place
Great Ocean Road (*see* p.42)

Top experience
Hot-air balloon over Melbourne
(*see* p.36)

Important dates
Victoria has more festivals and events
than any other state across Australia,
with something new going on every
single month. Plan your trip to check
out some of the best events, including:

- Australian Open (Jan)
- Melbourne International Comedy
  Festival (March)
- AFL Grand Final Parade (Sept)
- Australian Moto Grand Prix (Oct)
- Spring Racing Carnival (Nov)

Time zone
Victoria follows the Australian Eastern
Time Zone (GMT +10), with daylight
savings time (GMT +11) in effect
between October and April each year.

Stay connected & get featured
Follow @visitmelbourne for all the
inspiration and best places to
visit in VIC, and have your Victoria
photos featured by using hashtags
#visitmelbourne or #visitvictoria.

Helpful websites
- National Parks
  parks.vic.gov.au
- Caravan parks
  vicparks.com.au
- Public transport
  ptv.vic.gov.au

Victoria

Although it is Australia's second-smallest state, Victoria is overflowing with places to explore and a whole range of diverse landscapes. With an epic coastline and one of the best drives in the world along the Great Ocean Road (*see* p.42), and the mountain range of Gariwerd (Grampians, *see* p.46), as well as rainforests, an abundance of native wildlife and the Murray River (*see* p.50), Australia's longest river, each region of Victoria offers something unique and different to anywhere else in Australia.

Victoria is also one of the best places in Australia to experience all the different seasons, with heatwaves in summer so you can hit the beach, autumn colour lining whole towns with pretty orange, yellow and pink trees, snowfall in the winter giving incredible skiing conditions (*see* p.54), and a whole calendar of festivals in the spring, to make the most of the warm weather rolling around again.

No matter where you decide to visit, you're sure to have a great time exploring Victoria. It might be one of the smallest states in the country, but it's still bigger than all of the United Kingdom, so there's plenty to see and discover.

MELBOURNE

The Traditional Owners of Naarm (Melbourne) are the Wurundjeri and Bunurong people of the Kulin Nation

FOODIES

Where do we even start with Melbourne? Our home city, full of beautiful architecture and historical buildings, narrow laneways filled with ever-changing street art, underground bars and fancy boutiques, expansive parks and the Yarra River running right through the middle. Things are always changing in Melbourne, there's always a new place to eat, a new show to see or new exhibits to explore.

The perfect destination for a weekend getaway, Melbourne is full of surprises. It's the home of world-famous coffee and some of the most incredible breakfasts you will find around Australia, living up to its reputation of avocado on everything. It's also the home of sports in Australia, with AFL, cricket, tennis, soccer and rugby games.

There's always something going on in Melbourne, something new to see or explore, with rooftop bars popping up all over the place, boutiques and cafes, festivals and riverside events throughout the seasons. No two weekends are ever the same in this city, so check the events calendar before you visit.

PLAN YOUR TRIP FOR

Our favourite time to head into the city is during the **Melbourne International Comedy Festival** which runs for almost a month across March and April each year.

Other great times to visit Melbourne are during the **Australian Open** (Jan), **Lunar New Year Festival** (Feb), **Moomba** (Labour Day long weekend in March) and the **Melbourne Cup Festival** (Nov).

CAN'T MISS

Take a **hot-air balloon ride over the city at sunrise**, as the sun begins to light up the city.

To get your bearings, jump on the free **City Circle Tram** and do a lap of the city. It will take you past some of the top attractions in Melbourne, including Federation Square, the Princess Theatre, Parliament House, Docklands, Melbourne Museum and the Melbourne Aquarium.

Check out the famous **Melbourne Street Art**, found in many of the tiny laneways in the city. Some of the most colourful laneways you'll ever find are **Hosier Lane** and **AC/DC Lane**.

Explore the laneways, full of hipster cafes, tiny boutiques, hidden bars and some of the best treasures in the city. Start with **Centre Place**, the **Block Arcade** and **Hardware Lane** and see where they take you.

Check out some of Melbourne's famous markets, like **Queen Victoria Market** and **South Melbourne Market**, both of which are always worth a visit. The **Night Noodle Market** (Nov) and **Winter Night Market** (Wednesday nights from June to Aug) are also a lot of fun.

Visit the **Shrine of Remembrance** next to the Royal Botanic Gardens along St Kilda Road, built to honour the men and women of Australia who served in World War I.

Have some fun at **Luna Park**, sitting right on the beach in the heart of St Kilda. Luna Park is over 100 years old, with a mixture of heritage-listed attractions and new thrill rides.

Head to the famous brightly coloured bathing boxes at **Brighton Beach**, each uniquely painted and providing a cute backdrop for your beach day.

Visit the **National Gallery of Victoria**, with changing international and local exhibitions throughout the year and some truly beautiful permanent displays.

Shop up a storm with some of the best shopping in Australia found in Melbourne. The shopping culture here has always been big, but in the last few years it has absolutely exploded, with the opening of **Emporium**, renovations to **Melbourne Central**, and tiny laneway shops popping up all over the city. Start at **Bourke Street Mall** for the department stores, head to **Collins Street** for designer boutiques, or jump on a tram to **Chapel Street** in South Yarra and Prahran for unique boutiques and hipster thrift shops.

Take a ride on the **Melbourne Star**, a replica of the London Eye which offers a different viewpoint of the city.

Grab a sunset cocktail at one of the floating bars and restaurants found along Southbank on the Yarra River. **Pony Fish Island** and **Riverland Bar** have the ultimate floating vibes.

Melbourne

Watch an AFL game at the iconic **Melbourne Cricket Ground (MCG)**. Head here for a night game during the season (March to Sept) to experience the footy and soak up the atmosphere, but rug up with a lot of layers as it can get quite cool at the 'G'.

Have a unique outdoor movie experience during the summer months at **Moonlight Cinema** (Jan to March) on the lawns of the Royal Botanic Gardens.

Grab dinner in **Chinatown**, for a cheap delicious meal with cuisines from all over Asia. Bring a group of friends and BYO drinks for a great night, and don't forget to try the dumplings.

BEST PHOTO SPOTS
Head to the **Eureka Skydeck**, the tallest building in Melbourne, for some of the best views over the city, stretching from Flinders Street all the way to the coastline. For an extra adrenaline kick, step into the Edge, where you will be standing over the city in a completely see-through box.

Street art in Hosier Lane
Opposite Melbourne's infamous Bourke Street
Previous Sunrise at the 12 Apostles, Port Campbell

Where
Melbourne is in the south of Victoria, sitting at the top of Port Phillip.

Getting here
Melbourne Tullamarine Airport (MEL) is the main airport, just 30 minutes from the city. The easiest way to get into the city is with SkyBus, a direct bus between Melbourne Airport and the city centre which operates 24/7. A SkyBus ticket starts at $15 per adult to the city, which is significantly cheaper than a taxi ride (you're looking at around $60 depending on traffic).

Getting around
If you're not leaving the main city of Melbourne, it's easy to get around everywhere on the train and tram systems. Free trams run in the city centre, taking you to almost all of the top highlights around the city, as well as connecting you to the major train stations and shopping centres. You will need to purchase a Myki card which can be bought at major train stations, convenience stores and newsagencies, and can be reloaded with money to use on the trains, trams and some buses.

When to go
The summer months (Dec to March) are definitely the best time to visit Melbourne, with daylight savings giving you long warm days and light evenings to explore. It's the ideal time to take advantage of the rooftop bars, outdoor beer gardens and summertime events.

Where to stay
You can find plenty of great places to stay scattered around Melbourne's central business district (CBD), which are all within close walking distance of restaurants, shopping and sights. Look for a place to stay around South Yarra or Prahran to put you in the heart of the hipster scene, with plenty of cool bars and clubs.

For the most unique stay, book in at **Notel**, where you can stay in a redesigned 1970s airstream trailer on the rooftop of a carpark. You can't get more Melbourne than that.

Need to know
Melbourne is famous for having four seasons in one day, so it's always a good idea to check the weather report and have a jacket with you, as you never know when the weather is going to suddenly change.

Get planning
To plan your visit, head to visitmelbourne.com or whatson.melbourne.vic.gov.au for a guide to all the upcoming events, and check out @visitmelbourne, @whatsonmelb and @cityofmelbourne for all the best spots around the city.

YARRA VALLEY & DANDENONG RANGES

Immerse yourself in nature and wine

FOODIES | NATURE LOVERS

Only a short drive out of Melbourne are two of Victoria's favourite weekend destinations, the Yarra Valley and Dandenong Ranges. Both equally unique and special destinations on their own, combine them for the ultimate weekend getaway, exploring soaring forests in the morning and sipping on delicious wines in the afternoon.

The Yarra Valley is Victoria's premier wine region, with more than 80 cellar doors to explore, offering delicious menus filled with produce from the local area, and beautiful views over the valley. It feels like each restaurant in the Yarra Valley is prettier than the last, with beautifully designed dining rooms overlooking endless rows of vines.

Just down the road, the Dandenong Ranges offers a completely different experience where you can immerse yourself in nature, with winding scenic drives taking you to tiny hilltop villages, incredible gardens to wander around and the iconic Puffing Billy Railway, one of the most well-preserved steam railways in the world.

Whether you choose just one to explore on your weekend, or road trip between both destinations, there's always something to see in the Yarra Valley and Dandenong Ranges.

PLAN YOUR TRIP FOR

Visit during September and October for the **Tesselaar Tulip Festival**, where you can wander through a rainbow of almost a million tulips in bloom. The festival goes for about a month each year, with lots of different events and celebrations on each of the weekends throughout the festival. It's so colourful and pretty, you'll think you've been transported to Holland.

CAN'T MISS
In the morning:

Start your morning with a **hot-air balloon** over the Yarra Valley for breathtaking scenery and 360-degree views over the valley and the vineyards. It's a great contrast to Melbourne's hot-air balloon views, with rolling hills, green landscapes and maybe even some kangaroo sightings. The valley views are so much prettier from the air.

Head to **The Piggery** in Sherbrooke for breakfast or lunch, found amongst the stables and piggery of the historic Burnham Beeches Estate. It's a great place in the summertime, with outside tables to soak up the sunshine, or meet up with a group of friends for a game of lawn bowls, croquet or bocce. We love the seasonally rotating menu that has plenty of fresh and healthy choices, created from the best Australian ingredients and local produce.

A favourite for kids and families is to jump onboard the iconic **Puffing Billy steam train** that winds its way through the forests and fern gullies of the Dandenong Ranges for 24 kilometres. The carriages are open on the side, so you can dangle your legs out the door as you take in the beautiful scenery. There are even special journeys which include lunch or dinner in enclosed first-class dining carriages, if you want a truly memorable experience.

Stock up on juicy fruit fresh from the source, with plenty of fruit picking farms around the Dandenong Ranges. Head to **Cherryhill Orchard** (late Nov to early Jan) to grab fresh cherries. It's also a beautiful spot to visit in spring (between late Sept and early Oct) when the cherry blossoms are in bloom. **Blue Hills Berries & Cherries** grow strawberries, raspberries, blueberries and cherries as they season throughout the year, but make sure you check the fruit repot before you go to see what's in season.

Take a stroll around **Alowyn Gardens** in the Yarra Valley, a beautiful garden with plenty of great spots for pictures, which is actually where my husband and I got married! Alowyn includes six very different garden areas, all extending from the magnificent 100-metre-long wisteria- and rose-covered arbour, a site to see all on its own.

Opposite Aerial views over TarraWarra Estate

The Dandenong Ranges is also home to a handful of cool-climate gardens, that are even prettier if you visit during spring and autumn. The **Alfred Nicholas Gardens** is home to beautiful waterfalls and water features, as well as an ornamental lake and picturesque boathouse. **William Ricketts Sanctuary** shares the message of Aboriginal philosophies, with more than 90 sculptures bringing together the connections between humans, nature and the earth.

In the afternoon:
Spend an afternoon hopping through the unique beautiful wineries of the Yarra Valley. Dating back to 1838, it's Victoria's oldest wine region and is home to some great cellar doors, as well as restaurants with incredible menus. **Zonzo Estate** is our personal favourite - great wines and delicious food, with stunning views over the vineyards and hilly countryside. Some of the other top wineries include **Stones of the Yarra Valley**, **Domaine Chandon**, **Yering Farm** and **TarraWarra Estate**.

Visit the **Yarra Valley Chocolaterie & Ice Creamery**, which combines striking architecture with unique food experiences, amongst iconic Yarra Valley views. The chocolaterie welcomes you with free entry, chocolate and ice-cream tastings, displays of thousands of premium chocolates and large viewing windows to watch the chocolatiers at work. What more could you ask for!

To taste test your way through more local produce, drop into the **Yarra Valley Dairy**, located in the original 100-year-old milking shed on the farm and known for producing award-winning fresh soft cheeses made in distinct Italian and French styles. You can enjoy free tastings of handmade cheese and locally produced wine, and grab yourself some of the delicious locally made jams and relishes.

Pop into **Healesville Sanctuary**, a bushland haven for Australian wildlife. The sanctuary is home to many iconic Australian animals and is a great place to meet koalas, kangaroos, platypuses, dingoes, wombats and emus. Healesville Sanctuary is also home to the **Australian Wildlife Centre**, a hospital which treats more than 2000 sick and injured native animals each year from around the area.

Check in for an afternoon of relaxation at the **Piaf Day Spa**. Sitting on a 10-acre rainforest, you can't beat the views from the spa's treatment rooms. Try a hot stone or aromatherapy massage, a custom facial, a full body cocoon, or a rejuvenating foot or hand massage that touches on all your pressure points, leaving you completely relaxed and ready for the week ahead.

In the evening:
Hit up some of the region's best distilleries and breweries to try some more of the Yarra Valley's best drinks. Head to **Four Pillars Distillery** to taste test your way through their popular gin paddles, or sign up to one of their gin or cocktail masterclasses. Check out **Coldstream Brewery** for beers and ciders brewed right in the Yarra Valley, and delicious pub meals for a great night out.

BEST PHOTO SPOTS

Visit **Alowyn Gardens** during October to see the Wisteria Arch blooming a beautiful purple colour. Although it's stunning at any time of the year, you can't go past a completely purple archway, with the light filtering through. Just around the corner, Zonzo Estate offers their tastings in a barn, with views overlooking the vineyards. You can't take a bad photo here, either!

Where
The Yarra Valley and Dandenong Ranges are located just an hour east of the city of Melbourne.

Getting here
The Yarra Valley and Dandenong Ranges are both only about an hour drive from Melbourne Airport (MEL).

Getting around
Pick up a rental car at the airport to give you the freedom to get around the region and zig-zag between the valley and the ranges for the ultimate weekend.

When to go
For the best weather, head to the Yarra Valley and Dandenong Ranges during summertime (Nov to March). It's the best season to enjoy a wine outside and take advantage of the warmer weather to explore more of the gardens and vineyards of the region.

Main towns
To make the most of your visit, base yourself in Healesville. Within just 20 minutes of both the Yarra Valley and Dandenong Ranges, it's the biggest town in the area and a great place to spend a weekend. There are lots of good accommodation options in Healesville, with hotels, caravan parks and cute Airbnbs dotted around the town.

Get planning
Head to visityarravalley.com.au and visitdandenongranges.com.au to plan your visit, and check out @yarravalleydandenongranges on Insta for all the best spots you can't miss.

Wander the stunning Alowyn Gardens
Opposite Don't miss a visit to Zonzo Estate's cellar door

GREAT OCEAN ROAD

One of the world's most scenic coastal drives

NATURE LOVERS

The Great Ocean Road is one of the best places for a weekend getaway, a spectacular stretch of coastline with beautiful beaches, holiday towns and nature walks. Whether you want to explore the whole coastline or take it at a more leisurely pace, there are just an endless amount of places to visit along Victoria's most scenic driving route.

Living in the western suburbs of Melbourne, the Great Ocean Road was always my go-to if I needed to get away. Only an hour down the road, with awesome surf beaches and an abundance of wildlife, it's one of my favourite places in the state.

Beginning in Torquay and winding all the way along the southern coast of Victoria to Allansford, the Great Ocean Road is more than 100 years old, celebrating its centenary birthday in 2019. The road was originally planned during World War I as a way to create jobs for returning soldiers, then built as a memorial of the war and loved ones who had not made it home.

The iconic drive is long and windy, and takes several hours to get from one end to the other, especially if you're stopping to explore along the way. A weekend is the ideal amount of time to dedicate to discovering this beautiful stretch of road, giving you plenty of time to visit the little towns along the way.

BEST PHOTO SPOTS

You can't go past **Teddy's Lookout** in Lorne at sunset for some of the most iconic views over the twists and turns of the Great Ocean Road, as well as Saint George River and the surrounding mountain ranges.

The winding Great Ocean Road from Teddy's Lookout, Lorne

CAN'T MISS

There are two ways to explore the Great Ocean Road. You can either choose to base yourself in one spot for the whole weekend, or explore the coast from town to town. To make the most of your visit, we recommend that you choose one end to start at and slowly make your way along the scenic drive. This way you can spend more time exploring and less time on the road, travelling to and from your base.

In the morning:

Start your morning in **Torquay**, with breakfast right on the beach at **Growlers**, and a quick look through the surf shop outlets at Surf City.

Take in the views from the clifftops overlooking the surf beaches of **Bells Beach** and **Jan Juc**, famous for their fantastic surf conditions and annual international surf competitions, like the Rip Curl Pro, held at Bells Beach each April. If you've never surfed before, you can take a lesson at **Go Ride A Wave Surf School**. They have locations all along the Great Ocean Road, with Torquay being one of their biggest branches.

Pop into the **Great Ocean Road Chocolaterie and Ice Creamery** for a sugary fix. With free entry, free chocolate and ice-cream tastings and a huge showroom full of chocolate to tempt you, you can't go wrong with a visit here.

Stop in at the Sunday **Anglesea Riverbank Market**, where more than 150 stalls selling beautiful handmade local goods descend on the bank of the river. The market is on at least one Sunday a month, but somewhat sporadically, so make sure you check when it's on.

Try your hand at a game of golf at the **Anglesea Golf Club**. Open seven days a week, the golf club is surrounded by beautiful bushland, and is home to hundreds of kangaroos. If golf isn't your thing you can also jump on a **Guided Kangaroo Tour** at the golf club, which run between 10am and 4pm for about 30 minutes, getting you close enough for the perfect candid kangaroo photo.

Stop at Fairhaven to snap a photo with the iconic wooden Great Ocean Road sign, that marks the beginning of the road.

Head to **Erskine Falls**, one of the most popular and impressive waterfalls along the Great Ocean Road, just a few minutes out of the town of Lorne. It's accessible by a steep flight of stairs and a careful walk over a rocky landscape, but the views are worth it, with the falls plunging 30 metres down into the lush tree-fern gully of the Erskine River.

Take a hike along the **Cumberland River Walk** to Jebb's Pool to take in more of the Great Ocean Road's bushland. The track is about 6 kilometres return, with lots of river crossings and climbing over rocks around the falls. **Sheoak Falls** and **Swallow Cave** is another popular waterfall spot, with an easy 1 kilometre walk from the carpark.

In the afternoon:

Grab a coffee from the **Wye River General Store** and then drive a little further on to visit the **Kennett River Koala Walk**, known for being one of the best places in Australia to see koalas in the wild. There are many large colonies of koalas here, so you're almost guaranteed a close sighting. The Koala Walk starts behind the Kennett River Caravan Park and continues around Grey River Road. You can walk or drive along the trail, just watch out for tourists that might wander in front of your car and keep an eye on the tops of the trees.

Apollo Bay is one of the best places to explore **Otway National Park** which actually stretches from Torquay all the way to Princetown. To immerse yourself in the rainforest, go to the **Otway Fly**, where you can take a treetop walk along the canopy walkway, which stands 30 metres off the ground. There's also a zipline tour which includes eight cloud stations and six flights around the treetops.

Head to the famous **12 Apostles** at either sunrise or sunset to visit one of the Great Ocean Road's most iconic attractions in the best light. There are only eight of the rock formations left these days, with several of them having eroded and crashed into the ocean. Walk down the **Gibson Steps** to get even closer to the Apostles, and really get an understanding for their immense size. Check at the visitors centre if the beach is open before you head down there, as it can be closed at different times of the year due to extreme winds and weather. While you're here, pop into **Loch Ard Gorge** just down the road, a beautiful secluded beach that has great views from the carpark above.

In the evening:

Spend an evening in Aireys Inlet, a sleepy coastal town between Anglesea and Lorne, that is home to the **Split Point Lighthouse**, made famous from the '90s kids show *Round The Twist*. The lighthouse was built in 1891 and is perched on the cliffs 70 metres above sea level. It's a great little beach to watch the sunset from, before heading into the **Aireys Pub** for a great meal and welcoming community vibe.

Sunrise at the 12 Apostles, Port Campbell
Opposite top Koala on the Kennett River Koala Walk
Opposite middle The Great Ocean Road cutting
through the green Otways
Opposite bottom The quiet beach at Loch Ard Gorge

Where
Located on the southern coast of Victoria, the start of the Great Ocean Road is about 103 kilometres out of the city of Melbourne, about an hour and 15-minute drive.

Getting here
Avalon Airport (AVV), followed by Melbourne Airport (MEL), are the closest options if you're flying into Victoria.

Getting around
If you're driving from Melbourne, take the Westgate Freeway onto the Princes Freeway, continue onto the Geelong Ring Road and follow the signs for Torquay and then for the Great Ocean Road.

The V/Line train service also connects Melbourne to either of the regional cities of Geelong or Warrnambool, stopping along the way in many of the hinterland towns which are connected by the local bus service.

When to go
The warmer months (Dec to March) are the best time to visit the Great Ocean Road, when the weather is warmer and you can take advantage of all the great beaches. Due to its coastal location and those southerly ocean winds, it's usually a bit cooler along the Great Ocean Road than it is in Melbourne.

Main towns
Along the Great Ocean Road, the main towns to stop in are Torquay, Anglesea, Lorne, Apollo Bay and Port Fairy, although you will also find shops and services in some of the smaller towns like Aireys Inlet.

Where to stay
Arguably the most popular destination along the Great Ocean Road, Lorne is a great place to base yourself. It's right in the heart of the action, about halfway along the twisting road, with lots of accommodation options, cute cafes and restaurants popping up all the time, boutique gift stores and one of the best beaches along the Great Ocean Road, right in the middle of it all.

Need to know
It might be one of the most scenic and beautiful drives in the world, but it can also be one of the most dangerous. The Great Ocean Road follows the coastline of Victoria while also winding in and out of rainforest and around coastal towns. The speed limit changes often along the road, due to the changing conditions, and frequent roadworks, so make sure you're always taking note of the road signs. These signs will also give you an idea of the type of bend that is ahead of you, so you can see if it's going to be a sharp turn or just a slight bend. If you're travelling slowly and taking in the scenery, be mindful to take advantage of the roadside pullouts so you can pull over and let faster drivers overtake you.

Always swim between the flags at patrolled surf beaches along the Great Ocean Road, as these beaches are open ocean. Rips in the ocean are very prevalent and if you're swimming in an unsafe area you could be swept into danger before you know it.

If you're hoping to spot wildlife, make sure you're out and about exploring early in the morning. This is when koalas and kangaroos are at their most active and often still hanging around near the beach or napping on lower lying tree branches.

Get planning
The main Great Ocean Road Visitors Centre is in Apollo Bay, but there are several smaller centres in towns along the way, including Port Campbell, Port Fairy, Portland, Torquay and Warrnambool. The visitor centre in Lorne also includes a small exhibition on the building of the Great Ocean Road.

Head to visitgreatoceanroad.org.au to plan your visit and follow @visitgreatoceanroad for all the best spots.

GARIWERD (GRAMPIANS)

Home to the best views in Victoria

NATURE LOVERS

A trip out to the mighty Gariwerd (Grampians) is another of Victoria's favourite weekend getaways. A stunning mountain range and forest that rises out of nowhere in the farmland of country Victoria, and offers spectacular hikes, beautiful views, an abundance of wildlife, Aboriginal history and art sites, and everything you need for a great long weekend.

The Djab Wurrung and Jardwadjali people have been connected to these mountains for more than 22,000 years. Dotted across Gariwerd, there are more than 60 rock art sites (five of which are open for you to visit) and 4000 motifs, sharing Dreaming and creation stories about the land.

A weekend in the mountains is the perfect way to immerse yourself in nature, disconnect from technology and deadlines and enjoy life at a slower pace. Whether you choose to camp amongst the wildlife or check into one of the unique Airbnbs, it's a weekend getaway that will leave you relaxed and recharged.

DAYTRIPS
From Gariwerd (Grampians) you can explore the famous **Silo Art Trail**, where beautiful colourful murals have been painted on silos across country Victoria. The 200-kilometre-long trail takes you through six small towns that now make up one of the country's biggest outdoor galleries. A daytrip along this trail will also give you plenty of time to explore the cute little towns along the way.

PLAN YOUR TRIP FOR
On the first weekend in May the **Grampians Grape Escape** takes over Halls Gap, a weekend wine and food festival that showcases the best local produce and live music from the region. More than 120 market stalls pop up across the village, as well as cooking demonstrations, live music, masterclasses and guest chefs.

Sunrise at The Balconies

CAN'T MISS

The best way to spend your time here is to get yourself into nature! Take a couple of hikes, check out the views from the breathtaking lookouts, and explore the many waterfalls scattered around the national park.

In the morning:
Head out early to catch the sunrise at **Reed Lookout** and **The Balconies.** The Balconies is one of our favourite spots in Gariwerd (Grampians), where you can really watch the mountains light up as the sun rises. It's a short and flat 2 kilometre walk from the carpark, keep an eye out for the local friendly fox who likes to roam around this area. Reed Lookout is accessible by wheelchair from the carpark and has great views across Victoria Valley, Serra Range and Mt Difficult Range.

Straight after sunrise, head out on **The Pinnacle Walk**, one of the main hikes that offers beautiful views across Halls Gap and the mountains throughout the whole trail. There are several different starting points, depending on how long you want to hike for. Starting from Sundial carpark is the easiest route (about 45 minutes, 2.1 kilometres), it gets a little tricker with more inclines if you leave from Wonderland carpark (about 90 minutes, 2.1 kilometres), or for the biggest challenge, you can leave from the Halls Gap Caravan Park and hike the whole trail (five hours, 9.6 kilometres).

Mt William is the highest point in the Grampians National Park and provides outstanding 360-degree views over the mountain range and open plains. The walk is quite steep and takes about 45 minutes, but is a must-do for anyone wanting to see the entire range from one lookout.

In the afternoon:
Visit one of Victoria's largest waterfalls, **MacKenzie Falls** which flows all year round, with fresh water tumbling over the huge cliffs and into the deep pool below. There's an easy 1 kilometre walking path to the viewing platform of the falls, or you can get up close and personal by taking the steep staircase right to the base of the falls (about 30 minutes one way). Some of the other great waterfalls in the park are **Silverbend Falls, Splitters Falls** and **Beehive Falls.**

Boroka Lookout can be found on Mt Difficult Road and is a great lookout in the afternoon, only a short stroll from the carpark. It has stunning panoramic views over Halls Gap and the eastern side of the ranges, with two lookout platforms offering views every which way.

Check out the **Aboriginal Art and Culture sites**, which are some of the oldest and most important Aboriginal sites in Victoria. Some of the most impressive rock art sites are **Bunjil's Shelter** to see Bunjil, the traditional creator of the land, and **Ngamadjidj's Shelter** to see Ngamadjidj's

spirit dancing with white figures on the walls. To learn more about these sites and the history they hold, you can either jump on a guided tour or visit the **Brambuk Aboriginal Cultural Centre and Visitors Information Centre**, where you can paint your own boomerang and watch insightful presentations on these ancient traditions.

Eat and drink your way around the region, with plenty of wineries to visit that are home to grape vines that date back more than 150 years. Jump on a **Grampians Wine Tour** to explore the nearby Great Western wine region and spend an afternoon taste testing some of the best wines and grazing platters in the area.

In the evening:
Head to the **Royal Mail Hotel** for dinner, which is regularly voted one of the best dining destinations, not just in Victoria, but in all of Australia! There are two restaurants here, with casual dining at Parker Street Project (Wed to Sat) and fine-dining at Wickens at Royal Mail Hotel (Thurs to Sat). Both take the farm-to-table concept to the next level, with an orchard, olive grove, chickens, sheep and cows right on the property.

Sunset at Lake Bellfield
Opposite Views over Gariwerd (Grampians) and country Victoria

BEST PHOTO SPOTS
You can't go past the **Balconies** and **Boroka Lookout** for some of the best easy-to-access views. Visit either at sunrise or during the golden hour to see the countryside and mountain ranges glow in the prettiest colours.

Where
Gariwerd (Grampians) is located just under three hours west from Melbourne, towards the border of South Australia.

Getting here
Fly into Melbourne Airport (MEL), pick up a rental car from the airport and then follow the Western Freeway from the Ring Road out through Ballarat - the whole drive takes just under three hours. You can also get to Gariwerd (Grampians) with public transport, although this does take longer (approximately 3 hours and 40 minutes, not including wait time). From Southern Cross Station in Melbourne, catch the V/Line train to Ballarat Station, switch to the V/Line bus that heads towards Stawell, and then from Stawell catch the Halls Gap Bus that will drop you right in the middle of town.

Getting around
Driving is definitely the easiest and most efficient way to explore the region, especially since travelling by car is really the only way to get to all the different lookouts, waterfalls and trails of the mountain ranges.

When to go
Autumn and spring are the most popular times to visit, when the weather is generally quite pleasant, while avoiding the extremes of summer heatwaves and heavy rain. To avoid the biggest crowds, it's always a good idea to not travel during the Victorian school holidays or public holiday long weekends, when Gariwerd (Grampians) is overflowing with visitors and accommodation often books out well in advance.

Main towns
Halls Gap is the best base for exploring the mountains, located just at the bottom of the mountain range, with a village that offers all the accommodation, dining and shopping options you need. Most of the hiking and driving trails start from Halls Gap, placing you literally in the heart of the action.

Need to know
Be extra careful when driving around dawn or dusk. The area is home to heaps of wildlife, and you can regularly spot kangaroos and deer walking around the town and crossing the roads as they please, so always keep your eyes peeled.

Get planning
To start planning your visit to Gariwerd (Grampians), head to visitgrampians.com.au and check out @thegrampians on social media for all the inspo.

MURRAY RIVER

Australia's longest river

NATURE LOVERS

Creating the border between Victoria and New South Wales (NSW) is the mighty Murray River. Measuring in as Australia's biggest river, the Murray crosses over three states, running 2530 kilometres from Mount Kosciuszko in NSW all the way to the Southern Ocean near Goowla in South Australia. Home to countless country towns, an abundance of native wildlife, great fishing, and plenty of free camping, it's a wonderful place to relax, unwind, and take a step back from big city life.

More than 60 million years old, and with Aboriginal history that dates back for at least 60,000 years, the Murray River is a very special place. It forms a major arm of the Murray-Darling Basin, which is the driest major water system in the world, is home to Australia's largest freshwater fish, the Murray Cod, and the world's largest River Red Gum forest grows along its banks. Boasting more sunny days than the Sunshine Coast in Queensland and beautiful warm weather all year round, what are you waiting for!

The Murray River is a great place to take your first weekend camping trip, where you can immerse yourself in nature, enjoy life at a slower pace and see a completely different side of country Victoria. There are lots of great places along the Murray to free camp, so it can be a super-cheap option for a weekend getaway. Get together a group of friends, find yourself a little beach along the riverbank, pitch your tent or roll out a swag and enjoy life off the grid for a couple of days.

Aerial view of the Murray River
winding across the country

CAN'T MISS

In the morning:

Take a step back in time at the historical **Port of Echuca**, a pioneer town on the banks of the Murray in Echuca that has been preserved since the 1860s. Here you can learn all about the history of Australia's inland river systems, the paddle steamers the town is famous for, and how they once connected the communities of the Murray River with the rest of the country.

Head to the **Echuca Farmers Market** on the first and third Saturday of the month (8am to 12pm) to sample some of the best local produce in the region, with many growers, producers and wine makers coming out to sell their goods. It's a great place to stock up on fresh food for the weekend.

For morning tea in Echuca, cruise down the mighty Murray River on the iconic **PS Emmylou**, where you can snack on delicious scones and jam as you slowly make your way down the river. There are actually a few paddle steamers that you can take a cruise on, including the **Pride of the Murray** and **PS Canberra**, with some even offering overnight packages for a complete experience.

Hit up the local **fishing spots**, wherever you're camping, and try and catch yourself a metre-long Murray Cod. They're rare and hard to catch, but they are definitely in there somewhere, a little bit of a creepy thought when you're going for a swim!

One of our favourite activities to do with a group of friends and family is buy some ridiculously oversized, colourful floaties - you know, swans, unicorns, sparkly donuts, the bigger the better - and enjoy an afternoon floating along the Murray River. Walk a while upstream from your campsite, jump in the water and then let the current float you back to camp. It's so relaxing on a warm summer's day, just make sure you wear lots of sunscreen.

Head to the **Pioneer Settlement** in Swan Hill where you can step back in time and experience the best of pioneer life, with old-fashioned cars, horse and carts and historical old stores. From the settlement, you can jump on a luxury cruise on the **PS Pyap** that will take you upstream past the historical Murray Downs Homestead.

Tick off another of Australia's 'big things' with a visit to the **Big Strawberry** just out of Tocumwal. Whether you want to pick your own strawberries or come to try their strawberry desserts, it will definitely be a very sweet visit!

In the afternoon:

You can't miss popping into **Cactus Country** near Strathmerton, one of our favourite spots along the Murray. This amazing garden is home to more than 4000 species of cacti and succulents from around the world, and is Australia's largest cactus collection. From the minute you walk through the door it feels like you've been transported to country Mexico. After working up an appetite exploring the gardens, grab yourself a frozen margarita and a plate of nachos to refuel - delicious!

Check out the epic **Lake Mulwala** just at the end of the main street in Yarrawonga. The bridge across the river takes you from Victoria to New South Wales, or vice versa, and both sides of the river offer a huge range of water activities to try, from water-skiing and jet-skiing to kayaking and boating. There are also lots of great pubs along the main street of Yarrawonga to grab some lunch when you need a break from the water.

Jump on a winery tour with **For The Love of Grape** in Echuca, where you can choose your own wineries and local speciality food producers to create a personalised tour of the region. It's a great way to explore, you don't have to worry about directions or organising anything and they can take you to all the best spots.

Take a stroll along the river on the **Chinaman's Island Walking Track** near Yarrawonga, which takes you on a 2 kilometre walk from the Yarrawonga Yacht Club carpark. It's a great way to see a little more of the river and bushland if you choose to stay in accommodation in town rather than camping along the river.

Explore the national parks that lie around Mildura, offering an abundance of wildlife, pink lakes, sand dunes and four-wheel drive tracks. The main parks are **Murray Sunset National Park**, and **Hattah-Kulkyne National Park**, only about 45 minutes out of town, where you can find sand dunes, multi-coloured lakes and plenty of wildlife.

In the evening:

Spend a night at the spectacular **Heartbeat of the Murray** show in Swan Hill, a dramatic laser and sound show that tells the epic story of the Murray River against the backdrop of a 9-metre-high water screen. The show starts each evening just after the sun has set (around 9.15pm) and everything comes to life under the bright stars of the night.

Murray River

Spend an afternoon at Cactus Country, Strathmerton

Where

The Murray River is at the very top of Victoria, creating the northern border with New South Wales.

Getting here

Depending on which part of the Murray River you're visiting, it can be anywhere from about two and a half hours to about six hours away from Melbourne. A couple of the closest towns to Melbourne include Echuca (2.5-hour drive) and Yarrawonga (3-hour drive). You can also fly directly to Mildura Airport (MQL) from Melbourne, Adelaide and Sydney on Qantas (from MEL and SYD) and Rex Airlines (from MEL and ADL) to visit some of the further parts of the Murray River region.

When to go

For any towns from Echuca to Albury Wodonga, the best time to visit is during the summertime and the shoulder seasons, when the weather is nice and hot and you can spend your days swimming, floating and water-skiing down the Murray. For the more rural locations, from Swan Hill over to Renmark, the summer is almost unbearably hot, with temperatures regularly hitting and staying over 40°C. Visit either during the spring or autumn for the best weather, when the more extreme temperatures have calmed down a little bit. No matter where you're planning to visit along the river, school holidays and Victorian long weekends are always absolutely crazy, with thousands of people flocking there to take advantage of the warmer weather. If you're planning to travel during this time, make sure you book ahead and get up there early.

Main towns

There are plenty of towns along the Murray River. From east to west, some of our favourites include Yarrawonga, Echuca, Cohuna, Swan Hill, Mildura and then Renmark across the South Australian border (*see* p.102 for more about the SA Riverland).

Where to stay

One of the biggest and most popular towns along the Murray River, Echuca is a great place to base yourself to explore lots of different spots along the river. It's a beautiful stretch of the river, with a town rich in great restaurants, historical architecture, music festivals and of course the iconic river vibe. There are hotels, motels, caravan parks and free camping spots along the river, as well as lots of holiday houses and cute Airbnbs to rent for your stay. Or to spend even more time on the water, rent a houseboat for the weekend to explore a little further and sleep on the river.

Need to know

If you are planning to free camp along the Murray River or even just come for an afternoon, always make sure you take every piece of your rubbish with you and leave your campsite exactly the way you found it. Do not leave any bits of toilet paper behind trees, it's just disgusting. It's important to protect the environment, and to keep the Murray River free and clean for everyone.

Get planning

To find out more about the Murray River region and plan your visit, head to murrayriver.com.au

MT HOTHAM & THE SNOWFIELDS

Victoria's ultimate winter wonderland

ADVENTURERS

As the highest alpine village in Australia, Hotham boasts tall snowy mountains, stunning views and a huge choice of ski runs to get your adrenaline pumping for a winter weekend. Whether you're a keen snowboarder or prefer to sit by a fireplace with a mulled wine and watch the action fly past the window, it's the perfect getaway to immerse yourself in the snow.

The only resort in the Southern Hemisphere where the village is located right on the top of the mountain, Hotham gives you the winter vibes that Aussies mostly just see in movies. It's where you put your skis on in the morning as you step out of your accommodation and ski to grab a coffee; where you can step in a soft patch of snow and sink right down to your knees; where the heaters are so warm and toasty in the bars that you'll end up wearing a T-shirt – even though it's snowing outside.

Hotham is the ultimate place to head for a weekend of winter sports, with unique and unforgettable experiences that will make even the biggest cold weather cynic fall in love with the snow.

Welcome to Mt Hotham
Opposite Views over the Mt Hotham snowfields

CAN'T MISS
In the morning:
If it's your first time to the snow, this is a no-brainer - book yourself in for a ski or snowboarding lesson with Hotham's **Ski and Ride School** before you attempt to hit the slopes. No matter how many kids under five glide past you on their skis, making it look exceptionally easy, don't be fooled. Skiing and snowboarding can be super hard (I'm terrible at it), especially if you're trying it for the first time; it's so much easier to get on top of if you take a lesson. You'll be zig-zagging across the black diamond runs before you know it.

Explore more of the mountains with a snowmobile ride with **SnowStuffPark**. Jump onboard for a scenic snowmobile ride across the mountains, from 10-minute to half-day tours, as well as toboggan hire, petrol-powered snowboards and kiddie snowmobiles for hire. We loved the 30 minute back-country sled tour, which takes you across Wire Plain, Davenport and Slatey Cutting Area.

In the afternoon:
Grab a seat near the fire for a cheese platter and mulled wine, a great way to spend the afternoon while the snow is falling. There are lots of places to eat around Hotham Village, with cute cafes and laid-back pubs to choose from, all of which will give you a warm toasty break from the chilly snow fields.

After a long morning of skiing, snowboarding and maybe falling over a few times, replenish your muscles at **The Onsen Retreat and Spa** at Dinner Plain. It has an outdoor pool that's heated to 40°C, which is lovely for soaking in after a long session on the slopes, as well as a whole menu of treatments with massages, facials, private baths, and mineral detoxes to choose from.

Slide through the snowy back country on a sled dog tour, run by a remarkable team of Siberian Huskies. You can find the **Howling Husky** team behind the Wire Plain hut, and there are a few different options to choose from, starting from 45 minutes.

Enjoy the drive down **Great Alpine Road**, one of the most scenic drives in Victoria which stretches from Wangaratta over the mountains and Hotham Heights and down to Omeo on the other side. This windy road offers you some beautiful

views of the mountain tops, snow-covered trees and just all-round epic views as you make your way to the alpine village right at the very top.

Give yourself plenty of time to stop and admire the views of the Hotham mountains. I can't even tell you how many times I asked Thom to pull over so I could take more photos. Some spots can be particularly cold and windy when you get out of the car, so make sure you always have a beanie and a big coat close by to grab as you're getting out.

In the evening:
For the most unbelievable experience, spend the evening with **Alpine Nature Experience** on their **Snowshoe to Fondue** experience (*see* p.58). Take a scenic snowshoe walk through the snow to a stunning little eco-village for a night of mulled wine by the bonfire and a three-course dinner made up of French cheese fondue. After dinner, it's a short snowshoe walk back to Wire Plain, under a beautiful view of the stars and the night sky.

Experience the mountains like never before, with **night skiing and snowboarding** sessions every Saturday and Wednesday night during the snow season. Ski your heart out under the stars with slopes open at the Big D and Dinner Plain.

DAYTRIPS
Victoria actually has five alpine resorts dotted around the mountains. If one weekend in the snow isn't enough, here's some of Victoria's other favourite mountains:

Mt Buller: Only a 3-hour drive from Melbourne or Mt Hotham, Mt Buller is a favourite for a daytrip from Melbourne. It's a great place to learn the basics if you've never tried skiing or snowboarding before, but it also has plenty of black diamond runs for the skiing pros.

Falls Creek: About a 4.5-hour drive from Melbourne or 2 hours from Mt Hotham, Falls Creek is Victoria's largest alpine resort and is the go-to for cross-country skiers. One of the best things about Falls Creek is that it closes its roads to cars, giving you the ultimate ski-in, ski-out experience, so you can get around without even taking your skis off.

Mt Baw Baw: One of the smaller mountains, Mt Baw Baw is only a 2.5-hour drive from Melbourne (4.5 hours from Mt Hotham), and is a great place for beginners and intermediate skiers. It's also the perfect destination if you don't care about skiing, and just want to enjoy some time in the snow.

Where

Mt Hotham is in the Victorians Alps of the Great Dividing Range.

Getting here

Sitting along Great Alpine Road, Hotham is accessible from Harrietville and Omeo. Fly into Melbourne Airport (MEL) and pick up a rental car from the airport. It's about a 4.5-hour drive from Melbourne, by taking the Hume Highway to Wangaratta and then the Great Alpine Road directly to Hotham, or the Snow Road if you want to go through the pretty towns of Myrtleford, Bright and Harrietville.

Getting around

Hotham Alpine Village offers a free shuttle bus to effortlessly get you around the mountain. There are bus stops located all over the mountain, including at most of the main carparks and ski lifts. The bus service generally operates in winter from 6.45am until 1.45am daily, but may finish earlier in the shoulder seasons. The Dinner Plain Bus Service also runs between Mt Hotham and Dinner Plain, for easy access for those not staying right in the village.

When to go

The ski season at Mt Hotham generally runs from the beginning of June until the end of September, depending on the snow conditions.

Where to stay

If you stay right in Hotham Village, it's the ultimate ski experience, where you can ski-in and ski-out from your front door, straight onto the slopes! There's a whole range of options available for all kinds of budgets, from backpacker hostels and communal lodges, to luxury retreats and holiday houses big enough to fit a whole group. For a little bit more of a relaxed experience, Dinner Plain offers all sorts of accommodation options, including house and apartment rentals for groups. Dinner Plain is only about 10 minutes from Hotham Village, and is still completely covered in snow for that winter wonderland vibe.

Need to know

Any vehicles stopping in Hotham Alpine Resort are required to purchase a resort entry pass. Day, multi-day and season passes are available, with rates starting at $50 per vehicle. Resort entry is complimentary between 3pm and midnight on the day of your arrival - so if you arrive after 3pm on a Friday for a weekend trip, you'll only need to pay resort entry for two days!

If your car runs on diesel, you need to make sure you fill up with alpine diesel before you start to head up the mountains. This is important for any alpine region in Victoria, not just Mt Hotham. Regular diesel that you fill your car with in the city or around any coastal or country areas have different cold temperature properties than alpine diesel, and can freeze around your engine when your car is left outside for several hours or overnight in alpine regions. If this happens, your car will literally freeze like a block of ice on the inside and it won't start again until the diesel has melted.

Get planning

Head to mthotham.com.au for everything you need to plan your visit to the snow, or check out @hothamalpineresort for all the inspo.

Camping in the snow at Alpine Nature Experience
Opposite top Views over the Mount Hotham snowfields
Opposite bottom Snowshoe walk through the snow

Alpine Nature Experience

The Alpine Nature Experience is, without a doubt, a night that will stay with your forever. A sleepover in the snow, complete with mulled wine, cheese fondue and good conversation over a roaring fire makes for a winter wonderland.

Nestled amongst the snow gum trees in the wilderness of Mt Hotham (*see* p.54), you can find the little eco-village that is home to this unforgettable nature experience. Carefully designed and created by Jean-François Rupp, the Alpine Nature Experience is unlike anything else you will find at the snow. It's an evening of mulled wine, cheese fondue, making friends, sharing stories, and watching the stars from your bed in your cosy snow-dome tent.

The first part of the evening is called Snowshoe to Fondue, and includes a leisurely walk through the snow to the Nature Experience's eco-village in a pair of snowshoes. You arrive at the eco-village around sunset, where you'll be greeted with a roaring warm fire and a cute little bar serving delicious mulled wine. It's the ultimate winter wonderland, with a thick layer of snow coating the ground, the trees and everything around you, as you enjoy your drink in the snow fire-pit, swapping stories with the rest of the group.

When it starts to get too cold, you'll move into the main tee-pee where a roaring Coonara fireplace keeps everyone warm for the night. To prepare for dinner, Jean-François gives you a short cooking class to learn how to make the perfect French fondue. The food is simply delicious, with homemade pumpkin soup from the local Harrietville Bakery, cake for dessert, a traditional French shot of liqueur and many wines.

As dinner comes to an end, and everyone is absolutely full of wine and cheese, head to your cute snow-dome tent and settle in for the night. Each snow-dome has a woodfire heater inside as well, which was lit for us before we arrived so our dome was already lovely and warm. The snow-domes also have a clear roof, so if you have a clear night you can see the stars and the night sky from your cosy bed. Temperatures might be in the minuses outside, but the beds are so warm and cosy that you don't even feel a breeze for the whole night.

Wake up for the sunrise in the morning, before breakfast in the tee-pee and a snowmobile ride back to the village where your experience ends. It's truly such a magical way to experience the Victorian snowfields.

IMPORTANT INFO

The Alpine Nature Experience evenings run in winter from Wednesday to Sunday, starting at about 4.30pm in June and July and 5pm in August and September. You return back to Wire Plain around 10.30am the following morning.

Your experience includes the guided snowshoe walk through the snow, a glass of mulled wine on arrival, the three-course dinner including a French cheese fondue cooking class, overnight accommodation in the snow-domes, all bedding (including a -10°C sleeping bag and cosy fur blankets), a cooked breakfast in the morning, hot drinks and a scenic ski-mobile tour back to Wire Plain.

The eco-village is completely off-grid, a great place to disconnect from the rest of the world, but they have catered for everything you might need. The power in the snow-domes works off batteries, so while it's a little limited, there's still definitely enough to charge your phone. There's 4G phone reception, credit card facilities to pay for any extra drinks you might have in the tee-pee, as well as dry toilets.

MORNINGTON PENINSULA

The prettiest beaches in the bay

FOODIES | NATURE LOVERS

The Mornington Peninsula, sitting at the edge of Port Phillip, is one of Melbourne's most popular spots for a quick beachside getaway. Home to some of the prettiest beaches in the bay, with cute colourful bathing boxes lining the shoreline and crystal clear sparkly water, it's a great place to explore on a weekend getaway.

The peninsula is dotted with sleepy beachfront towns, from Mount Eliza around to Portsea, that boast boutique shops, art galleries, more cellar doors than you can visit in a weekend, and of course the famous natural hot-springs, offering all kinds of wellness experiences and spa treatments. There is no shortage of great places to have dinner on the Mornington Peninsula, which kind of feels like an extension of Melbourne when it comes to the food scene. There are all kinds of restaurants scattered around the peninsula with cuisines from around the world, served in unique and wonderful places.

As a bonus, as well as the calm blue beaches of the bay, many of the little towns also have a back beach which faces out towards the ocean. Lots of the back beaches are full of rockpools and hidden caves to explore, as well as having great surf breaks to catch a wave on. The peninsula is the ultimate weekend getaway for anyone who loves the water.

PLAN YOUR TRIP FOR

For quite a different weekend, plan your visit to the Mornington Peninsula in January and grab yourself a ticket to the **Portsea Polo**. Get dressed up and feel like a royal at the polo, surrounded by Aussie celebrities and TV personalities, fancy marquees, great food and wine and a warm summer's day to top everything off. Bring a group of friends, sip on a frozé, and strike up a conversation with someone famous.

The rockpools at Sorrento Back Beach

CAN'T MISS

In the morning:

Start your morning with breakfast at one of the many cute cafes around the Mornington Peninsula. No matter where you're staying, there's always a great place nearby, with some of our favourites including **Commonfolk Coffee** in Mornington, **Merchant & Maker** in McCrae and **Georgie Bass Café & Cookery** in Flinders.

Spend your morning completely immersing yourself in the natural thermal pools of **Peninsula Hot Springs**. With private pools and larger bathing areas, the hot-springs are lovely to visit at any time of the year, with all kinds of treatments and experiences on the menu to leave you feeling completely relaxed and renewed. Try a Turkish steam bath, an underground sauna, or a hilltop pool with amazing views over the entire Mornington Peninsula region. It's just magical. To take the pampering one step further, pop into the Spa Dreaming Centre, where you can get a facial, massage or exfoliating scrub to really leave feeling like a new person.

Head to **Sorrento Back Beach** early in the morning to explore the many rockpools that dot the shoreline before the crowds arrive. Take a walk around the rocky cliffs and you can often find you have a rockpool all to yourself, full of starfish, crabs and all kinds of pretty shells. Just down the road from Sorrento Back Beach, **Diamond Bay** is a much less-known favourite, giving you a piece of European paradise right here in Melbourne with white cliffs surrounding a rocky beach with bright turquoise water. It's a great beach if you're looking for a surf break and has some good waves without the crowds, as it faces out to the ocean instead of into the bay. The back beaches are unpatrolled and often have dangerous rips in the water.

In the afternoon:

Pay a visit to the **Red Hill Cherry Farm**, Victoria's oldest cherry farm, where you can pick your own delicious cherries (between mid-Nov and early Jan). The cherry farm is great for those Insta shots, with trees that are maintained at the perfect height for picking.

There are so many incredible wineries on the Mornington Peninsula, with more than 50 cellar doors to choose from. **Montalto Vineyard and Olive Grove** is one of our favourites and a beautiful spot to stop at, with views overlooking the rolling hills covered in vineyards as you lunch on woodfired pizza and taste test the wines. A few of the other great wineries to add to your must-see list are **Pt Leo Estate**, **Jackalope** and **Paringa Estate**.

Spend an afternoon enjoying the sun at the **Mount Martha Pillars**. A hidden beach spot that definitely gives you all the vibes of Europe, only an hour out of Melbourne CBD. Follow the tiny path from the road along the edge of the cliffs and down to the rocky beach for a spot unlike any other in Victoria.

Hike out to Cape Schanck and visit the **Cape Schanck Lighthouse** which has been standing tall over the ocean since 1859, the second lighthouse ever to be built in Victoria. There is a great viewing platform in the lighthouse with views across the Cape, and daily guided tours between 10am and 4pm. While you're here, don't miss the nearby town of **Flinders**, a pretty town with boutiques and eateries, an historical general store that's worth a visit, and one of our fave cafes on the peninsula, **Georgie Bass Café & Cookery**.

Right at the end of the bay is **Point Nepean**, the infamous Tip Of The Bay in Mornington Peninsula National Park. After more than 100 years of the national park being closed to the public, you can now visit and explore the history that lies here and dates back to the 1880s. If you're in the mood for deeper exploration and a bit of a history lesson, **Fort Nepean** at the very very last point of the bay is where you can find a preserved 18th-century fortress, complete with tunnels, World War II battlements and other military defence displays.

In the evening:

Take a ride on **Arthurs Seat Eagle** chairlift at sunset for the best views over the Mornington Peninsula in your own private gondola, combined with the added delight of happy hour! On Saturday nights the Eagle offers an extra package at sunset, where you can watch the view change colours while snacking on a grazing platter with a glass of sparkling wine.

Head to **Morgan's Beach Shack** in Sorrento for Mexican and burgers, **Red Gum BBQ** in Red Hill for South American barbeque, **DOC Pizza and Mozzarella Bar** in Mornington for delicious Italian dishes, and the iconic **Hotel Sorrento** in the town of the same name for a delicious pub meal.

BEST PHOTO SPOTS

You can't go past the bright colourful **bathing boxes** that line many of the beaches around the Mornington Peninsula. You can find them at Mount Martha, Dromana, Rosebud and Portsea, but they're all completely unique, so make sure you find your favourite before snapping a photo.

Top Sunrise at Sorrento Back Beach
Middle Bathing boxes can be found at lots of beaches along the Mornington Peninsula
Bottom Mount Martha Pillars

Where

The Mornington Peninsula is along the coastline of Victoria, at the end of Port Phillip.

Getting here

Book your flight into Melbourne Airport (MEL) and grab a rental car when you arrive at the airport. It's just over an hour's drive from the airport to the Mornington Peninsula, with freeways linking you the whole way. There are toll roads on the way to the peninsula though, so it's a good idea to ask your car rental company how they charge for tolls to avoid any unnecessary processing fees.

When to go

Make the most of the region by heading to the Mornington Peninsula around the warmer months of the year (Nov to March). With long hot days in the summertime, you can really make the most of the beautiful beaches and rockpools to hop around, although you will need to book accommodation and some dining in advance as it can get very busy during this time.

Main towns

There are plenty of towns along the peninsula, including Sorrento, Portsea, Mount Martha, Mornington, Mount Eliza, Dromana, Rye and Rosebud, just to name a few. Each little town has its own unique style, often a couple of different beaches and everything you need for a great weekend away.

Where to stay

Base yourself near Ocean Beach Road, the main street in Sorrento, to really soak up the Mornington Peninsula's vibe. One of the oldest seaside communities in Melbourne, there's an instant holiday feel in Sorrento, with an unmatched authentic charm. You'll be only a short walk from some of the prettiest beaches, close to great restaurants and cafes, plenty of great chain and independent stores, galleries filled with artwork from local Australian artists, and wellness centres so you can try the latest treatments.

If you're camping or caravanning, Mornington Peninsula Shire offers designated campsites right along the beach, which means you can wake up to the ocean on your doorstep. The campsites are all centrally located, close to local shops, cafes and walking trails and have shower and toilet blocks. For casual camping, you can fill out the Book A Campsite form on the Mornington Peninsula Shire website (mornpen. vic.gov.au/Activities/Camping/Book-a-campsite) with powered and non-powered sites available.

Get planning

To plan your visit, head to visitmorningtonpeninsula.org and check out @officialmorningtonpeninsula for all the best spots.

PHILLIP ISLAND

Home to the famous Penguin Parade

NATURE LOVERS

Phillip Island isn't really one of Victoria's hidden gems – it's pretty popular with families and visitors to the state but it might just be one of Victoria's most underrated places. While it is only a small island, taking no more than 25 minutes to drive from one side to the other, it's overflowing with activities, experiences and fun things to do that will keep you entertained for the whole weekend.

Home to an insane abundance of wildlife, visitors flock here to see the fairy penguins waddling in from the beach at dusk, koalas lazily snoozing in gum trees, fur seals playing together in the ocean, as well as stingrays, kangaroos, pelicans and more. There's wild hiking trails around the coastline, with stunning views over the rugged cliff-faces, heritage farms that give you a glimpse into a lost way of life, and chocolate treats that will keep you on a sugar high for days.

Whether you're coming to relax or to immerse yourself in nature, Phillip Island is a great weekend destination to escape the hustle and bustle of the city.

Cowes Main Beach
Opposite Sunrise at Cape Woolamai by Dean Faulkner

CAN'T MISS
In the morning:
Head out early to hike to **The Pinnacles** at Cape Woolamai for sunrise. The walking trail for The Pinnacles begins in The Surf Life Saving carpark, and is about 2 kilometres long. Once you get to the lookout, follow the small path down to Boulder Beach for some of the most beautiful views over this rocky coastline. It is pretty spectacular, especially at sunrise or sunset, with the whole world glowing golden. **Cape Woolamai** is also a fantastic surf beach, with some of the best breaks on the coastline. Bring your board or sign up for a surf lesson to take advantage of these ideal conditions.

Take a walk around the tree-top boardwalks at the **Koala Conservation Centre** to see Australia's most-loved furry creature in its natural habitat. Since koalas are often curled up in the tallest branches of gum trees, the boardwalks get you close to the koalas in this beautiful wetland setting.

Learn more about Antarctica at **Nobbies Ocean Discovery**, which plunges you into the world of the Southern Ocean and Antarctica through a number of interactive and immersive experiences. Feel the freeze in the Antarctic Chill Zone, check out thermal imaging, explore the Sound Lab and Research Station to learn more about the sights and sounds of Antarctic wildlife, and throw yourself right into the heart of the action with a spectacular multimedia experience.

Step back in time with a visit to **Churchill Island Heritage Farm**, an important site in Victorian history which is recognised as the site of the first agricultural pursuits in Victoria. Since the 1850s, Churchill Island has been continuously farmed with all kinds of local produce. You can experience the way life used to be, with cow milking, sheep shearing, whip cracking and wagon rides. You can also just walk around the farm and meet some of the local highland cattle, Clydesdale horses and baby animals.

In the afternoon:
Head to **San Remo Pier** at 12 noon each day to watch the pelican feeding. There's lots of different wildlife around the pier as well, so you might even be able to spot some stingrays along the shoreline.

Eat and drink your way across Phillip Island, with fresh seafood and local produce served up at some of the best foodie hot spots. Head to **Phillip Island Winery** or **Purple**

Hens Wines to try their signature cool-climate wines, or to Ocean Reach Brewing for local tap beers with a lunch menu to match. Grab a meal overlooking the ocean at The Cape Kitchen or Saltwater Phillip Island, and head to BEANd Roastery for an early morning coffee fix.

Meet the local wildlife on an EcoBoat Adventure Tour, where you can get up close and personal with Phillip Island's own colony of fur seals, playing with each other and swimming around off the shore. This 90-minute boat ride will take you along the beautiful coastline, before pulling into a secluded inlet to get a closer look at the seals that live here. The tour also takes you to see the Nobbies sea-cave which is only visible from the water, and the Cat Bay National Surfing Reserve famous for its longboard break.

Try a little bit of everything at Panny's Amazing World of Chocolate. With endless entertainment, attractions and free samples, the chocolate factory has created a series of experiences dedicated to sharing the story of chocolate, with the world's largest chocolate waterfall, a chocolate carving machine and the one tonne chocolate challenger. You're sure to roll out in a chocolate coma.

Take your kids or indulge your inner child with an afternoon at A Maze'N Things, home to astounding illusions, insane puzzles, maxi mini golf and their signature giant 3D maze. Confuse yourself in the Magic Manor, get shrunk down to be super tiny on Puzzle Island, or see if you can make your way out of the giant maze.

Get your adrenaline pumping at the Phillip Island Grand Prix Circuit, home to some huge motor racing events each year, including the Australian Motorcycle Grand Prix (Oct), the Superbike World Championship (Feb) and the V8 Supercar Series. Get into the action by taking a speedy drive around the track with a real race car driver, or for something a little calmer, you can drive a go-kart around a smaller replica of the circuit.

In the evening:
Head to the Penguin Parade, that takes place every night at dusk, for the chance to see the cute little penguins waddling out from the ocean and back to their nests on the shore. The Penguin Discovery Centre has built a fantastic boardwalk so that you can watch the penguins finding their nests, feeding their babies and interacting with each other on the shore. The penguins start to emerge from the ocean at sunset each evening, and access to the viewing areas opens about an hour before the estimated penguin arrival time.

Where
Phillip Island sits along the southern coastline of Victoria, connected to the mainland by Phillip Island Road.

Getting here
It's a 2-hour drive from Melbourne Airport (MEL). Pick up a rental car from the airport and then take the Monash Freeway out of Melbourne, before heading along the South Gippsland Highway until you hit the Bass Highway. Follow all the road signs that lead to Phillip Island and you can't miss it.

When to go
Head to Phillip Island during the summer months (Dec to March) to take advantage of the warmer weather and the longer days, thanks to daylight savings. Like anywhere around the southern coast of Victoria, the weather on Phillip Island can be quite temperamental, as well as a bit colder than in the city. Bring a jacket and some warmer clothes options for your visit, especially for the Penguin Parade and going out in the evening.

Main towns
The very cute main town of Cowes is the hub of Phillip Island. Here you can find everything you might need for your stay, including the Visitors Centre, grocery store and petrol station. The main street of Thompson Avenue has all the local restaurants, bars and cafes, with plenty of different options to choose from offering you cuisine from around the world. There are also lots of surf shops and boutique gift shops, so you can shop up a storm during your visit.

Where to stay
There are lots of accommodation options right in the heart of Cowes, with caravan parks that lead right onto the beach, cute holiday houses and Airbnbs for groups and large families, and hotels right on the main street.

Get planning
To plan a visit to Phillip Island, head to visitphillipisland.com.au and check out @phillipisland on socials for all the best spots.

GIPPSLAND

Home to the longest beach in the
Southern Hemisphere

NATURE LOVERS

One of Victoria's largest regions, Gippsland stretches all the way eastwards from Western Port Bay, to the border of New South Wales along the East Coast. This huge region is often overlooked by visitors for some of Victoria's more famous regions, but there is so much to explore and discover here. From beautiful beaches, to some of the state's best snowfields in winter, there is a huge amount of different landscapes to experience. Gippsland is full of vineyards and wineries, all kinds of farms and dairies, national parks and quiet little beach towns.

Gippsland is actually broken down into four distinct regions, known as East, West, South and Central Gippsland. It covers an area of 41,566 square kilometres and is home to 14 national parks and more than 20 per cent of Australia's milk production. It's an enormous area by any measure! Get off the beaten path for the ultimate weekend getaway, with so many great places to visit, especially along the East Coast.

At the southernmost tip of Australia's mainland you will also find Wilsons Promontory, home to thick bushland, huge granite mountains and lots of native Aussie wildlife, surrounded by stunning coastlines full of white sand beaches. It's a great place to disconnect from the world for a few days, with multi-day hikes to the untouched side of the island, with completely deserted beaches at the end of the trail.

Sunset at Jemmys Point Lookout,
Lakes Entrance

CAN'T MISS

In the morning:

Head to **Ninety Mile Beach**, one of the longest beaches in the Southern Hemisphere, that stretches from Port Albert all the way to Lakes Entrance. Along its ninety miles, you can discover beautiful golden shores, coastal sand dunes and great surf waves crashing in from the ocean. It's a great place to relax and unwind on your weekend getaway, where you can walk, swim or fish, or even spot whales, dolphins and pelicans right from the shore. Ninety Mile Beach is predominately a surf beach though, so make sure you swim between the flags at Seaspray, Woodside Beach and Lakes Entrance where life guards are on patrol during the summer months.

Explore the **Gippsland Lakes** by renting a boat in Metung or Paynesville and hopping your way along some of the waterside cafes that line the lakes. The three lakes that make up the Gippsland Lakes are Lake Victoria, King Lake and Lake Wellington, which are fed by rivers that begin in the High Country and cover more than 600 square kilometres with a network of lakes, marshes and lagoons. You can also take a ferry to **Raymond Island** (free for pedestrians) to see its local koala colony, or across to **Rotamah Island,** home to heaps of kangaroos and wallabies.

Pop into **Mallacoota**, right at the very top of the pointy part of Gippsland, which is bouncing back after being decimated by some of the harshest bushfires in history at the beginning of 2020. This pretty little town is found on Mallacoota Inlet and is right next to Croajingolong National Park. It's a sleepy little town, with an airy beach vibe and is a great place to spend some hours outdoors. Get up close to a family of local kangaroos at Gipsy Point, take a dip in the popular Betka Beach, or hire a boat, canoe or kayak from Gipsy Point Lodge and hit the Genoa River.

In the afternoon:

Lakes Entrance is known as the seafood capital of Victoria, due to the large number of fishing trawlers that operate in the area, and is a great place to try some of the local seafood. You can even catch your own fish for the freshest seafood experience. Lakes Entrance is also home to Australia's largest inland network of waterways, is where the Gippsland Lakes meets the Southern Ocean, and is full of accommodation options, dining choices and aqua experiences to get you trying something new.

Wind your way along the **Gippsland Food & Wine Trail**, which offers some of the best culinary experiences from Port Albert to Mallacoota. Taking you through the East, West and Southern regions of Gippsland, the trail includes all kinds of cafes and restaurants, cellar doors and breweries, offering award-winning wines, delicious farm-fresh cheeses, craft beers and gins and menus overflowing with all kinds of local produce. Some of the highlights include **Narkoojee Winery, Prom Country Cheese, Lightfood & Sons, Tinamba Hotel, Loch Brewery & Distillery** and **Toms Cap Vineyard Retreat**.

Croajingolong National Park is about a 7-hour drive from Melbourne and one of the lesser-known national parks in Victoria, but it is an absolute playground for people who like the outdoors. It is one of Victoria's largest parks and is home to secluded white sand beaches, thriving rainforests, more than 300 bird species and some pretty spectacular fishing. If you're visiting for the first time, some of the best experiences include sleeping under the stars at a beach campsite, the epic views from the **Wilderness Coastal Walk**, and whale-watching from the Gabo Island Lighthouse or Point Hick Lighthouse in the park.

DAYTRIPS

Give yourself at least a day to explore **Wilsons Promontory National Park**, one of the most popular and favourite places to visit in Gippsland. Wilsons Prom is Victoria's largest coastal wilderness area, covering more than 50,000 hectares. The whole park is overflowing with walking trails, white sand beaches, eucalyptus forests and an abundance of native wildlife. Much of the park is only accessible by hiking, with some of the best and most beautiful beaches reserved for those who are willing to put in the most effort to visit them. While you're here, make sure you go to Squeaky Beach, Lilly Pilly Gully and Tidal River, and you can even catch an outdoor movie in Tidal River on Wednesdays and Sundays during the summer months.

Sand dunes on the beach in Wilsons Promontory National Park
Opposite Koalas are often spotted in Gippsland

Where

Gippsland lies along the whole east coast of Victoria, from Wilsons Promontory in the south all the way around to Mallacoota at the NSW border.

Getting here

Depending on where you're planning to visit in Gippsland will really impact the travel time and the best way to get there, with the closest locations starting about three hours away from Melbourne by car. Wilsons Promontory National Park, one of the most popular highlights of Gippsland, is about a 3-hour drive from Melbourne, or it's about a 4-hour drive to get to the coastal town of Lakes Entrance.

Getting around

Gippsland is fairly easy to navigate, with long flat roads and plenty of signage for exits, upcoming towns and attractions and highlights in the region.

When to go

During the summer months (Dec to March), is generally the best time to visit Gippsland, when the sun is out and the days are long and hot. Gippsland weather is generally a few degrees cooler than the nearby inland areas, being closer to the coast and the ocean winds. Keep in mind that the summer months are also the busiest time to visit, with families flocking to Gippsland during the school holidays. If you're visiting during this time, make sure you book in advance to avoid missing out on accommodation.

Where to stay

Lakes Entrance is a great place to base yourself in Gippsland, with plenty of choices for accommodation, cafes and restaurants and activities, as well as being a central location to explore a lot more of the Gippsland region. **The Esplanade Resort & Spa** is our favourite in Lakes Entrance, with hotel rooms, as well as self-contained apartments, a day spa, and an awesome lagoon pool that's perfect to come back to after a day of exploring.

Get planning

To plan your visit to Gippsland, head to visitgippsland.com.au and check out @visitgippsland for all the best spots along the way.

Can't-miss place
Kangaroo Island (*see* p.80).

Top experience
Swimming with sea lions and great white sharks in Port Lincoln (*see* p.84).

National Parks Pass
A multi-park pass gives you access to all the national parks in SA for $44 for two months or $99 for 12 months. It gives unlimited vehicle entry into Belair National Park, Bool Lagoon Game Reserve, Coffin Bay National Park, Deep Creek Conservation Park, Ikara-Flinders Ranges National Park, Gawler Ranges National Park, Innes National Park, Lincoln National Park (including Memory Cove Wilderness Protection Area), Mount Remarkable National Park, Ngarkat Conservation Park and Para Wirra Conservation Park.

Important dates
To make the most of your visit to SA, some of the top events include:

- Adelaide Fringe Festival (mid-Feb to mid-March)
- Adelaide Cup (second Monday of March)

Time zone
South Australia follows the Central Australian Time Zone (GMT + 9.30), with daylight savings time (GMT + 10.30) in effect between Oct and April each year.

Stay connected & get featured
Follow @southaustralia for all the inspiration and best places to visit, and have your SA photos featured by using hashtags #southaustralia or #seesouthaustralia.

Helpful websites
- Fire ban updates and fire safety cfs.sa.gov.au
- Outback road closures in SA dpti.sa.gov.au/outbackroads

South Australia

South Australia (SA) might just be the most underrated state in the whole of Australia. Often overlooked by its high-profile neighbouring states, South Australia is an amazing weekend destination.

From incredible desert road trips to dramatic coastlines, peninsulas full of secluded beaches, stunning remote islands, beautiful wine regions and the beginning of Australia's iconic Nullarbor drive, there's an endless amount of places and experiences to discover in South Australia, most of which is largely untouched and lacking the crazy crowds you often find on the East Coast.

You could come to South Australia for a dozen different weekends throughout the year and have a completely different experience every single time. If you're flying in, there are plenty of incredible places to explore only a short drive out of Adelaide. Places like the Barossa Valley, famous for its wineries (*see* p.74), and the Fleurieu Peninsula (*see* p.77) with some of the state's most beautiful beaches. And you can't miss Kangaroo Island (*see* p.80), one of our favourite places in the state. In this chapter is everything you need to create an amazing itinerary for your visit to SA.

ADELAIDE

The Traditional Owners of Tarndanya (Adelaide) are the Kaurna people

FOODIES | CULTURE BUFFS

Feeling a little more like an overgrown country town than a capital city, Adelaide is more laid-back than you would expect. It's a place where lifestyle comes first, where almost everything in the city is closed on a Sunday, seemingly forcing you to relax and unwind. It definitely doesn't have the 'go go go' attitude of other cities around the country.

A city beside the beach, one of the best things about Adelaide is that you're never more than 20 minutes away from the coast. You can explore the boutiques of the laneways in the afternoon, and still make it to the beach to watch the sunset with a cocktail in the evening. With towns like Glenelg and Port Adelaide only a short tram ride away, you can get the best of both worlds.

PLAN YOUR TRIP FOR

Without a doubt, the best time to come to Adelaide is in February and March during the annual **Adelaide Fringe Festival**. Lasting for almost a month, the Fringe Festival is a celebration of art, culture and creativity, with more than 800 events across the city, including comedy shows, live music, theatre, drive-in performances, open-air amphitheatre shows, light displays and art installations. The city absolutely comes to life during the Fringe Festival, and it's a great time to get amongst the action.

CAN'T MISS

Head to the **Adelaide Central Markets** for fresh local produce, including meat, seafood, organic fruits and vegetables, cheese, flowers and all kinds of food delicacies. Right next door you will also find **Chinatown** with lots of great Asian restaurants and cuisines.

Take a walk down **Rundle Mall** and make sure you check out the **Adelaide Arcade** which dates back to 1885. It's such a beautiful historic piece of the city.

Enjoy a cocktail at **The Mosely Beach Club** in Glenelg, where you will feel like you've been transported to a tropical beach club overseas. Everything is super cute and Instagrammable, and you can even order a cocktail in a pineapple. YUM.

Explore **Hahndorf**, Australia's oldest German town, that has retained all its charm and character. There are plenty of German restaurants and stores to explore, with more kransky sausages and sauerkraut than you can eat. Stop in at the **Hahndorf Inn** for lunch to soak up the atmosphere.

Visit **Haigh's Chocolate Factory** that has been making chocolate in Australia since 1915, to see chocolates being made and maybe even try a few cheeky samples. Don't forget a stop at the gift store to stock up on all kinds of delicious treats.

Pop into **Adelaide Zoo**, where you can meet the only giant pandas in Australia, Wang Wang and Fu Ni. You can also jump on a VIP tour to go behind the scenes and meet the pandas, as well as learn more about the conservation and breeding program at the zoo that is working to protect the pandas from extinction.

Head to **Adelaide Oval** to watch a game of footy or cricket. If sports aren't really your thing, you can actually climb the roof of the Adelaide Oval for some of the best views over the city.

Pick up an electric scooter and ride your way around the city. It's a great way to explore and so much fun.

Adelaide

Sunset at The Moseley on Glenelg Beach
Opposite Rundle Mall
Previous Rockpools at Greenly Beach, Eyre Peninsula

Where
Adelaide is on the south coast, sitting within St Vincent Gulf.

Getting here
There are frequent daily flights to Adelaide Airport (ADL) from every major city around Australia.

The airport is only a 15-minute drive from the heart of the city, so it's easy and affordable to catch an Uber or a taxi from the airport. The Adelaide Metro Bus service also offers an express double-decker bus called JetBus, which travels between the airport and the city, as well as out to coastal towns like Glenelg and West Beach. You only need a metro ticket for the JetBus, which costs $5.70 for a single trip.

Getting around
Being quite a small city, it's relatively easy to get around Adelaide. There are buses, trains and trams that can connect you to anywhere you need to go. They all run on the Metro service, so one ticket will allow you to use any form of transport. Grab yourself a Metro Visitor Pass when you arrive, which will give you three days of unlimited travel for just $25, and includes a discount compared to single-day passes. Explore the streets of Adelaide by jumping on one of the city scooters. They can be found all over the city - just download the app and you can be off in a couple of minutes.

When to go
For the best weather in Adelaide, visit during the warmer months (Nov to April). During the summertime, the city comes to life with street parties in beach towns, festivals all around the state, and an abundance of sunshine, giving you the best South Australian experience.

Where to stay
The question is always the city versus the beach when you come to Adelaide. To stay in the heart of the city, choose accommodation within walking distance of Rundle Mall, and to give yourself easy access to shopping, restaurants and bars, without needing to worry about a ride home. If you're looking to soak up more of Adelaide's beach vibe, Glenelg is definitely the place to be, with one of the top beaches in Adelaide. Glenelg has a great main street leading up to the beach, full of boutique shopping, cute cafes, and great places to eat and drink during your stay. Grab yourself a room with a balcony overlooking the beach - it's delightful.

Get planning
To plan your trip to Adelaide, head to explore.cityofadelaide. com.au or southaustralia.com/destinations/adelaide and check out @cityofadelaide and @findingadelaide on Insta, for all the best pop-up spots around the city.

DAYTRIPS
Adelaide is in a great location, only a short drive from world-renowned wine regions and a collection of beaches that perfectly encapsulate the South Australian vibe.

For food and wine, head out to McLaren Vale, the Barossa Valley (*see* p.74) or the Clare Valley, some of Australia's favourite wine regions with countless cellar doors, tastings and menus built on local produce.

For remote beaches with incredible views, take a drive along the Fleurieu Peninsula (*see* p.77), where every beach is prettier than the last.

To experience nature, head into the Adelaide Hills, where there are endless cute little towns, and koalas can often be spotted in the trees along the road. Head up to the top of **Mount Lofty** for spectacular views across the city. There are plenty of great cafes and distilleries across the Adelaide Hills, as well as the **Cleland Wildlife Park** where you can cuddle a koala.

BAROSSA VALLEY

Home to some of Australia's favourite wineries

FOODIES

Just an hour north of Adelaide, the Barossa Valley is internationally renowned as one of Australia's best wine-growing regions. It's home to some of the oldest vines in the country, with generations upon generations of winemakers creating delicious blends and flavours across the 150 wineries of the Barossa Valley.

There are more than 80 cellar doors scattered across the green lands here, all offering their own wines to taste, as well as menus created with local produce, and cheese and antipasto platters to nibble on. Not to mention, there are stunning views across vineyards and the countryside to give you the ultimate winery experience. Whether you're coming as a group of friends or looking for a romantic weekend away, the Barossa Valley is the perfect getaway from Adelaide.

If you're feeling more adventurous, you can also visit the Barossa Valley as part of South Australia's Epicurean Way road trip, leading you through four of SA's favourite wine regions, including McLaren Vale, Clare Valley and the Adelaide Hills. Taste testing your way across all the best food and wine that South Australia has to offer, you're sure to leave this weekend in a bit of a food coma.

PLAN YOUR TRIP FOR

The **Barossa Vintage Festival** held in April every second year, is a five-day celebration of culture, heritage, food, wine and community. From long lunches and degustation dinners, to parades, markets and masterclasses, it's a lovely way to soak up the Barossa life.

CAN'T MISS
In the morning:
Start your morning with an early **hot-air balloon ride** for some of the most stunning views over the sweeping valley as the sun is just beginning to rise. **Balloon Adventures** takes you on a beautiful aerial tour of the Barossa Valley, followed by a gourmet breakfast with views over the **Penfolds Stonewall** vineyards, complete with a sparkling wine toast.

Stock up on local products at the **Barossa Farmers Market** (Sat 7.30am to 11.30am), with growers and producers from all over the region coming to sell fresh fruit, vegetables, dairy, meat, baked and sweet treats, oils and jams, drinks and flowers. Follow it up by checking out the **Butcher, Baker Winemaker Trail** for some of the other artisan food producers and local delicacies in the area, with freshly baked bread at the **Apex Bakery**, handmade cheese from the **Barossa Valley Cheese Company**, and **Schulz Butchers** where you can grab some traditionally smoked sausages for a barbecue dinner.

Pop into the **Barossa Valley Chocolate Company** to watch chocolatiers hand-making artisan chocolate, join in on a chocolate making class, or try their curated chocolate and wine pairing experience at their cellar door. Grab a freshly made gelato at their ice-creamery before you go.

Rent a bicycle from **Barossa Bike Hire**, who will give you a map and highlights on the way to explore the best of the Barossa Valley on a self-guided bicycle tour. The **Barista, Brewer, Wine Cycle Tour** is a top favourite, taking you through privately owned vineyards, with stops at artisan coffee markets, boutique breweries and some of the smaller wineries.

In the afternoon:
Obviously, all afternoons spent in the Barossa Valley should be spent hopping your way across as many wineries and cellar doors as possible. Home to both quite established and newly emerging winemakers, some of our favourite spots to visit include:

Seppeltsfield is one of the country's oldest and most iconic wineries. You will find it at the end of a long road perfectly lined by palm trees that encapsulates the Barossa Valley. They are the only winery in the world to release a 100-year-old single vintage wine every year, as well as offering a 'Taste

Your Birth Year Tour' where you can try a wine from the year you were born.

First Drop Wines is the first place we started to enjoy red wine - you can't go past their Mother's Milk Shiraz. A very young brand in comparison to others in the region, First Drop Wines breathes a youthful energy into cellar doors, with fun wine labels, a super-cute cellar door and easy wines to sip on, with tastings from just $5.

Whistler Wines holds Summer Sessions (second Friday of each month Nov to March, 5 to 9pm), with a big lawn and festoon lights really creating a great vibe. For something sweet and tasty, try their Fruit Tingle Frizzante. It's fun and refreshing and not like any other wine in the region.

Jacob's Creek is renowned as one of Australia's favourite wines, and you can't go past a visit here. With tasting experiences from $5, you can try some of their most popular wines, as well as blends that are exclusive only to the cellar door. You can also book a picnic out by the vines, where all the produce is sourced from local farmers, giving you a real taste of the whole Barossa Valley region. Or, book a spot with a group of friends at their ping-pong table overlooking the gardens for some friendly competition.

In the evening:
Splash out on a fancy dinner date at one of the countless award-winning restaurants found in the Barossa Valley, with menus curated to the wines on offer, and everything designed for an incredible culinary experience. **Harvest Kitchen** has a menu that is designed around the seasons, choosing quality produce from the Barossa and South Australian regions, as well as stunning views across the vines surrounding it. **Appellation Restaurant** is one of Australia's finest regional dining experiences, with most of the produce grown in their own kitchen garden.

Palm trees and vines along Seppeltsfield Road

Where
The Barossa Valley is about 70 kilometres north of Adelaide.

Getting here
The Barossa Valley is an easy one-hour drive from Adelaide. If you're coming from interstate, fly directly into Adelaide Airport (ADL).

Getting around
You can pick up a rental car at the airport to give yourself the freedom to explore as much of the Barossa Valley as possible.

When to go
Visit the Barossa Valley during the summer months to make the most of the warm weather and outdoor dining and picnic spots. Many of the cellar doors have regular events during the summer that really give you the best opportunity to soak up life amongst the vines.

Main towns
The main towns of the Barossa Valley are Tanunda, Nuriootpa, Angaston, Lyndoch and Williamstown, which are all pretty close together. There are plenty of cellar doors within a short distance of each of the towns, so you're never far away from a new, exciting wine.

Where to stay
The Villas – Barossa offers luxury eco-villas surrounded by bushland, where you will feel completely immersed in the environment whenever you need a break.

Kingford Homestead will make you feel like you're staying in a castle, with heritage elements and outdoor baths overlooking the surrounding gardens.

Barossa Valley Apartments is a great option for groups and families, with two-bedroom apartments and free wi-fi, and it's right in the heart of the action.

Get planning
Head to barossa.com to learn more about all the wineries and cellar doors, as well as the events calendar for your visit, and to book your accommodation and experiences. On socials, check out @mybarossa, @barossawines and @visitbarossavalley for all the inspo.

BEST PHOTO SPOTS
You can't beat the **Seppeltsfield Road**, stretching for 10 kilometres and lined with tall, picturesque palm trees. It's an iconic trademark of the Barossa Valley.

Top Wine tastings at First Drop Wines, Nuriootpa
Bottom Vines as far as the eye can see in the Barossa

FLEURIEU PENINSULA & MCLAREN VALE

The perfect combination of beaches and wine

FOODIES | NATURE LOVERS

The Fleurieu Peninsula and McLaren Vale is where the vineyards meet the sea. They are destinations that can be explored together or separately, with some of SA's prettiest beaches only minutes away from one of the state's top wine regions. What could be better?

One of the most easily accessible peninsulas to visit from Adelaide, the Fleurieu Coast stretches from Noarlunga in the north, all the way around the peninsula to Goowla and Lake Alexandrina in the east. It encompasses all the little beach towns along the way, including Deep Creek Conservation Park in the south. Only a few minutes inland, McLaren Vale lies alongside, with wines to suit every palate, secret cellar doors, menus made up of locally made produce and more than 160 vineyards growing grapes of all different colours.

Surrounded by beautiful rolling hills that seem to be yellow and brown in the summer months and green during the winter months, the Fleurieu Peninsula is really one of the most picturesque coastlines around. Whether you want to bring a group of friends to camp on the beach, your lover for a romantic weekend, or your kids for a playful getaway, it's an idyllic destination for all, and a region where you can really create your own perfect holiday.

Second Valley Beach

CAN'T MISS

In the morning:

Head to the **Willunga Farmers Market** (Sat 8am to 12pm) to stock up on food and goodies for the weekend. Farmers and specialty food producers sell their produce directly to customers, so it's always fresh and there's always something new to try. It's a great place to start before all those beach barbecues you've been planning.

Get the four-wheel drive into action and explore **Deep Creek Conservation Park**, one of the more rugged and remote national parks around. At the bottom of a bumpy track you'll come across Blowhole Beach, which is a great hidden gem in the park. On a clear day you can spot Kangaroo Island (*see* p.80) across the water, and there are often dolphins jumping around in the ocean and kangaroos hopping around on the shore.

Hop across the many beaches of the Fleurieu Peninsula, each one prettier than the last. **Port Noarlunga South Beach** has a huge sandbar in the middle that gets bigger and smaller depending on the tide throughout the day, and is surrounded by white limestone rocks that lead into deep red cliffs. **Carrickalinga Beach** has some of the clearest blue water along the coast, and if you're keen for some exploring, there are plenty of rockpools to be found if you search hard enough.

And don't forget about **Port Willunga**, where little square caves have been carved out of the limestone cliffs, providing a lovely spot for you to set up for the day, with the remnants of an old jetty, also known as 'the sticks', standing tall in the ocean in front of you.

In the afternoon:

Taste test your way across the **wineries of McLaren Vale**, trying new flavours and refining your wine-tasting skills. There are about 74 cellar doors in the McLaren Vale region, all offering their own signature wines and specialties. A great place to start is at **Hugh Hamilton Wine**, whose great-great-grandfather started South Australia's first winery in 1837. Some of the other highlights include **D'Arenberg**, **Samuel's Gorge**, **Wirra Wirra** and **Paxton Wines**. Renting bicycles is a great way to explore more of the region, allowing you to get out to a few more of the cellar doors and still have a wine.

Take a drive along the beach at **Sellicks Beach**, one of the biggest and most popular beaches along this coastline. The sand here is super hard, making it possible for even the smallest of cars to drive on and experience beach driving. It's a great spot for a picnic or a barbecue lunch, and you can take frequent dips in the ocean to cool down.

Get out and explore **Onkaparinga Gorge National Park**, which sits right alongside McLaren Vale. There are heaps of great hikes around the park, including the Punchbowl Lookout Walk, River Hike and Sundews Ridge Hike that show you some of the best views of Onkaparinga and a different perspective of the area.

In the evening:

You can't go past **Down The Rabbit Hole** on Friday nights, where there is live acoustic music, great wine and a delicious menu to enjoy as you watch the sun go down over the vineyard next door. Get down there a little early for a wine tasting on their impeccably renovated big, blue double-decker bus before grabbing a woven throw and a picnic spot on the grass to enjoy the evening. It's just like stepping straight into the perfect photo. Fridays are magical here, and they even let you bring your pets.

DAYTRIPS

On the other side of the Fleurieu Peninsula you can find **Victor Harbour**, a very popular holiday spot from Adelaide and a larger town along the coastline. The beachfront town of Victor Harbour sits alongside Encounter Bay, where you can find Granite Island floating in the bay, home to resident fairy penguins and beautiful views of the town. A historical Clydesdale horse-drawn tram takes you between the island and the main beach, where you can often find camel rides as well.

Horseshoe Bay just 10 minutes down the road is one of the prettiest little beaches over here. It's in the neighbouring town of Port Elliot, with a jetty to jump from and inviting water to swim in.

BEST PHOTO SPOTS

The tiny little bay of **Second Valley** is one of the most photogenic spots along the whole South Australian coastline. A small beach hidden amongst the surrounding cliffs, it offers sparkling crystal-clear water, a small jetty for fishing and if you venture a little further around the cliffs, amazing rockpools and coastal views. Follow the steep path behind the beach up over the cliffs and above the bay for a beautiful sunset picnic spot.

Where
The Fleurieu Peninsula and McLaren Vale sit along the southern coastline of SA, only a short drive from Adelaide.

Getting here
Adelaide Airport (ADL) is only a 45-minute drive away from the Fleurieu Peninsula and McLaren Vale, with direct flights to every major city around Australia.

Getting around
Pick up a rental car from the airport and make the easy drive out to the region, where there are plenty of great places to base yourself.

When to go
The summer months are the best time to visit the Fleurieu Peninsula, when the days are long and hot - ideal for hopping across beaches and sipping wine outdoors. Anytime between October and April can offer great weather conditions and sunny days, while the winter months are quite cool and better spent at cellar doors with fireplaces.

Main towns
Port Noarlunga South is one of the larger towns, where you can find a shopping centre and plenty of entertainment. But if you're coming to escape the rat-race look for stays in Willunga, Aldinga and McLaren Vale.

Where to stay
You can find great places to base yourself all along the Fleurieu Peninsula, depending on what you want to be closest to.

If you're caravanning or camping, Rapid Bay is a great place to camp right on the beach. There's not much in Rapid Bay except for the campground, but the beach here is absolutely beautiful, surrounded by all the hills and with caves to explore and squid to be caught. It gives you those ultimate holiday vibes as soon as you spot the water as you're coming over the hill.

Get planning
Start your visit by heading to fleurieupeninsula.com.au and mclarenvale.info, and check out @officialfleurieupeninsula and @mclaren_vale on Insta for all the best spots and inspo for your visit.

Top Horseshoe Bay, Port Elliot
Middle Live music and sunsets at Down the Rabbit Hole
Bottom Camping on the beach at Rapid Bay

KANGAROO ISLAND

Bringing together the best of South Australia

ADVENTURERS | NATURE LOVERS

Kangaroo Island was one of the places that made us fall in love with the idea of travelling around Australia. Our first visit to the island, affectionately known as KI, made us feel like this is exactly where we were meant to be. Having visited three times now, it is always one of the places we recommend to anyone looking for a new destination to head off to on a weekend getaway around Australia.

Found just off the coast of SA, Kangaroo Island offers all kinds of landscapes, from soaring cliffs and dense national parks, to towering sand dunes and untouched white sandy beaches. There is an abundance of wildlife, amazing farm-to-table produce, beautiful untouched spaces and something different to explore at every turn.

There is an unmistakable holiday vibe on Kangaroo Island, while locals also make you feel like you're part of the community. Bring your car over to the island and experience the best of it at your own pace – off-the-beaten track and completely immersed in the rugged natural beauty this little island has to offer.

BEST PHOTO SPOTS
Flinders Chase National Park is just overflowing with great photo spots. Some of the best are along the hilly main road through the park that is surrounded by an endless horizon of trees - you can see this view when you are driving into the park and the iconic Remarkable Rocks.

Opposite The main road in Flinders Chase National Park

CAN'T MISS
In the morning:
Spend your mornings beach hopping across Kangaroo Island, with a new remote beach everywhere you turn. One of the places that keeps us coming back to KI again and again is **Vivonne Bay**. This spot is one of our favourite beaches in all of Australia, with the brightest blue water, made all the more stunning alongside the contrasting red dirt road that leads you there. It's the ideal spot for a picnic lunch, an afternoon of fishing off the jetty, or to check out the marine life snorkelling in the shallows. Just around the corner, try the famous whiting burger at the **Vivonne Bay General Store**. When you arrive in the carpark for **Stokes Bay**, it might look like you're in the wrong spot, but follow the signs to the beach, through the cracks of the rocky cliffs that surround it, for another KI favourite hiding away from view.

Head to **Seal Bay Conservation Park** to jump on an early morning guided tour when the sea lions are often most active, emerging from their burrows in the sand dunes and making their way to the ocean for their morning swim and sunbake. This is home to Australia's largest colony of more than 1000 wild sea lions, and a great place to watch them play and interact together.

Pop into **Hanson Bay Wildlife Sanctuary** where koalas are free to roam around the trees, coming and going as they like. Each time we have visited there has always been more than 30 koalas in the trees, with lots of little joeys around too.

In the afternoon:
Head to some of the island's best distilleries and eateries in the afternoon to experience the local cuisine. Known for their award-winning botanical gin, **Kangaroo Island Spirits** also creates some unique vodka and whisky. They have free tastings, as well as a delicious cocktail menu, at their cellar door in Cygnet River.

Emu Bay Lavender Farm is a great lunch spot, with a delicious menu, as well as lavender-themed snacks if you're on the go (try the lavender scones)! Make sure you stop in at their shop, selling all kinds of wellness products made from their lavender. If you're not sure what to choose, try the lavender sleep balm - you'll thank me later.

For locally brewed beer, head to the **Kangaroo Island Brewery**, where a tasting paddle will allow you to sample

four of their best local brews. **Dudley Wines** also has great wines, food and panoramic views, giving you an excellent place to soak up some of the northern end of KI.

Visit **Kangaroo Island Wildlife Park** to meet all kinds of Australian native wildlife. You can also hand-feed kangaroos, koalas and baby wallabies. This park quickly became one of the biggest rescue and rehabilitation centres for wildlife during the devastating 2019/20 bushfires, keeping their own animals safe as the fires advanced on them from every direction, as well as taking in more than 700 injured koalas and other animals who were rescued from fire around the island.

Unexpectedly, a small pocket of KI is covered in tall, white sand dunes. Head to **Little Sahara**, a featured attraction on the island, where you can grab yourself a sandboard or toboggan and go sliding down the dunes. After a couple of times it's a real mission to get back up to the top, but the slide down is worth it!

In the evening:
Grab a group of friends, stock up on food and drinks and head to **Emu Bay**. The long, flat Emu Bay is one of the best for beach driving right along the water's edge, and it's never hard to find a place to yourself here. It's the perfect spot for a sunset dinner and a campfire on the beach.

DAYTRIPS
Taking up the whole west side of the island, **Flinders Chase National Park** is home to some of Kangaroo Island's top natural attractions and is worth a whole day visit. The **Remarkable Rocks** stand tall on a granite cliff, having been formed over 500 million years of wind, rain and pounding waves. They stand in unique shapes at the end of the park overlooking the ocean, and are a great place for creative photos. Just down the road, the **Admirals Arch** was also formed from thousands of years of erosion, and is now home to hundreds of local seals.

Remarkable Rocks in Flinders Chase National Park
Opposite The beautiful Vivonne Bay

Where

Kangaroo Island is just 15 kilometres off the south coast of South Australia.

Getting here

SeaLink operates a vehicle and passenger ferry service daily (with the exception of Christmas Day) between Cape Jervis on the mainland and Penneshaw on KI. The trip across takes about 40 minutes, with a departure generally every 45 minutes to an hour. Dogs are allowed onboard SeaLink, and you can also bring your caravan, boat or trailer across.

For those who prefer to fly, Kangaroo Island has its own airport - Kingscote Airport (KGC). There are regular daily flights departing from Adelaide Airport with Rex Regional Express, touching you down to KI in just 30 minutes. QantasLink also offers a direct service from Melbourne Airport a couple of times each week.

Getting around

By far the best way to get around Kangaroo Island is exploring with your own car, giving you the freedom to check out every nook and cranny of the island. You can bring your own car across on the ferry, or grab a rental at either Kingscote Airport or Penneshaw when you get off the ferry.

There are several unsealed roads around the island that take you to some of the best beaches and hidden hot spots, so if you have a rental car, make sure there are no issues with taking it onto unsealed roads.

Petrol stations are few and far between around the island, so before you head out for the day, always make sure you have enough fuel to keep you going. The main fuel stops can be found in Kingscote and Penneshaw, with smaller stations available at Vivonne Bay, Parndana and KI Wilderness Retreat (near Flinders Chase National Park).

When to go

The summer months (Dec to Feb) are the most popular times to visit, especially if you're hoping for some sunny weather. If you're travelling during these peak times, make sure you book your ferry tickets and accommodation in advance though, as the whole island can completely book out. The shoulder seasons through spring and autumn are also lovely times to visit, with the slightly cooler weather allowing hiking and exploring to be a little more comfortable.

Main towns

Kingscote and Penneshaw are the two main towns on Kangaroo Island. At both you can find petrol stations, supermarkets, car rental, cafes and restaurants, and other shops.

Kingscote is the main town on KI and is a great place to base yourself. Here you can find petrol stations, the biggest supermarket on the island, cafes, souvenir shops, the island's airport, restaurants and anything else you might need.

Where to stay

There are seven different regions on Kangaroo Island, which all offer different accommodation options, beautiful landscapes and iconic attractions. KI offers accommodation options for every budget, from luxurious rental houses to campgrounds, with a range of hotels, resorts and even farm stays in between. Kingscote in particular is where most accommodation options are located, with a few others dotted throughout the island.

Around the island you can find a number of different campgrounds, all of which have reopened following the summer 2019/20 bushfires. Campsites are allocated on a first-come, first-served basis, and reservations can't be made in advance. Fees apply for each location when you arrive and are made onsite via a self-registration booth.

Need to know

The size of Kangaroo Island is often underestimated. It takes 2 hours and 20 minutes to travel across the whole island, from Cape Willoughby in the east to Flinders Chase National Park at the western end of the island. From north to south you're still looking at about a 45-minute drive, from Stokes Bay to Vivonne Bay.

Outside of the main towns there is very limited phone reception, with much of the island being quite remote. Telstra has the most coverage across the island, although internet access is very limited.

Get planning

Head to tourkangarooisland.com.au to plan your visit, or @authentickangarooisland on social media for all the best inspiration and spots to check out.

EYRE PENINSULA

Australia's seafood frontier

The Eyre Peninsula is one of the most beautiful places in all of South Australia. Home to remote little towns overlooking sweeping, isolated beaches, there is so much more to see and explore around the Eyre Peninsula than you might expect. It's home to stunning national parks, including Coffin Bay National Park and Lincoln National Park, that offer remote camping spots right on the beach, with emus and kangaroos that leisurely stroll across the road like they haven't even seen your car.

Covering a huge amount of land, from Port Augusta on the east all the way to the beginning of the Nullarbor Plain in the west, the Eyre Peninsula has once-in-a-lifetime wildlife and marine experiences, colourful silo art and dynamic landscapes. It's also one of Australia's biggest seafood hubs, with more than 65 per cent of Aussie seafood coming from this region.

Surprisingly, no matter where you visit along this remarkable piece of coastline, you often find that you have the beaches all to yourself, with not another soul around for miles. Spend your weekend hopping through rockpools, driving on white sand beaches, fishing right off the shore, and you'll be surprised how few other people you'll be sharing these epic places with.

PLAN YOUR TRIP FOR

It's all about the wildlife experiences on the Eyre Peninsula. Come down from April to June for the best great white shark sightings; May to August to see the annual whale migration along the southern coast; and June to July to swim with giant cuttlefish in Whyalla. It's a good idea to book wildlife experiences, such as swimming with sea lions or great white sharks in advance for your dates, as tours often completely book out weeks before they depart.

Opposite Crystal-clear pools at Greenly Beach

CAN'T MISS

Given the Eyre Peninsula covers such a large area (in fact, it's roughly the size of Switzerland!), plan out your itinerary to make sure you have enough time to fit in everything you want to see.

In the morning:
For one of the most memorable and amazing experiences during your visit to the Eyre Peninsula, book yourself in for a morning **swimming with the sea lions**. There is a huge wild sea lion colony in the area, who are definitely some of the ocean's cutest and most playful residents. Book a morning trip with **Adventure Bay Charters**, who will take you out to Hopkins Island, where dozens of sea lions are waiting to play.

To get your adrenaline pumping a little higher, you can go **cage diving with great white sharks** from Port Lincoln. Considered the great white shark capital of Australia, there are almost daily reliable shark sightings in the waters around Port Lincoln, with an underwater observatory on board for those who might feel the cage is a little too up close. Makes you nervous about jumping into the beach now, doesn't it?

For an early morning swim, head to **Greenly Beach**, one of our favourite beaches in SA and one you're likely to have mostly to yourself. It's a beautiful spot, with lots of free camping spots and bright blue water that just looks so inviting. Climb over the rocks at the western end of the beach to find huge rockpools to swim in, filled with starfish, crabs and all kinds of marine creatures, in calm pools protected from the crashing waves.

Check out the **colourful art murals** that can be found all over the small coastal town of Tumby Bay. There are murals covering half of the surfaces in town, including on the silos, shop walls, alleyways and even the rotunda on the beach.

In the afternoon:
Take a drive down **Whalers Way** to see some of the Eyre Peninsula's most dramatic coastline, peppered with beautiful rockpools, huge crevasses, deep caves and dramatic beaches all the way around. Some of the highlights along the way include the **Swimming Hole**, **Cape Wiles**, **Baleen Rockpool** and **Blowhole**, **Old Whalemans Grotto** and **Red Banks**. Stop by the Visitor Information Centre on Adelaide Place in Port Lincoln before you go to grab a permit and a key for the gate.

Eyre Peninsula

Grab lunch at **The Fresh Fish Place** in Port Lincoln, a mix of a fresh fish store, fish and chip restaurant and fish wholesaler. They have every type of seafood you could want to try here, and it's literally as fresh as it gets. You can eat in or take-away, or grab some fish to cook up yourself later.

A little further along the coastline, **Locks Well Beach** is thought to be one of the most reliable places to catch salmon right off the shore. There are often huge swells with king waves crashing onto the shore, that are meant to be full of great fish. Due to the power of the waves here though, don't swim.

Head out in the afternoon to explore **Port Lincoln National Park**, a wilderness protection area full of secluded beaches, emus running around and dolphins jumping off the shore. One of the highlights here is **Memory Cove**, which only allows 15 vehicles to visit per day to conserve the environment. With plenty of places to explore, you're sure to find that you have a beach or a lookout all to yourself.

DAYTRIPS

Take the time to explore the beauty of **Coffin Bay**. Home to some of the most popular and renowned oyster farms in the world, as well as the stunning **Coffin Bay National Park** filled with sand dunes and baby emus, Coffin Bay is an especially beautiful part of the Eyre Peninsula. Jump on a farm tour with **Coffin Bay Oysters** and learn about how oysters are grown and harvested, how to shuck your own oyster, and taste test some straight from the ocean. After lunch at **Oyster HQ**, head into Coffin Bay National Park to explore remote secluded beaches (**Alamonta Beach** is a great place to start) and sweeping white dunes overlooking the Great Australian Bite.

Sunset at the Woolshed Cave
Opposite Swim with the sea lions from Port Lincoln

Eyre Peninsula

Where

The Eyre Peninsula is along the southern coastline of South Australia, about halfway across the state.

Getting here

There are multiple daily direct flights to Port Lincoln Airport (PLO) from Adelaide with both QantasLink and Rex Airlines. It's only a 50-minute flight, with connections from Adelaide to the rest of Australia.

If you're travelling by car, it takes about 6 hours (647km) to drive from Adelaide to Port Lincoln. Take the Princes Highway to Port Augusta and then follow the Lincoln Highway south to Port Lincoln.

Getting around

Rent a car from the airport or road trip down in your own vehicle to explore the best of the Eyre Peninsula. With plenty of the attractions within a short drive of Port Lincoln, having your own car is the ultimate way to explore, where you can truly create your own itinerary.

When to go

The summer season (Nov to March) is considered the best time to visit the Eyre Peninsula. During summer the days are warm, giving you the best weather to explore the beaches and beautiful coastline, as well as get in the water for some of the incredible marine wildlife experiences here.

In the winter, the weather can turn a little nasty, with strong winds from the ocean and much cooler temperatures. However, this can be considered a great time for shark and whale sightings, with incredible whale-watching experiences along the Eyre between May and August each year.

Main towns

Port Lincoln is the ideal place to base yourself on a weekend in the Eyre Peninsula. It's right in the middle of the region, so you're never too far away from where you need to go. It's actually quite a large town by country South Australian standards, with everything you might need during your visit. Port Lincoln has award-winning restaurants, its own beautiful beaches, great fishing, and a lot of maritime and pioneering history.

Where to stay

All types of accommodation can be found in Port Lincoln, including hotels, holiday apartments and caravan parks. Once you leave Port Lincoln most towns are incredibly small, or non-existent the further you move west. There are plenty of free camping spots if you are self-sufficient along the coast, as well as campgrounds in the national parks and along many of the beaches.

Need to know

When you arrive at Port Lincoln, head straight to the Visitor Information Centre. Open seven days a week, you need to head here if you want to visit Whalers Way, Memory Cove or the national parks, as many of these places require a permit and key to access, and camping spaces need to be confirmed before you go. You don't want to get all the way out there before you realise that!

Get planning

To start planning your Eyre Peninsula adventure, head to eyrepeninsula.com and portlincoln.com.au, and check out @eyrepeninsula, @visitptlincoln and @port_lincoln for all the inspo.

BEST PHOTO SPOTS

Some of the best photo spots can be found a little further along the Eyre Peninsula, but are easily accessible by a short road trip. You can never get a bad rockpool photo at **Greenly Beach**, with some of the largest, clearest pools along the Eyre. Head west along the coast to find **Talia Rock Pools** and the **Woolshed Cave** overlooking the ocean, or head further inland to **Murphy's Haystacks**, a group of uniquely shaped granite boulders rising from the red dirt and standing up to 3 metres tall which offer great photo opportunities.

Travelling on
The Ghan

A weekend travelling across Australia by train, departing from the top in Darwin, down through the centre, to arrive down south in Adelaide, is an experience unlike any other. The Ghan exceeded our expectations in every single possible way.

From the minute you step on board *The Ghan*, you are transported to another world, where everything is taken care of for you, meticulously planned down to the finest detail. All you need to do is sit back, relax and enjoy the journey.

The Ghan Expedition is a 4-day, 3-night journey, stopping along the way in Katherine (*see* p.157), Alice Springs (*see* p.150) and Coober Pedy (*see* p.96). At every stop, you can choose from a selection of carefully curated experiences, offering you one-of-a-kind activities that have been designed by the team at Journey Beyond, from a sunset barbecue dinner at the Alice Springs Telegraph Station, to an underground lunch in a Coober Pedy opal mine. Everything about the trip is all-inclusive, so there's no need to worry about a thing once you step on board. The drinks are flowing and the food is absolutely incredible, the menu expertly created to reflect the region of Australia you're passing by. No two meals are ever the same on *The Ghan* and every dish we ate was exquisite.

Inside the train you have your own compartment and ensuite to retreat to when you want to just sit back and watch the world go by. During the day, your compartment is set up as a lounge suite, giving you plenty of space to move around, and then while you're having dinner each evening it is transformed into bunk beds, ready for you to fall asleep to the slow sway of the train and sound of the tracks. When you want to be a little more social you can head to the Outback Explorer Lounge, where you can have a couple of drinks, chat with other travellers and watch the changing landscape as you cross the country.

The Ghan is considered one of the world's greatest rail adventures, with visitors from all over the world coming to explore the Centre of Australia. It gives you a perspective of the outback that is completely special and unique to travelling on a train. Even though we had spent a lot of time in Central Australia, and driven ourselves from Adelaide to Darwin, completing the journey by train was just such a special and memorable experience. We simply cannot recommend a journey on *The Ghan* highly enough.

IMPORTANT INFO

The train leaves from Darwin each Wednesday, with a second service departing on Saturdays between June and August. Find all the details online (journeybeyondrail.com.au) and make sure you look for the current deals and promotions, because you can often score yourself a discount.

If you caught the bug for train travel after your trip on *The Ghan*, Journey Beyond also offers a few other trips across the country, with the equally iconic Indian Pacific travelling between Perth and Sydney and the Great Southern Rail travelling between Brisbane and Adelaide.

FLINDERS RANGES

Home to some of the oldest landscapes on Earth

NATURE LOVERS | ADVENTURERS

Take a trip back in time in Ikara-Flinders Ranges National Park, with landscapes that are more than 800 million years old and First People's history that dates back more than 49,000 years. Start your stay by joining the Welcome to Country ceremony at the Wilpena Pound Resort reception area. Each evening, one of the local Adnyamathanha guides welcomes visitors in their Yura Ngawarla language, sharing creation stories, information about the family bloodlines in the area and some background into the lives of the Yura people. Learning about the Ikara-Flinders Ranges region through the eyes of a local is such a powerful experience, and gives you a much greater understanding of the land you're exploring and awareness of any important cultural protocols, including sacred areas which may have restricted access.

Ikara-Flinders Ranges National Park is the gateway to the South Australian outback. This part of the land is filled with history and culture, as well as spectacular natural beauty, with mesmerising gorges, some of the world's oldest geological and fossil sites, and many significant and sacred sites of the local Adnyamathanha people. Stretching over more than 90,000 hectares and spanning from Hawker in the south to Parachilna in the north, Ikara-Flinders Ranges is an extremely special place for a weekend away.

BEST PHOTO SPOTS
Head to **Stokes Hill Lookout** at sunset and Razorback Lookout at any time of the day for that iconic Ikara-Flinders Ranges National Park view.

CAN'T MISS
In the morning:
Before heading out to explore the Flinders Ranges, stop by the **Wilpena Pound Resort Visitors Centre** (open 8am to 6pm daily) to check in with some of the local Yura guides who can recommend places to visit. It's definitely worth popping in for a chat before you go out exploring.

Then, start your day with a quick 20-minute **scenic flight over Ikara (Wilpena Pound)** to really get the whole picture of this incredible place. Ikara (Wilpena Pound) looks like a huge crater, and seeing it from the sky gives you a greater perspective of the land, the stories of the Traditional Owners, and the whole outback.

Hike up to Arkaroo Rock to see some beautiful Aboriginal rock art that has been preserved here for hundreds of years. This is an amazing site, with images clearly distinguishable on the wide rock face. The walk takes about an hour each way and is best done in the early morning, before the weather gets too warm.

Bushwalk your way across the ranges with **walking trails** that will lead you to some of the best lookouts not accessible by car. During the summer months a number of the walking trails are closed due to the extreme heat, so bushwalking season is best between April and October when everything is open. **St Mary Peak** and **Mount Ohlssen Bagge** offer some of the most beautiful views over the pound, but you're definitely going to have to work for them.

In the afternoon:
Jump on a **cultural tour** with a local Adnyamathanha guide to learn more about Ikara-Flinders Ranges. Throughout the tour, your Yura guide will share creation stories, information about their land, how they understand and learn from it, and stories from their families growing up in this area. The **Time Travel & Gorgeous Gorges 4WD tour** run by Wilpena Pound Resort is our favourite for a wonderful cultural experience.

Visit the **Sacred Canyon & Adnyamathanha Engravings**. This is best visited on a tour with a local guide, as the sacred site has so much meaning and significance to the Yura people. This canyon was described to us by our guide as their cathedral - a place of true beauty and meaning that makes them feel at peace when they visit.

Take a four-wheel drive to visit **Bunyeroo Gorge** and **Brachina Gorge**. The gorges themselves are just beautiful, but the drives along the way have just as much to see and explore.

In the evening:

Visit as many of the lookouts in the ranges as you can. **Razorback Lookout** is our clear favourite, with views over the mountain ranges, as well as the iconic sharp-bending road through the pound. Head to **Stokes Hill Lookout** at sunset, to watch the ranges change colour as the sun sinks behind the mountains. You can also find some impressive views at Hucks Lookout, Rawnsley Lookout, Arkaba Hill Lookout and Elder Range Lookout. All of these lookouts you can drive right up to, so take a couple of picnic chairs and some drinks to enjoy while you watch the sun go down.

Have a unique Aussie dinner at the iconic **Parachilna Prairie Hotel**, known in the outback as the best place to try dishes that include emu, kangaroo, goat and camel. For dessert, you can't go past their signature quandong pie, made from a native wild peach. Yum!

DAYTRIPS

Take a daytrip up to **Arkaroola** at the far-northern tip of the Flinders Ranges. There are more epic landscapes out here to explore, with gorges to hike, waterfalls to swim in, and rare yellow-footed rock wallabies to be found. You can take a self-guided four-wheel drive tour around the ridge of the gorge, where you can find some of the best lookout spots in the northern parts of the Flinders Ranges. Arkaroola is also home to Australia's largest privately owned **astronomical observatory**, a great place to come and experience the incredible starry night sky.

Sunsets in Ikara-Flinders Ranges National Park

Where
The Flinders Ranges is located about 500 kilometres north of Adelaide.

Getting here
From Adelaide it's an easy 5-hour drive to the Flinders Ranges, via the National Highway A1 and Flinders Ranges Way.

Alternatively, Rex Airlines will connect you to Port Augusta airport with a 55-minute flight from Adelaide, followed by an hour and 45-minute drive. Flights between Adelaide and Port Augusta are available several times each week, with connections to all other major cities around the country.

Getting around
To make the most of your weekend in the Flinders Ranges, it's best to have your own car. A four-wheel drive is recommended to get to some of the more remote locations, however a regular car will still give you plenty of freedom to explore. The only petrol station in the national park can be found at Ikara (Wilpena Pound), so always make sure you fill up before you head out for the day.

When to go
During the cooler months (April to Oct) is the best time to visit the Flinders Ranges, when the temperatures are a little bit cooler.

For safety reasons, many of the bushwalking trails are closed from the end of November until the beginning of March, including the popular St Mary Peak hike, as they can be very dangerous if attempted in hot weather, so avoid these months if you're hoping to go on some of the hiking trails.

Where to stay
To really make the most of your experience, stay at **Wilpena Pound Resort**, the only accommodation that is actually located within Ikara-Flinders Ranges National Park. Wilpena Pound Resort offers all kinds of accommodation options, including bush campgrounds with powered and unpowered sites, resort-style rooms and their stunning Ikara safari glamping tents if you're looking for something a little more special. Within Wilpena Pound Resort you can also find the local visitors centre, an IGA Xpress convenience store, a bar/bistro, restaurant, swimming pool and the only petrol station within the ranges.

Need to know
Vehicle entry fees apply within Ikara-Flinders Ranges National Park. A day entry permit costs $11 per vehicle and gives you access to the entire park. Ikara-Flinders Ranges National Park is also covered by the South Australian Parks Pass (*see* p.70).

We found that within the Wilpena Pound Resort we had full 4G phone reception, including at our campsite and the resort restaurant and pool. However, as soon as we left the resort we didn't find service anywhere else in the park. Keep this in mind if you need reception and are considering other places to stay.

Get planning
To start planning your visit to Ikara-Flinders Ranges National Park, head to wilpenapound.com.au for the most reliable updates, information and experiences to book. Also look at parks.sa.gov.au/parks/ikara-flinders-ranges-national-park for specific park information and to pay your entry fee.

YORKE PENINSULA

More than 700 kilometres of picture-perfect coastline

NATURE LOVERS | OFF-THE-BEATEN TRACK

One of the more remote peninsulas in South Australia, the Yorke Peninsula gets you away from the crowds and straight into nature, with beach hopping, fishing and surfing the main activities for your weekend itinerary. Much of the peninsula is still undeveloped, with tiny little coastal towns dotted around and remote beaches, where you can often find a shipwreck washed up on the shore. There are lots of great places to eat scattered too, with more and more microbreweries, distilleries and modern restaurants popping up in the small towns along the coastline.

There are plenty of hiking trails around the Yorke Peninsula that range in distance, time and levels of difficulty, from 600 metres to 11 kilometres long – you could easily spend a weekend hiking around here and taking in all the incredible coastal views.

Sitting right at the bottom of the Yorke Peninsula is Innes National Park, the absolute highlight of the Yorke. This little park is packed with beautiful beaches, rocky cliffs overlooking the ocean, great fishing and camping spots and heaps of native Australian wildlife. With secluded campsites right near the beach and mobs of emus wandering around with their chicks, it's the ideal place to get off the grid for a weekend and enjoy the slow life.

BEST PHOTO SPOTS

Stop by **Ardrossan** on your way back to Adelaide, for a stunning photo backdrop, with bright red cliffs that lead straight down to the water. A great place to visit at sunrise or sunset, when the red cliffs are glowing extra bright in the sunlight.

Chinaman Creek free camp in Winninowie Conservation Park
Opposite Views from Razorback Lookout

CAN'T MISS

In the morning:

Spend your morning hopping through some of the best beaches and secret rockpools of **Innes National Park**. **Stenhouse Bay** was one of our favourite spots, with reefs lining the shore and families of emus wandering around the campsites. The sand here is bright white as well, making the hues of the ocean even more spectacular. There are more than 40 shipwrecks along the coastline of Innes, but the *Ethel* is one of the biggest and most visible from land. It was wrecked in 1904 during a severe storm and washed up on the beach here. It's not always 100 per cent visible throughout the year though, it does depend on the sand movements during your visit.

Head to **Pondalowie Surf Break** if you're hoping to ride some of the biggest waves on the Yorke Peninsula.

Gym Beach just outside the national park is another favourite of ours, a pretty little spot with large rocks creating the perfect little bay beach. Stop by **Shell Beach**, a little further down the coastline, at low tide for a swim in the Blue Hole rockpool, with clear still water sheltered from the crashing ocean waves, and where you can often find coral, crabs and starfish.

Learn more about the peninsula's history with a visit to **Innestown**, the historic abandoned ghost town surrounded by wild bushland.

In the afternoon:

The Yorke Peninsula is a popular area for **fishing**, so spend the afternoon at one of the 20 boat ramps and jetties and try your hand at catching King George whiting, bream, squid, tommies and blue swimmer crabs. Some of the best fishing spots can be found at Wallaroo, Moonta Bay, Ardrossan, Stansbury, Port Hughes and Marion Bay.

Jump on a working oyster boat with **Pacific Estate Oysters** to pull your own oysters straight out of the ocean. Learn all the tricks of the trade as you find oysters and learn how to shuck them, before enjoying a delicious oyster lunch.

Many of the peninsula's best foodie spots can be found in Wallaroo, with favourites including **Bond Store**, and **Coopers Alehouse Restaurant**. Coopers sits right on the water, with a big outdoor deck and great views. Both offer some of the freshest seafood in the world; there's no shortage of seafood grazing platters, stocked with oysters, cheeses and fresh fruits, and local wines to try.

Jump on an **Aboriginal Cultural Tour** to explore the Aboriginal township of Bookyanna (Point Pearce) with an experienced and knowledgeable Narungga guide. You can learn about the history of the settlement on a half-day tour, or extend to a full-day tour, taking part in cultural ceremonies and listening to Dreaming stories.

In the evening:

Stop by the **Cape Spencer Lighthouse** to watch the sunrise or the sunset, with beautiful views over the surrounding beaches full of bright turquoise water and rocky cliff-faces dropping into the glistening ocean. This is such a pretty spot, and when you visit at dawn or dusk you're likely to be sharing your picnic spot with some of the local kangaroos. Bring a throw rug and a picnic basket to make the most of this special spot as the sun goes down.

Red cliffs at Youngs Beach, Ardrossan
Opposite top Emus roaming in Innes National Park

Where
The Yorke Peninsula is right in the middle of the Eyre Peninsula (*see* p.84) and the Fleurieu Peninsula (*see* p.77), along the South Australian coastline.

Getting here
From Adelaide, Moonta Bay is the closest town of the Yorke Peninsula, just a 2 hour drive out of the city, or it takes about 3 hours, 20 minutes to get down to Innes National Park.

Getting around
If you're flying into Adelaide Airport (ADL), pick up your rental car from the airport to explore more of the park on your own. The park has proper bitumen roads throughout, so there's no issue with bringing rental cars down to Innes.

When to go
The summer months (Dec to March), as well as the shoulder season months on either side of summer are definitely the best time to visit the Yorke Peninsula. With the warmer weather during this time you can take advantage of all the beaches along this beautiful coastline. If you're visiting for bushwalking, autumn is considered the best time, with the cooler weather providing better conditions for hiking, and wildflowers blooming across the peninsula.

Where to stay
Base yourself in Innes National Park to make the most of your time on the Yorke Peninsula. The campsites around the park can either be booked in advance or when you arrive, depending on availability.

The **Stenhouse Bay Campgrounds** were our favourite, set right alongside the ocean, with emus roaming around and plenty of Telstra phone reception.

You can also find smaller campgrounds at Browns Beach, Cable Bay Beach, Casuarina, Gym Beach and Shell Beach.

Need to know
Vehicle entry fees apply within Innes National Park. A day entry permit costs $11 per vehicle and gives you access to the entire park. If you're spending more time in SA, Innes National Park is also included in the South Australian Parks Pass (*see* p.70).

Get planning
Plan your visit to the Yorke Peninsula by heading to yorkepeninsula.com.au, and check out @yorkepeninsula on socials for all the best places to visit.

COOBER PEDY

The opal capital of Australia, where life happens underground

ADVENTURERS | OFF-THE-BEATEN TRACK

Coober Pedy might just be one of the wildest and most unique places in Australia. A small remote town, surrounded by the desert plains that sweep across the middle of South Australia, people come to live in Coober Pedy for a reason. Some are searching for wealth and riches, hoping to strike it big in the famous opal mines. Others are looking to get lost in a place where they will be left alone. No matter what they've come for, there are some very interesting characters to meet here.

The name Coober Pedy was taken from the Antakirinja words 'Kupa Piti', which mean 'whitefellow burrow' – the description given to the opal miners' houses by the local Antakirinja people. It's a place where temperatures regularly sit above 40°C for days on end in the summertime, so most of the town lives in underground dugouts to escape the heat. You can stay in an underground hotel room, or even an underground campsite and experience the unique life that happens under the ground.

While at first it might seem like a small, quiet desert town, there is a whole world happening underground in Coober Pedy. There's no other place like it – it's crazy and random, in all the best ways, and definitely worth a weekend visit for something a little out of the ordinary.

PLAN YOUR TRIP FOR
The biggest event on the Coober Pedy social calendar is the annual **Opal Festival**. Held in June, the festival celebrates the vibrant and culturally diverse community that calls Coober Pedy home, with parades, live music, markets, games and a huge fireworks display. There are also plenty of opals for sale at the festival, a great time to grab yourself a bargain.

Opposite **Views at Kanku-Breakaways Conservation Park**

CAN'T MISS
In the morning:
Take a photo with the iconic **Coober Pedy sign**, found just before the entrance to town when you're driving north from Port Augusta. It's not really a trip to Coober Pedy without this photo!

Try and find your own piece of opal with a bit of **noodling or fossicking** before it gets too hot. Noodling is when you try your luck digging through the mounds of sand, rock and dirt that have been discarded from the opal mines, and fossicking is when you wander around and just try to spot something shiny on the ground. You just never know what you're going to find out here, it's always worth a quick try. If you do go out to the opal fields be extremely careful where you step - there are open mines all over the place and you do not want to fall down one of them.

If you don't have any luck, head to some of the **opal stores** on the main street, where you can buy yourself an authentic Coober Pedy opal. There is jewellery, as well as just loose stones which you can use to create something special yourself.

Explore life underground. While it might not look like it from the road, so much of the town lies below the surface, with an **underground church** filled with incredible stained-glass windows, **underground bars** for a beer, and **underground shops** to keep you cool while you choose your own sparkly opal souvenir.

In the afternoon:
Take a self-guided tour of the **Old Timers Mine**. A definite highlight on any Coober Pedy visit, this is an original hand-dug mine that dates back to 1916. For some reason it was filled and abandoned, until it was rediscovered in 1968, when an underground house extension broke through the walls, into the mine, and found a whole heap of opals! A historical dug-out house has also been preserved in the museum, which is a little creepy.

The **Umoona Museum & Opal Mine** is also worth checking out. It has displays that take you through some of the Aboriginal history of the area, fossilised seashells from the great inland sea that is thought to be under much of Australia, and even dinosaur skeleton remains that have been found in the area.

Coober Pedy

Head to **Josephine's Gallery & Kangaroo Orphanage**. It sounds like a strange combination, but the gallery is full of local Aboriginal artwork, in all kinds of beautiful colours and patterns, that you can view or buy. Out the back of the gallery is a small kangaroo orphanage, with kangaroos that have been rescued from road accidents in outback SA, and you can meet them at their feeding times, at 12pm and 5.30pm each day.

See part of the iconic **dog fence**, famous for being the longest fence in the world. The fence stretches over 5300 kilometres from Queensland, through New South Wales and all the way down to South Australia. It was originally built in the 1880s to prevent dingoes entering sheep grazing country in the south and killing livestock, and has become a historical part of Australia.

In the evening:
Watch the sun set at the **Big Winch**, Coober Pedy's very own 'big thing'. The Big Winch stands tall on a hill in the middle of town, and offers some of the best views across Coober Pedy's main streets, all the way out to the opal fields.

Catch a movie at Coober Pedy's **outdoor drive-in cinema**, which hosts one movie each week on a Saturday night. Bring a deck chair, and there is a delicious sausage sizzle before the movie that's run by local volunteers.

Have dinner at the **local RSL** on a Sunday. Built in a shipping container, this is not like the RSL clubs you're used to at home, but they have a fantastic home-cooked barbecue menu on Sundays and so much community spirit, you'll feel like you're part of the town.

Main street of Coober Pedy

BEST PHOTO SPOTS

Explore **Kanku-Breakaways Conservation Park** and the iconic views of **the Breakaways**. Visit at dusk, about an hour before sunset, to see these insane landscapes changing colours, and you'll feel like you've stepped right onto Mars. The best lookout can be found by following the small sign that says *Angkata* down the dirt track. The Breakaways is part of the traditional land of the Antakirinja Matu-Yankunytjatjara people and is an important part of Coober Pedy. Make sure you stay on the pathways and follow the instructions of any signs you come across so you don't disturb the natural environment. The Moon Plains are also worth a visit, a bizarre landscape that truly makes you feel like you've left Earth.

Where

Coober Pedy is located about 850 kilometres north-west of Adelaide, in the north of South Australia.

Getting here

You can take a 2-hour flight from Adelaide directly into Coober Pedy Airport (CPD), with Rex Airlines. There are three or four flights per week, with a regularly changing schedule. Alternatively, it's a long 9-hour road trip along the Stuart Highway from Adelaide. The road is easy to drive, although it is quite boring if Coober Pedy is your sole destination.

When to go

Avoid visiting during the summer months (late Nov to mid March), when temperatures are at their most extreme. We visited Coober Pedy in February, and although the weather wasn't too hot while we were there, one of the shopkeepers told us that they had a run of more than 10 days in December where the temperature never dropped below 45°C, hitting the low 50s a few of the days!

Where to stay

For the complete Coober Pedy experience, check yourself into one of the underground motels and live life the way the locals do. Underground rooms are cool during the day and night, and they are a kind of pitch black that you do not experience above ground. There is even an underground campground, where you can pitch your tent or your swag in the same way you would above ground.

There are also plenty of above ground choices too, with hotels and motels along the main street and a number of caravan parks with cabins and pools to choose from.

Need to know

Coober Pedy has a fun movie-making history, with films such as *Priscilla, Queen of the Desert* and *Pitch Black* filmed around the area. You can see the spaceship from *Pitch Black* out the front of the Opal Cave, and lots of the Priscilla filming sites around Kanku-Breakaways Conservation Park.

Get planning

To start planning your visit, head to cooberpedy.com for everything you need to know. Check out @cooberpedysa for all the best spots to visit and for town updates.

LIMESTONE COAST

A coastline of natural wonders

NATURE LOVERS

The coastal part of South Australia that runs from the border with Victoria in the east, all the way to Lake Alexandrina and the Murray River Mouth in the west is known in SA as the Limestone Coast. It is said to have taken 26 million years to create the Limestone Coast and, wow, the wait was definitely worth it.

Covered in countless stunning white sand beaches, water that is a mixture of bright blue and green, and landscapes that are full of caves, sinkholes and underground cenotes created on a volcanic plain, there is so much to explore in this little pocket of SA. The Limestone Coast also makes up one section of South Australia's Southern Ocean Drive, lots of natural wonders to see and more than 40 cellar doors offering delicious wine and local produce to try, as well as cute beachside towns such as Robe and Beachport and the dynamic Naracoorte Caves National Park.

To make the most of your visit to the Limestone Coast, fly into Mount Gambier and make your way along the coastline, before flying out of Adelaide. This will give you plenty of time to stop at lots of different places along the way, without having to double back when it's time to go home. It's also an easy drive from Victoria, with Mount Gambier just a four-and-a-half hour drive from Melbourne.

BEST PHOTO SPOTS
You can't go past the **Umpherston Sinkhole** in the early morning light for some truly beautiful shots.

The beautiful garden in Umpherston Sinkhole

CAN'T MISS

It's a good idea to do a little bit of planning before you head to the Limestone Coast. Most of the best natural attractions are hidden away, so if you don't know what you're looking for, it's easy to miss them.

In the morning:
Start your morning at the **Umpherston Sinkhole**, also known as the Sunken Garden, where a beautifully green and vibrant garden has grown out of a crater in the middle of Mount Gambier. The pathway from the top spirals around the garden, offering lots of different viewpoints on the way down. If you visit early in the morning, you can often have the sinkhole all to yourself.

Take a hike up **Mt Schank** (only a 15-min drive out of Mount Gambier), Australia's 'youngest' volcano that erupted just 4500-5000 years ago. It's a big one, but climb up the steps to enjoy extensive 360-degree views across the region, all the way out to the ocean.

Visit the **Blue Lake** in Mount Gambier, which turns the most vibrant blue colour between December and March. Sitting in an extinct volcanic crater, the colour of the water is so vibrant, it's crazy to think that it returns to an unexciting grey colour for the rest of the year. There's a 3.6-kilometre walking trail around the lake, which takes you to each of the lookout platforms around the lake.

Follow it up with a visit to the **Little Blue Lake**, which has one huge bonus over its Mount Gambier counterpart - you can swim here. About 11 kilometres out of Mount Gambier, there's nothing around the Little Blue Lake, it's just a deep sinkhole surrounded by the dry countryside of SA. The lake is a cool 12°C all year-round though, so not one for those who don't like cold water.

Immerse yourself in a completely different type of underwater world, **diving in some of the sinkholes** that lie around the Limestone Coast. **Kilsby Sinkhole** is a top choice, world-renowned as one of the best sinkhole dive sites with fantastic visibility and clear water. **Piccaninne Ponds** and **Hells Hole** are also favourites around the region, with scuba-diving and snorkelling tours from Mount Gambier. You need to join a guided tour to dive in the sinkholes, but most offer snorkelling on the spot.

In the afternoon:
Drive out to **Carpenter Rocks**, a very quiet fishing town known for its dramatic rocky coastline and the remains of the *SS Admella* shipwreck that washed up on the beach. Start at the **Cape Banks Lighthouse** and then make your way down to the beach to see the shipwreck still lying at the water's edge.

Stop in to **Beachport** for a quick visit, one of our favourite towns along the coastline. Beachport has some of the prettiest coloured sea water along the coast, as well as being a charming little town full of shops selling windchimes and colourful gifts.

Grab an afternoon drink at a local winery, with more than 24 cellar doors that produce world-famous cabernet sauvignon and shiraz both inland and along the coast. Whether you have time for a quick taste test or to stop for a little longer, the reds that are made in this region are absolutely delicious. You can't go past **Cape Jaffa Wines** in Mount Benson or **Katnook Coonawarra Cellar Door** in Coonawarra.

Spend your afternoon exploring the best of Robe's four-wheel drive tracks with a visit to **Little Dip Conservation Park**. Follow the sandy tracks off the main road to find some of Robe's best-kept secrets, including Stoney Rise, a peaceful little beach with clear water and a jagged coastline. If you're sand driving, make sure you lower your tyre pressure and carry recovery tracks to get you out of a jam - we saw plenty of cars that got stuck.

From Robe, head inland a little to visit South Australia's only UNESCO World Heritage Site - the **Naracoorte Caves National Park**. The caves gained World Heritage status in 1994 for being home to 21 fossil sites that have preserved the bones of megafauna that became extinct more than 60,000 years ago. Also in the area, **Tantanoola Caves Conservation Park** is another very popular spot for exploring SA's cave system.

Explore the wetlands of **Coorong National Park**, which is home to Lake Alexandrina, the last stop on the Murray River's journey before it finally reaches the ocean after winding its way across three states and thousands of kilometres. At the Murray River Mouth, fresh water and salt water mix together in a very unique blend of colours before running into the ocean. Jump on a cruise with **Spirit Australia Cruises** to see the best of Coorong National Park, and they'll take you all the way to the mouth of Lake Alexandrina.

In the evening:
Head to **Kingston S.E** (also known as Kingston South East), best known for **Larry The Lobster** - another in Australia's collection of 'big things'. After snapping your selfie, find a restaurant for dinner along the beach where you can sample some of the local seafood. This is primarily a fishing town, and you know you're getting some of the freshest fish in SA when you order in Kingston S.E. The crayfish is highly recommended, sorry Larry!

Where

The Limestone Coast runs from the border with Victoria, along the coast to the Murray River Mouth.

Getting here

Fly to Mount Gambier Airport (MGB), with direct flights from both Adelaide and Melbourne on Qantas and Rex Airlines. The flight takes just an hour and 5 minutes from both directions, with connections onwards to the rest of the country.

Alternatively, Mount Gambier is pretty much right in the middle of Adelaide and Melbourne, with about a 4 hour and 40 minute drive to reach either city.

When to go

Head to the Limestone Coast during the summertime, roughly from November to March to take advantage of the warmer weather and all the activities that come with it. Weather along the Limestone Coast can be a little temperamental all year round, but summer has the most consistency of warm weather and sunny days.

Main towns

There are a couple of main towns in the Limestone Coast region, with Mount Gambier inland and Robe along the coastline. Both have everything you could need for your visit, including lots of different accommodation options, supermarkets and plenty of great places to eat. Both towns will have you feeling like you're a local in no time.

Get planning

Head to discovermountgambier.com.au to find out everything the Limestone Coast has to offer, and check out @discover_mount_gambier and @limestonecoast on Insta to find all the best secret spots.

Time for a dip in Little Blue Lake

RIVERLAND

Immerse yourself in life on the river

NATURE LOVERS

On the South Australian side of the border, the Murray River region is known as Riverland, the ultimate weekend destination to get wet and dirty, and enjoy life under the sun and the stars. It's a place where time moves a little slower, where nothing feels like it's super urgent or important, and you have all the time in the world to just laze by the riverside and enjoy your weekend.

The Riverland is dotted with quiet riverside towns, a thriving fruit industry and plenty of ways to get out on the water. Renmark and Berri are two can't-miss spots, with the Murray running right through the heart of both towns. From the spot where Victoria and New South Wales meet South Australia, the Murray River runs for 362 kilometres, all the way down to the bottom of the country, where it then escapes into the Indian Ocean through Lake Alexandrina.

Riverland

PLAN YOUR TRIP FOR
Head to Renmark on the last weekend of January to get caught up in the craziness of the **Dinghy Derby**, where locals race their pimped-out dinghies across the river at up to 80 kilometres per hour. Find yourself a spot along the river to watch the race and enjoy the action and excitement. The **Riverland Wine & Food Festival** held in Berri in October each year is another great weekend to visit, where local food, wine and entertainment come together on the banks of the Murray River, sharing the best of the Riverland region.

Opposite The Murray River winding through Riverland

CAN'T MISS
In the morning:
Rent a kayak and explore the river from the water. There are lots of self-guided trails around Renmark, offering an insight into the river region and taking about an hour each to complete. You can organise a kayak rental from **Canoe the Riverland**, who also offer moonlight tours, foodie tours with **Taste of Riverland Day Tours**, overnight camping tours and basic kayaking skills sessions.

Check out the *PS Industry*, one of the oldest paddle steamers on the Murray River, dating back to 1911. It still fires up on the first Sunday of every month, as well as on random long weekends throughout the year, and you can pop inside and learn about a piece of history.

Keep an eye out for colourful fruit stalls along the side of the road, selling seasonal fruit from around the region. **Aggies Fresh Fruit Stall** in Glossop is a favourite, a lovely place to stock up on fruit and grab a cute photo. You can also get local produce at **Flavours of the Riverland** in Barmera, with a large selection of gourmet foods made from local produce and a taste of the region's famous Backyard Bread.

Step back in time millions of years with a visit to **Ngaut Ngaut Conservation Park**, home of the Nganguraku people. With soaring cliffs sitting on the edge of an extinct sea bed, and ancient rock art sites, this is an important Dreaming and cultural site and the birthplace of the Black Duck Dreaming story.

Pop into **Berri**, another of the larger towns of the Riverland, home to unique shopping boutiques, a beautiful green riverfront and lots of outdoor beer gardens and alfresco dining. It's a quiet little town for a swim or a spot of fishing on the river, with a friendly community vibe.

In the afternoon:
Stop for lunch at the **Wilkadene Woolshed Brewery** and try one of their famous hard lemonades. Located right on the water, the balcony of Wilkadene looks straight over the Murray River, and is such a peaceful spot to spend a few hours, disconnect and relax in the sunshine.

Try the local at **Twenty Third Street Distillery**, which has been standing strong in Renmark since 1914. Creating all kinds of spirits, including gin, brandy, whisky and vodka, there is a range of delicious drinks to try. You can take a tour of the

distillery or maybe join a cocktail masterclass to create some of your own signature drinks.

Visit **Berri Estate Winery & Cellar Door** in Glossop, one of Australia's largest wineries, crushing more than 220,000 tonnes of grapes to produce more than 100 million litres of wine each year. WOW. Come for a tour or a tasting, and meet some of the locals here who have been passionately producing wine here for decades.

Have an off-road adventure with a visit to **Loveday 4×4 Adventure Park**, where you can explore the four-wheel drive tracks of this 8000 acre private property. With all kinds of terrains from smooth clay flats, to creek beds, stony hills and sandy Mallee scrub, test your skills on the trails before hitting the Loveday Tavern for a well-earned drink at the end of the day.

In the evening:
Head to the *Murray River Queen* in the heart of Renmark for happy hour on the Murray. With discounted drinks between 4pm and 6pm, grab a seat on the top deck where you can people-watch on the river all evening. It's also a great place to watch the sunset, as the sky glows bright beautiful colours at dusk.

Try your luck at catching an elusive metre-long **Murray Cod**, a challenge to locals and visitors alike. The Murray River has great fishing conditions, with redfin, trout, catfish and callop also regularly caught in the Riverland. Dusk seems to be a popular time for fishing, so see how you go along the bank as the sun goes down.

BEST PHOTO SPOTS
A can't-miss photo stop in Riverland is **Big Bend**, found just near Paringa (an Ngarrindjeri word meaning 'big bend in the river'), where you can see the towering red and orange cliffs that line the Murray River. Bring a big blow-up swan or sparkly donut for a fun shot floating down the river.

Big Bend near Paringa
Opposite Road tripping down the Oodnadatta Track

Where
Riverland runs from the South Australian border with Victoria and New South Wales in the east, all the way down to Lake Alexandrina in the south where it feeds into the ocean.

Getting here
From Adelaide, the Murray River region can be reached in as little as an hour and 15 minutes at Mannum, or just under 3 hours to get to Renmark at the other end.

Getting around
Pick up a rental car from Adelaide Airport (ADL), and it's an easy drive along the Sturt Highway.

When to go
Riverland is a great region to visit, with its inland location giving it warm sunny days all year round. Renmark and the more northern parts of Riverland can be particularly hot in the summer, with temperatures regularly hitting over 40°C, so for more comfortable temperatures visit during the shoulder seasons in autumn and spring.

Main towns
Renmark is one of the biggest towns in Riverland, and is a great place to base yourself to explore the SA side of the Murray River. It's also only a short drive to the other towns that make up Riverland, making it an easy and convenient spot to explore the river system from.

Where to stay
In Renmark, you can find accommodation to suit every type of traveller, from free camps along the river to luxury retreats overlooking the river.

Get planning
Find out more about the Riverland region by heading to destinationriverland.org.au or check out @riverlandsouthaustralia for all the best places to go.

Riverland

OODNADATTA TRACK

One of Australia's most epic outback drives

OFF-THE-BEATEN TRACK

So you might need longer than just one weekend for this one, but if you have a few extra days up your sleeve, the Oodnadatta Track is absolutely worth the effort. Known to be one of Australia's most iconic drives, the Oodnadatta Track is the best way to really explore the outback of South Australia and immerse yourself in life off the grid.

Stretching across the desert plains of South Australia, the actual Oodnadatta Track is a 617-kilometre-long unsealed dirt road between Marla in the north-west and Marree in the south-east. Depending on your plans – where you're coming from and going to – you might drive along the whole thing, or just part of it, connecting it with other road trips and destinations.

It's a trip that you don't make lightly though, with long drives between any towns and little access to water, fuel or phone reception along the way. It can be hard on your car, and even harder on your van, but it also gives you a unique insight into the outback landscape, a part of the country that few choose to travel.

Before embarking on the Oodnadatta Track, make sure you find yourself a Pink Roadhouse Mud Map. We absolutely lived by this map when we were driving along the track. On one side there is a mud map, showing you every single thing there is to see along the track, and on the other side there is a little bit of information about all the different stops, including what you can expect to find there and their UHF channel if you need to contact them. You can get the map from the Pink Roadhouse in Oodnadatta, as well as most other information centres in Outback SA.

WHERE TO STOP ALONG THE WAY

Start your journey in **Coober Pedy** (*see* p.96), the wild little opal hunting town in the middle of the South Australian outback. Make sure you leave with plenty of drinking water and fuel, as this will be the largest town you see for a long while. Follow the signs that point to Oodnadatta, right through the heart of the Moon Plain, and the most amount of nothing you will ever come across. The Moon Plain is known for land that is a little bit bouncy, as well as sparkly in the light from all the gypsum in the earth. Along the way you'll also see signs for the Painted Desert, where hills pop up from nowhere that literally look like they have been painted in colourful stripes.

A teeny tiny country town that gives this iconic drive its name, the only thing to see in Oodnadatta is the iconic **Pink Roadhouse**, where literally everything is pink - from the general store to the petrol pumps and even the picnic benches out the front. It's a good place to stop for fuel and a bite to eat, and of course to pick up a Mud Map if you haven't found one yet.

A great place to stop for the night, there's free camping at the **Algebuckina** waterhole alongside the river. It's not very inviting to swim in, looking much more like a murky swamp than a river, but it's a good spot to get off the road for the night. Algebuckina also has one of the best-preserved bridges from the Old Ghan Railway, the historical first railway line for *The Ghan* that ran through the outback from Adelaide to Alice Springs. The railway line changed its route in 1980 to avoid the floodplains along the Oodnadatta Track, where the original line was often washed away during heavy rain.

Roughly the halfway point along the Oodnadatta Track, the town of **William Creek** is pretty much just a pub. In fact, only 12 people live here. The William Creek Hotel is a great stop though, quirky and interesting, with lots to look at. The whole roof and lots of the walls are covered with all kinds of business cards, school IDs and expired driver's licences left behind by travellers who have passed through. If you do get the chance to visit, see if you can find our card, with a cute little illustration of our van stapled near the bar! There's phone reception here, as well as fuel if you need to fill up. Grab a drink and a toastie from Rose behind the bar before you continue on your way.

A favourite spot for many in the middle of the outback, **Coward Springs** is a little oasis with a natural spa of springwater to have a quick swim. After long days of driving in the outback, there is nothing better than breaking up your trip with a refreshing dip in the spa. Coward Springs is open from 10am to 4pm for day visitors, with a $2 fee to be paid into an honesty box for your swim. There's also a camping ground here, although it is quite expensive for very little. Stop

for a swim but find another place to camp for the night, with plenty of free camps (marked on WikiCamps app) just down the road.

A can't-miss spot along the Oodnadatta Track, **Kati Thanda (Lake Eyre)** is Australia's largest salt lake, as well as the lowest point in Australia. Most of the time it's pretty much dry, with little-to-no water in the lake at all. But when it's full it is quite spectacular, bringing visitors from all over the country, and the small towns that surround it are absolutely pumping. There's a good lookout point to stop at, where you can walk down to the lake and actually walk across it if you like. To see the greatness from the sky, you can also organise a scenic flight from William Creek or Marree.

Marking the end of the Oodnadatta Track, **Marree** is where the unsealed dirt road ends and the bitumen resumes as you drive onwards to the Flinders Ranges (*see* p.90). But stop here for a celebratory drink - YOU'VE MADE IT! Hang out with the friendly locals at the Marree Pub, who offer free camping out the back, or hotel rooms inside and plenty of entertaining stories about local life in Marree and the outback. Take advantage of their swimming pool to cool down and finally have a shower to get all that red dirt off you.

Top Swim stop in the natural spa at Coward Springs
Bottom Camels in the SA outback
Opposite Pit stop at the Pink Roadhouse in Oodnadatta

Where
The Oodnadatta Track is right in the middle of SA, connecting Marla in the north-west and Marree in the south-east.

Getting here
From Adelaide it takes around 8 hours and 40 minutes (or 5 hours and 20 minutes from Port Augusta) to get to Coober Pedy and the beginning of the Oodnadatta Track. On the other side, it takes about 7 hours to get from Marree back to Adelaide (or 4 hours to get back to Port Augusta) through the Flinders Ranges (see p.90). It's a huge amount of driving to explore this track, but it's just incredible out there.

Getting around
Before you embark on this outback drive, make sure you have done enough planning and preparing to keep you safe for the whole journey. Some of our top survival tips are:

Always make sure you check the road closures and track conditions before you leave for your trip, particularly if it has been raining or in times of extreme heat. Bookmark this website: dpti.sa.gov.au/outbackroads and check for updates regularly before and during your trip to keep up to date with what's happening in the region. You really don't want to get stuck out here.

Make sure you have a good quality, high-gain UHF radio and antenna for your car that can reach far distances.

Fill up with petrol every time you see it. You never know what can happen in the outback and it's better to fill up more often than to find a town out of fuel when you need it.

Lower your tyre pressure before you hit the dirt roads. Generally, 25psi is a good pressure for any off-road driving for the average tyre.

Slow down when you're passing other drivers to prevent rocks kicking up into their car and/or caravan.

When to go
The cooler months of the year are considered the best time to travel the Oodnadatta Track, particularly from around April to October. During this time, the weather is significantly cooler, making your drive a lot more comfortable. That being said, we drove the track in February and absolutely loved it. We didn't have any extreme temperatures, mostly in the low 30s or so each day, so it was comfortable to drive and sleep.

Where to stay
Download the WikiCamps app before you go, which lists all the different campsites, including free camps along the way, as well as any of the pubs and hotels that have rooms to stay in. If you're visiting during the peak season, book your stops ahead of time to avoid missing out, particularly if you're going to be staying in hotel rooms.

Get planning
For more about the Oodnadatta Track and planning advice, head to traveloutbackaustralia.com/oodnadatta-track.html, a great resource for any outback drives around Australia.

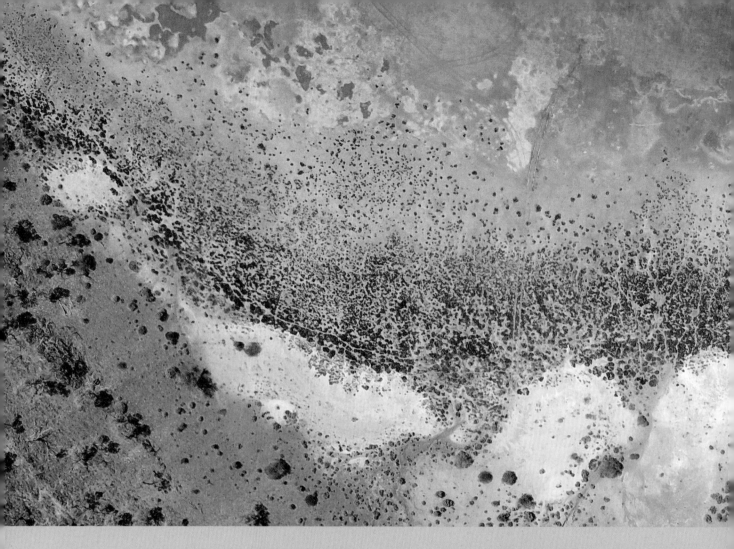

Can't-miss place
Esperance and Cape Le Grand National Park (*see* p.120).

Top experience
Swimming with whale sharks on Ningaloo Reef (*see* p.115).

National Parks Pass
An All Parks Pass provides unlimited entry into any WA national park. The pass covers one vehicle from $25 for a 5-day Holiday Pass, and $120 for a one-year All Parks Pass. You can purchase your pass at shop.dbca. wa.gov.au/collections/park-passes or at visitor centres around the state.

Visiting Aboriginal Lands
Permits are essential for travel on Aboriginal Lands in WA. The Outback Way, between Laverton and Uluṟu, is patrolled and fines will be issued if you don't have a permit. Permits are also required to travel across sections of the Canning Stock Route, Gunbarrel Highway and Anne Beadell Highway. Apply for a permit from the Department of Planning, Land and Heritage (daa.wa.gov.au/en/entry-permits). When travelling through Aboriginal Lands, drivers are prohibited from diverting off the main road, and alcohol is not allowed to be carried through Aboriginal communities.

Important dates
• Western Australia Day (first Monday of June)

Time zone
Western Australia follows the Australian Western Standard Time Zone (GMT +8).

Stay connected & get featured
Follow @westernaustralia for inspiration and have your photos featured by using hashtags #thisiswa or #justanotherdayinwa.

Helpful websites
• Road conditions and distances mainroads.wa.gov.au
• National Parks dpaw.wa.gov.au

Western Australia

Covering almost a third of Australia, and almost like its own little country in the west, Western Australia (WA) is a state unlike any other in Australia. It's a place where you can have some of the most beautiful landscapes, beaches and gorges all to yourself. Where you can drive for hours without passing another car on the road. Where you can explore for days or weeks or even months and only just scratch the surface. With a little planning, WA makes for many great weekends away.

Western Australia is distinctly different from the East Coast. The sun sets at an unreasonably early time, but the beautiful colours streaked across the sky make up for it. The supermarkets close at 6pm and even some of the larger towns are slow and sleepy, with shops closed on Sundays.

From the beautiful white sand beaches of Esperance (*see* p.120) and the Coral Coast (*see* p.124), to the vibrant red deserts (*see* p.139), WA is simply a magical place, overflowing with First Nations history, incredible environments, the delicious food and wine of Margaret River (*see* p.128), and of course the cheeky quokkas that are found on Rottnest Island (*see* p.112) – perhaps the most famous face of WA. It's a place where time moves at a slower pace, giving you the chance to explore more, see more and learn more about Australia's epic history and heritage.

PERTH

The Noongar people are the Traditional Owners of Boorloo (Perth)

CULTURE BUFFS

One of the most isolated major cities in the whole world, Perth is thousands of kilometres away from the next closest city. On the West Coast of Australia, Perth is in fact closer to Bali than it is to Canberra. With sunsets over the ocean and the largest city park in the world, even larger than Central Park in New York City, Perth also boasts more sunshine than any other Aussie city.

It's a city of great food and drinks, with an ever-expanding line-up of rooftop bars, pubs and restaurants, night markets, art galleries and shows, and beachside suburbs along the Indian Ocean. Perth is a lovely weekend getaway and also the gateway to so many incredible destinations in WA.

Perth is the first stop on many Western Australian road trips, plus only a short ferry ride from the shore you can be taking selfies with quokkas on Rottnest Island, one of the happiest animals in the world.

PLAN YOUR TRIP FOR

Visit Perth between mid-February and early March for the **Perth Festival**, Australia's longest-running cultural festival that is three weeks of music, dance, outdoor movies, theatre, visual arts, food, wine, celebrations and more. There are heaps of shows, performances and exhibits, with artists from all around the world.

CAN'T MISS

Take a dip in the beautiful **Cottesloe Beach**, one of the most famous beaches in Perth.

Pack a picnic lunch and enjoy an afternoon exploring **Kings Park** and the **Botanic Gardens**.

Jump on a **whale-watching tour** (Sept to Dec) to see humpback whales swimming by on their migration.

Take advantage of the sunshine and hop your way across the city's best **rooftop bars**.

Learn about Noongar culture and history on a walk with a Traditional Owner with **Nyungar Tours**.

The **Perth Cultural Centre** will keep you busy. It's home to the Art Gallery of WA, the Perth Institute of Contemporary Arts, the Urban Orchard, State Library and newly opened WA Museum.

Head to the beach at **sunset** to watch it set over the ocean.

Pop over to **Penguin Island** for a chance to spot wild penguins roaming around the island.

Eat your way through **Barrack Street**, home to a diverse range of restaurants and bars offering everything from Korean barbecue to pizza.

DAYTRIPS

Explore **Fremantle**, or Freo to the locals, the cute coastal city about 30 minutes out of Perth. With its signature weekend markets, cafes and bars, heritage streets, delicious food and great beaches, Fremantle makes for a lovely daytrip. Don't miss its famous brewery, **Little Creatures**, for an afternoon beer, or the heritage-listed pub for a bite to eat.

Jump onboard with **Captain Cook Cruises** and take a gourmet wine cruise to the **Swan Valley**. The cruise offers beautiful views of Perth from the water as it leaves Barrack Street Jetty, and once you get to Swan Valley you can either take a coach tour to see more of the region, exploring wineries, breweries and even the local chocolate company, or have a more in-depth afternoon at **Sandalford Estate**, with a delicious lunch, wine tastings and a winemaking tour.

Perth

Top The famous Crawley Edge Boatshed
Bottom Fremantle Markets
Opposite View from Kings Park
Previous Where the pink lake meets the desert,
Lake Ballard

BEST PHOTO SPOTS
Don't miss the super-cute little blue boathouse that has become famous as the perfect photo spot in Perth. The **Crawley Edge Boatshed**, to use its actual name, is more than 90 years old, with a short jetty connecting it to the shore. It is along Mounts Bay Road, just a short drive out of the city.

Where
Perth is in the south-western corner of Western Australia.

Getting here
There are direct flights to Perth Airport (PER) from every major airport around Australia. From the airport, you can either pick up a rental car or jump on a shuttle bus service which operates between Perth Airport and the CBD. There are quite a few different shuttle bus services to choose from, with pick-ups from every terminal and plenty of stops around the city. Alternatively, a taxi or Uber will cost around $50 from the airport to the city.

Getting around
It's easy to get around Perth on its public transport system, with a network of trains, buses and ferries taking you everywhere you need to go. There's a free zone in the city centre for trains and buses, making it super easy to get between City West, Elizabeth Quay and Claisebrook stations. To use any public transport, including the free zones though, you need to grab yourself a SmartRider card (available from the airport and most newsagencies), which also gives you access to the public ferries.

When to go
Offering more sunny days than any other capital city in the country, Perth is a great city to visit all year round. Summers are nice and hot, with average temperatures of 29°C, while winter sees averages of 19 to 21°C. It is quite a windy city though, with the windiest months being across spring and summer.

Where to stay
To stay right in the heart of the action, base yourself in Perth's CBD, somewhere between Wellington Street and St Georges Terrace. This will put you within walking distance of plenty of shops, restaurants and bars, Elizabeth Quay and the Swan River.

For a more laid-back vibe and to be right near the beach, look for accommodation options in Fremantle, definitely a more bohemian vibe, with awesome weekend markets and beautiful historic streets to explore.

Need to know
Perth is warm but can get exceptionally windy, so it's always a good idea to have a lightweight jacket on hand.

Get planning
To plan your visit to Perth, head to experienceperth.com for up-to-date planning advice or check out @destinationperth, @perthisok and @visitperth on Instagram for all the best places around the city.

ROTTNEST ISLAND

An island paradise

NATURE LOVERS

Rottnest Island is the ideal place to soak up the ultimate island vibes, with no cars at all on the island, and everything you need only a short walk away. Kick back and relax on one of the 63 incredible beaches and 20 bays dotted around the island, zip around on an electric bicycle, snorkel in the crystal-clear water, or enjoy the sunset views with a delicious cocktail at the beach club.

Affectionately known as Rotto, or Wadjemup to the local Noongar people, the island sits just off the coast of Fremantle, a short 30-minute ferry ride from the mainland. Best known for its famous quokka populations, people come from all over the world to try and snap a selfie with the cute smiling little quokkas that roam all over the island. They're definitely not shy, so you're likely to spot them everywhere from the main street to the beach club, and maybe even having a midday nap in the shade near your luxury glamping tent.

An easy weekend getaway from Perth, Rottnest Island feels like a whole different world, and is a can't-miss place for anyone heading to Western Australia.

BEST PHOTO SPOTS

Obviously, no trip to Rottnest Island would be complete without a super-cute photo of a quokka smiling up at your camera. For the best photo opportunities, try and find a quokka near the beach during the golden hour, and they are often spotted emerging at Pinky's around sunset. Quokkas have no fear of humans and if you sit still will often come right up to you. Keep a respectful distance when taking photos, and remember that there is a fine if you're caught touching or feeding them.

PLAN YOUR TRIP FOR

Rottnest Island is a great spot for humpback whale spotting (Aug to Nov) as they migrate south with their newborn calves. They spend lots of time hanging around the waters of Rottnest Island, so it's a great place to jump on a whale-watching cruise. **Rottnest Fast Ferries** has a seasonal two-hour whale-watching cruise, for your best chance of getting close to the action.

A Rottnest Island Iced Tea at Pinky's Beach Club
Opposite left Smiling quokkas are famous on Rotto
Opposite right Sunset over Pinky Beach and the Bathurst Lighthouse

CAN'T MISS

In the morning:

Rent an electric bicycle from **Pedal & Flipper** to quickly zip around the island, stopping whenever you like for photos or a quick dip, or jump on the **Island Explorer** for their hop-on, hop-off bus service. The **Discovery Bus Tour** also loops around the island, with a guided 90-minute tour of its cultural and historical heritage sites.

Beach hop across the island, stopping for a dip at as many of the beaches as you can. Head to **The Basin** early in the morning to get this stunning natural swimming pool all to yourself - definitely one of our favourite spots on the island, especially if you can beat the crowds. Some more great spots include **Fish Hook Bay**, **Pinky's Beach**, **Geordie Bay**, **Little Salmon Bay** and **Little Parakeet Bay**.

Jump on a daytrip with **Boutique Cruises** to experience the best of Rotto from the water, where you can snorkel around a shipwreck, see lots of the different bays and beaches and stop at a rocky little island to meet a colony of Australian sea lions.

Take a free guided walking tour with **Rottnest Voluntary Guides**, who have so much knowledge to share about the history of the island. Free tours depart from outside the Salt Store each day, with a whole schedule of different tours on offer.

In the afternoon:

Hire some snorkels from **Pedal & Flipper** and snorkel the **underwater self-guided snorkelling trails** at Little Salmon Bay and Parker Point to explore some of the beautiful marine life that surrounds Rottnest Island.

Climb to the top of the **Wadjemup Lighthouse** for the best views across the whole island, including the beautiful Pinky's Beach and the Basin nearby.

In the evening:

Grab a cocktail and settle in for the sunset at **Pinky's Beach Club**. Although the sun doesn't descend over the ocean, the sky still lights up in a beautiful swirl of pink, orange and yellow as the sun sets behind you. Enjoy the sky show with a tasty Rottnest Island Iced Tea, the beach club's specialty cocktail. Pinky's also serves dinner, with a delicious diverse menu each night.

Where

Rottnest Island lies 18 kilometres off the coast of Fremantle along the West Coast.

Getting here

Catch a ferry service from Fremantle to Rottnest Island with **SeaLink Rottnest Island**. The trip takes about 30 minutes from B Shed at Victoria Quay and there are multiple services throughout the day. A ferry ticket costs $51 per adult for a return fare, plus a mandatory $19.50 Government Admission Fee which contributes to the conservation of the island. Take advantage of SeaLink's luggage concierge, and let them know where you're staying when you check into the ferry. They will deliver your luggage straight to your accommodation, so you don't have to worry about lugging it around the island, and can start enjoying island life as soon as you set foot on Rotto.

Getting around

The main way to get around Rottnest Island is by bike, which you can rent from **Pedal & Flipper** on Bedford Avenue. The island is quite hilly and can also get a bit windy, so choosing an electric bike during your visit is the best way to go. It makes riding around the island quick and easy, with a little extra oomph to get you up those hilly roads. Pedal & Flipper also rent out snorkelling equipment, paddleboards, wetsuits, diving tanks, beach equipment and more. You can also jump on the **Island Explorer Bus** to get around the island, which has 19 different stops for you to get off and explore. A day pass will give you the freedom to hop on and off as many times as you'd like, which costs $20 for an adult ticket.

Dinner with a furry friend at
Discovery Parks Rottnest Island

When to go

For the best weather and to take advantage of the many beaches around the island, head to Rottnest Island between October and April, when the weather is warmer and the days are long and sunny. If you can, avoid travelling during the Western Australian school holidays, when families from Perth flock to the island and it's generally a lot busier.

Where to stay

Without a doubt, **Discovery Rottnest Island** is the place to stay. Sitting just behind the sand dunes of the iconic Pinky Beach, Discovery Rottnest Island has glamping-style accommodation, with luxury tents set up to give you the ultimate island experience. The beds are big and comfy, the tents are kitted out with their own bathrooms and small kitchens, there's a deck to relax on out the front, and the beach is only a few steps away. It's also home to Pinky's Beach Club, serving our favourite cocktails on the island, as well as complimentary breakfast during your stay.

Need to know

Droning for recreational use is not permitted anywhere on Rottnest Island. If you are desperate to drone during your visit, you will need to apply for a commercial photography or filming permit for approval, submit a risk-management plan, and if all that is approved, meet with the RIA Aerodrone Manager before you are able to get going. You can find all the information at rottnestisland.com/whats-on/filming-and-photography. Permits can take up to a month to be approved, so make sure you submit them well in advance.

Get planning

To help you plan your visit to Rottnest Island, head to rottnestisland.com or check out @rottnestislandwa for all the best spots to explore around the island.

EXMOUTH & NINGALOO REEF

Australia's whale shark capital

NATURE LOVERS

Sitting about halfway along the mighty Western Australian coastline is Exmouth, a sleepy little beach town that is the gateway to the incredible Ningaloo Coast UNESCO World Heritage Area. Ningaloo is the ultimate destination on the West Coast to immerse yourself in life underwater and the world's largest fringing reef. Stretching for 250 kilometres along Western Australia's North-west Cape, Ningaloo Reef is one of the only two coral reefs that have formed on the western side of a continent, and the reef can be found only a few metres from the shore in some places.

Receiving its name from the Wajarri language word 'Ningaloo', which means 'promontory', 'deep water' or 'high land jutting into the sea', the Ningaloo Coast has an Aboriginal history that dates back more than 30,000 years, encompassing the history of the Yamatji peoples of the Baiyungu and Yinigudura clans. It's such a special place to everyone who comes to visit.

At Ningaloo, you can find whale sharks, humpback whales, thousands of turtles, incredible corals and brightly coloured fish. It is one of the most important nesting grounds in the world for green and loggerhead turtles, and sees tens of thousands of whales pass by the coastline each year. With its own airport and daily flights from Perth, it's quickly becoming an ideal weekend getaway. Base yourself in the heart of Exmouth to take advantage of the relaxing beach resorts, great food and drinks and unbelievable views for the ultimate coastal holiday.

PLAN YOUR TRIP FOR

Visit the Ningaloo Coast to experience the whale shark season (April to July), where you can jump right in the water and swim around with these enormous majestic animals. There's also the annual **Ningaloo Whale Shark Festival** held in May with concerts, live bands, art exhibitions and cooking demos.

The blue waters of Ningaloo Reef are just incredible

CAN'T MISS

In the morning:

Jump on a **whale shark experience** to get up close and personal with these gentle giants in the only place in the world where whale sharks regularly swim close to land, and in such large numbers. Whale sharks usually arrive on the Ningaloo coast from early April and stay until the end of July each year.

After the whale sharks leave the Ningaloo Coast, the **humpback whales** waste no time taking their place. From June to November, more than 30,000 humpback whales migrate annually and are often spotted having a rest in the Exmouth Gulf before their long journey home. Book onto a whale-watching tour or head to the Vlamingh Head Lookout to see if you can spot them from the shore.

Pop into the **Jurabi Turtle Centre**, one of Australia's biggest breeding and nesting areas for sea turtles. Tours are run by the Department of Parks and Wildlife where you can head out onto the beach to observe these incredible creatures, with nesting season between November and March and hatching season beginning in February.

In the afternoon:

Spend an afternoon at the beautiful **Turquoise Beach**, where you can swim right out to the reef from the beach. The best way to experience the reef here is to drift snorkel - swim out a hundred metres from the southern side of the beach and then let the current drift you back to where you started over the beautiful colourful reef. The tide will keep you moving slowly along the beachline, while being calm enough to head back into the beach whenever you're done.

Take a hike in the remote **Kennedy Range National Park**, home to the popular Honeycomb Gorge right in the heart. Created from years of wind and water spray, the honeycomb name comes from a spattering of hexagon-shaped holes that have formed in the cliff-face. It's a great place for camping under the stars (bring your own camping gear, of course), connecting with nature and spending an afternoon hiking around.

Hop your way across some of Exmouth's best restaurants and bars, with plenty of outdoor dining with great views and cocktail menus to choose from. Some of the can't-miss spots include **Mantarays**, **Froth Craft Breweries**, **Whalers**, **The BBQ Father** and **The Social Society**.

Joy ride your way through the sky on a **microlight flight with Birds Eye View**. With 30-, 60- and 90-minute flight options, you can spot whale sharks, humpback whales, turtles and manta rays from the sky, while experiencing unparalleled views over the whole Ningaloo Coastline.

In the evening:

Marvel at the incredible views during the golden hour from **Charles Knife Canyon** in Cape Range National Park. The drive takes you along the ridge of the range and gives you stunning panoramic views over the gorges and out to the ocean. There are plenty of beautiful lookouts to stop at along the way.

DAYTRIPS

Take a daytrip out to the magical, breathtaking **Karijini National Park**, Western Australia's second-largest national park that covers more than 627 thousand hectares. It has insane dramatic landscapes, incredible gorges, waterfalls, lookouts and mountain ranges. Give yourself plenty of time to get around to the highlights, including Hancock Gorge, Hamersley Gorge, Oxer Lookout, Dales Gorge and Fortescue Falls.

BEST PHOTO SPOTS

All the best photos along the Ningaloo Coast are underwater, so grab yourself an underwater camera and take a selfie with all the turtles, whales, manta rays and colourful fish you find under the sea. But don't touch or disturb marine life, and swim calmly and slowly to avoid scaring them away.

Where
Exmouth is almost exactly in the middle of the Western Australia coastline, with the Ningaloo Coast extending for 250 kilometres along the coast.

Getting here
Qantas offers direct flights from Perth to Exmouth-Learmonth Airport (LEA), with connections onwards to the rest of the country. Alternatively, Exmouth is about a 13-hour drive (1250 kilometres) from Perth along the North West Coastal Highway.

Getting around
Book a car rental to pick up when you arrive at the airport to give yourself the freedom and flexibility to explore this dynamic region.

When to go
The best weather is during the dry season (March to Oct), when days are warm and sunny with minimal rainfall. During this time, you also have the most choice for activities and experiences, with many tour companies closing during the wet season. To experience whale shark season, visit between April and July.

Where to stay
There are plenty of great places to stay around Exmouth, with luxury resorts right on the beachfront, luxe holiday houses, glamping, and plenty of caravan parks to choose from. Whether you base yourself right in the heart of the city or towards the town beach, nothing is very far away, with easy access to the whole region.

Get planning
To plan your visit to Exmouth and the Ningaloo Coast region, head to australiascoralcoast.com/destination/exmouth and australiascoralcoast.com/region/ningaloo, and check out @australiascoralcoast on socials for all the can't-miss spots.

Snorkelling in Ningaloo Reef
Opposite Turtle hatchlings start appearing in February each year

Sal Salis Ningaloo Reef

We recommend camping under the stars at the luxurious glamping experience in Western Australia, Sal Salis. Overlooking the beautiful Ningaloo Reef, Sal Salis is the ultimate weekend to relax, unwind, disconnect and immerse yourself in nature.

A super-exclusive place, there are only 16 wilderness tents at Sal Salis, which means it's always quiet and peaceful, making it all the more personal. Located within Cape Range National Park and with the reef right on your doorstep, Sal Salis has been designed to work in tune with the fragile environment surrounding it, focusing on minimal impact and sustainability.

A completely immersive, all-inclusive experience, Sal Salis has thought of every tiny detail to make your stay extraordinary. You will indulge in an ever-changing menu, featuring seasonal local produce and accompanied by the best Western Australian beer and wines. Your days will be spent exploring the incredible surroundings, with tours that take you swimming with whale sharks and humpback whales, sea kayaking to secret spots on the reef, drift snorkelling along the shoreline and hikes through Mandu Mandu Gorge. The knowledgeable guides share the very best of the region with you.

The nights at Sal Salis are just as magical. If you've never experienced a truly dark night sky, this is the place to do it. With no light pollution to distract you out here, head to the designated Dark Sky area, with views of the Milky Way like you've never seen before and dinner by candlelight to keep everything as dark and as magical as possible. A place to truly experience just how little we are in the mighty universe.

IMPORTANT INFO

Sal Salis is located on the North-west Cape of WA, about an hour's drive from Exmouth, and is open from March through to November each year, often booking out months in advance. Definitely plan ahead if you're hoping to stay here. There is a two-night minimum stay at all times, three-night minimum if you book more than six months in advance.

There is no phone or internet reception at Sal Salis, giving you the complete feeling of disconnecting. The closest phone reception can be found in Exmouth, if you need it.

To find out more and book your stay, head to salsalis.com.au and check out @salsalisningaloo on Instagram to get all the incredible vibes before you even arrive.

ESPERANCE

Home to the famous Lucky Bay kangaroos

NATURE LOVERS

Esperance is home to what might be some of the most beautiful beaches in all of Australia. It is famous for beaches with bright white sand, crystal clear turquoise water, as well as the iconic Lucky Bay, where kangaroos hang out right on the beach, seemingly waiting to be in your perfect holiday photos. A huge 5 kilometre stretch of white sand, you can always find a spot to yourself at Lucky Bay, where you can drive your car onto the sand, bring a barbecue or picnic and really set up for the ultimate beach day.

But while many people may think that Esperance is only Lucky Bay, the region is actually made up of heaps of beautiful beaches. In fact, there are three or four just a short drive from the centre of town itself. And that's not even taking into account the many beaches that make up Cape Le Grand National Park down the road, with coastal walks linking some of the best beaches, bays and views together.

One of the most naturally beautiful coastal regions in Australia, the diverse scenery around Esperance will leave you speechless, where there's always a new beach to explore, trail to hike, or hidden secret to uncover. It's a rejuvenating destination to get you out of your normal routine and straight into the stunning natural surroundings for a weekend getaway by the ocean.

BEST PHOTO SPOTS

Head straight to Lucky Bay to get the ultimate Esperance photo hanging out with kangaroos on the beach. The kangaroos appear at all different times of the day, all along the beach, so just be patient and set yourself up for a great beach day while you wait. If you do spot some kangaroos make sure you approach them slowly so you don't scare them, and don't feed or pat them.

The incredible Hellfire Bay

Esperance

CAN'T MISS

In the morning:

Hike to the top of **Frenchman Peak** or Mandooboornup to the local Noongar people for incredible sunrise views over Cape Le Grand National Park and all the way out to the beaches. It's super pretty during the golden hour as the whole world shimmers to life. It's a very steep hike (grade 5 steepness, in fact), about 3 kilometres return (1 to 3 hours, depending on your fitness levels) and it can often be very windy on the climb up, so make sure you wear appropriate shoes and bring some water.

See the famous pink lake from the air with a **Lake Hillier Scenic Flight**. This bright pink lake sits on Middle Island in the Recherche Archipelago, with the bright blue water of the ocean sitting on the other side of the white shoreline. It's a great contrast and a beautiful photo and view from the air. On the way to and from Lake Hillier your scenic flight offers excellent views over Lucky Bay and Cape Le Grand National Park, as well as Esperance's township.

Jump on a **Kepa Kurl Eco Discovery Tour** with a Noongar guide to learn about how the Traditional Owners maintained their culture within the stunning area around Esperance. Learn about hunting and gathering practices, hike along the bush trails, see some of the local rock art and get a taste for bush food on either a half- or full-day tour.

In the afternoon:

Hop your way across the many, many **beaches of Cape Le Grand**, with some of the most beautiful water you have ever seen and backdrops that look like they're not even real. While **Lucky Bay** is the most well known of the park, the nearby **Hellfire Bay** and **Thistle Cove** are two of our favourite beaches in the whole country. They're absolutely beautiful, and so peaceful and calm with lovely warm water to go for a dip. There's a great walking trail along the coastline that connects Lucky Bay, Hellfire Bay and Thistle Cove, so you can easily spend a day wandering across all three beaches. Some of the other incredible beach spots around Esperance include Cape Le Grand Beach, Twilight Beach, Duke of Orleans Bay, Blue Haven Beach, Wylie Bay, Eleven Mile Beach and Wharton Beach.

Check out **Esperance Stonehenge**, the only full-size replica of Stonehenge from the UK in the world. It's only 15 minutes out of town, and is an interesting spot to stop on your way to or from the beaches.

Stop for a tasting paddle at **Lucky Bay Brewing**, Esperance's very own microbrewery with its own unique craft beer. There are eight different brews to try, live music on Fridays and Sundays and a menu full of wood-fired treats. Another of our favourite lunch spots is **Condigup Tavern**, with a chill beer garden and some huge burgers to fuel your afternoon.

In the evening:

Pop down to **Lucky Bay** to watch the sunset and see if the friendly kangaroos come out for the golden hour. Wildlife is often most active around dawn and dusk, so in the early evening is sometimes a great time to spot the cute little kangaroos on Lucky Bay.

Our other favourite sunset spot in Esperance is the **Rotary Lookout**, which offers 360-degree views over Esperance, the beaches and the Recherche Archipelago. It's a quiet, peaceful spot and a great place to watch the sun go down over the ocean.

DAYTRIPS

Take a ferry or private boat trip over to **Woody Island Nature Reserve**, where you can spend the afternoon swimming, bushwalking, snorkelling and fishing from this remote island. There is lots of wildlife to spot, and you can even stay out here if you're looking for something remote, with camping open between September and April.

Top Sunset at Cape Le Grand Beach
Bottom Views from Frenchman Peak Lookout
Opposite Kangaroos are often spotted on Lucky Bay Beach

Where

Esperance is on the south coast of Western Australia, the last coastal town before the Nullarbor Plain and the South Australian border.

Getting here

With its own small domestic airport, you can fly directly into Esperance Airport (EPR) from Perth, with connections to the rest of the country. There are several flights each day between Esperance and Perth with REX Airlines, which takes about an hour and 35 minutes. You can rent a car from the airport, and then it's only a short 20-minute drive into town. Alternatively, it's a 7-hour, 30-minute drive (697 kilometres) from Perth to Esperance via National Route 1.

Getting around

Rent a car when you arrive to give yourself the freedom to explore all the best corners of the Esperance region. Lucky Bay and Cape Le Grand National Park are about 45 minutes away from the main town of Esperance, and there are plenty of little beaches and bays to stop at along the way, so having your own car lets you stop wherever you like and create your own weekend schedule.

When to go

For the best weather, visit Esperance during the warmer months (Nov to March) and take advantage of the hot days to test the water at every single bay. The deep contrast between the vibrant blue water and the white sandy shores are best seen on a bright, sunny summer's day.

Where to stay

The best way to experience the Esperance region is with a stay at **Lucky Bay Campground**. With campsites that overlook the whole beach and kangaroos wandering around the campgrounds, it's a very special camping experience. Bookings are required (parks.dpaw.wa.gov.au/site/lucky-bay) and sites can often be booked out well in advance, so secure your spot as soon as possible. Sites cost $30 and are given out on a first-come, first-served basis, so when you arrive you're free to choose your favourite spot from any that are available.

For a little more luxury, another great spot is **Esperance Chalet Village**, where you can stay in a super cute triangle-shaped chalet that's close to the beaches and the main town. It's perfect for Instagram and offers complimentary bikes for you to explore on.

Need to know

You will need to purchase a National Parks Pass to visit Cape Le Grand National Park. You can choose between a day pass for $15 per vehicle for up to 12 passengers, a 5-day pass for $25, or Cape Le Grand is included in a WA All Parks Pass. There is a ticket booth at the entrance to the park where you can purchase a day pass, or pop into the visitors centre on the corner of Dempster Street and Kemp Street to pick up an annual pass.

Get planning

Head to visitesperance.com for everything you need to plan your trip to Esperance, or check out @visitesperance on socials for so many beautiful shots from the region.

CORAL COAST

The ultimate road trip destination

NATURE LOVERS

The Coral Coast is home to some incredibly diverse and different landscapes that date back hundreds of millions of years. From the yellow limestone Pinnacles, to vibrant pink lakes, white sandy beaches with bright turquoise water and the iconic red sand of Shark Bay. It also has the world's largest fringing reef with marine life from baby turtle hatchlings to whale sharks. The Coral Coast really is an absolute melting pot of adventure.

Start exploring the vast Coral Coast for a little perspective of how huge Australia really is. After leaving Perth and hitting the road for a Coral Coast road trip, you're likely to see very few people. In fact, sometimes you might not see any other cars at all for hours, making you feel like you're the only ones in the world road tripping along this epic coastline.

If you can, add a few extra days to your weekend to really immerse yourself in nature on a Coral Coast road trip. It's a wonderful place to experience where the red outback meets the most beautiful white sand beaches. A place to disconnect and spend your days in the sunshine and the ocean. A place where your soul feels happy and your heart sings.

BEST PHOTO SPOTS

Stop at **Hutt Lagoon** along the Indian Ocean Drive for one of the best pink lakes in Australia. Depending on the time of day you visit, the water can look bubblegum pink, lilac or even red, according to the sun's location throughout the day. It's a can't-miss stop along the Coral Coast, and one of the best photo spots in the country.

DAYTRIPS

Take a daytrip from Geraldton out to the **Abrolhos Islands**, about 60 kilometres off the coast of Geraldton and made up of 122 pretty little islands. It's an important marine area, with more biodiversity than almost anywhere in Australia and all kinds of water activities to enjoy, including fishing, swimming, snorkelling, diving, and marine and wildlife spotting.

The Pinnacles Desert in Nambung National Park

CAN'T MISS

In the morning:

Jump on a tour to **swim with sea lions** in Jurien Bay. The tours take you out to a small island where you get to jump into the water and play with these cheeky animals. It's good to note that the sea lions like to lie on the shore until they get warm, so it's a good idea to book on a warm clear day (for water visibility) and choose either a late morning or early afternoon tour for the most activity in the water.

Wander around the fascinating **Pinnacles Desert**, where thousands of limestone pillars are found in Nambung National Park. It feels like you've landed on a whole different planet, with a landscape that's completely out of this world. Follow the self-guided driving trail around the park, and stop as often as you like for some great photos.

Watch the friendly bottlenose dolphins swimming around **Monkey Mia**, one of the most reliable places for dolphin interactions in the world. Avoid the crowds during the feeding demonstrations and you're still likely to spot dolphins and turtles right off the shore, especially around the little jetty. Spend the day at the beach, jumping in and out of the water and grab a happy hour cocktail at the **Boughshed Restaurant**.

In the afternoon:

Spend an afternoon enjoying the beautiful little beach at **Coral Bay**. Everything about Coral Bay is absolutely picture perfect, a small little coastal town, seemingly in the middle of the desert, with one of the most incredible beaches right at its doorstep. With coral gardens only a few metres into the water, it's an amazing place to snorkel right off the sand, and you can often spot manta rays swimming by only metres from the shore.

Take a scenic flight with **Shark Bay Aviation** to see some truly spectacular views from the sky. **Francois Peron National Park** has some of the most incredible landscapes, particularly the Big Lagoon, and flying above just gives you the ultimate perspective. Witness the vibrant red sand tumbling into the turquoise blue bays.

Explore the incredible landscapes of **Kalbarri National Park**. Dating back more than 400 million years, carved from the harsh winds of the region, Kalbarri is home to some of the most dramatic coastal landscapes in the country. Take the short hike to **Nature's Window** to see some of the best views through the naturally forming rock arch, and from the **Kalbarri Skywalk** during the golden hour for spectacular cliff-top views over the gorges.

Pop into **Shell Beach**, one of only two beaches on Earth where teeny tiny shells completely replace sand along the shore. There are billions of beautiful tiny shells on the beach here, that stretches for more than 100 kilometres, which are all sublimely shaped and unique from one another.

Follow the **wildflower trail** (July to Sept) to check out some of the best wildflower country in Western Australia. Whole fields burst to life in a rainbow of pretty colours during these months.

In the evening:

Have an adventure under the stars on the **Didgeridoo Dreaming Night Tour** with **Wula Gura Nyinda Eco Cultural Tours** where you get to learn about the deep spiritual connection between the Nhanda and Malgana people and this beautiful region, hear Dreamtime stories, enjoy an incredible bush tucker dinner cooked on an open campfire and experience a sandalwood smoking ceremony. It's a great way to learn more about this ancient land, while also taking in the incredible night sky above.

Hutt Lagoon's bubblegum pink lake
Opposite The colours of Shark Bay

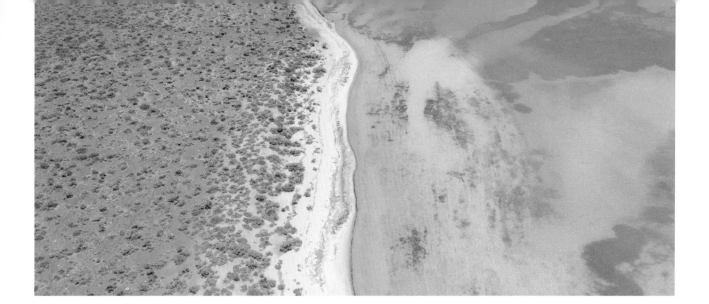

Where
The Coral Coast stretches for 1250 kilometres from Perth in the south all the way to Exmouth in the north.

Getting here
There are three airports along the Coral Coast, so where you fly into really depends on where you're planning to spend the most time. From Perth, there are direct flights to Geraldton Airport (GET) and Exmouth-Learmonth Airport (LEA) with Qantas, or Carnarvon Airport (CVQ) with REX Airlines.

Getting around
For the most freedom and flexibility, rent a campervan in Perth to explore the unique landscapes and highlights of the Coral Coast. It will give you more options of places to stay, with lots of camping grounds and free camps along the way, as well as getting you everywhere you need to go. **Travellers Autobarn** has some great deals. We rented through them and also saw their campers all along the coastline.

When to go
Your reason for visiting the Coral Coast will likely influence the time of year you choose to visit. For the overall best weather, visit outside of summer (March to Oct) when the weather is a little bit cooler although still warm and sunny most days. There are lots of different times to come for wildlife sightings, with whale sharks (March to July), humpback whales (July to Oct), turtle nesting (Dec to Feb), turtle hatching (Jan to March) all spotted off the Coral Coast, and to see the wildflowers in bloom (July to Sept).

Main towns
There are plenty of different stops and towns along the Coral Coast. The largest towns include Geraldton, Carnarvon and Exmouth, while some of the smaller towns are Jurien Bay, Kalbarri, Money Mia and Coral Bay. All offer places to stay, including campgrounds, caravan parks, hotels and motels and petrol stations. Other services like supermarkets, shopping and dining options differ from place to place.

Where to stay
One of our favourite places to stay on the Coral Coast is **RAC Monkey Mia Dolphin Resort**. Sitting within the Shark Bay UNESCO World Heritage Site, Monkey Mia feels like you've entered a whole different world. The ground is blinding bright white, the beach is turquoise and the ideal swimming temperature, and there are dolphins swimming along the coastline and under the pier all day long. There are resort-style rooms and apartments, as well as camping and caravan sites, with easy access to explore the incredibly diverse Shark Bay.

Need to know
You will need to purchase a National Parks Pass to visit Kalbarri National Park, Francois Peron National Park, Shell Beach Conservation Park, Cape Range National Park and Nambung National Park. Choose a holiday pass for either five days, 14 days or four weeks that gives you unlimited access to all the parks in WA during your stay. You can grab them online (dpaw.wa.gov.au).

Get planning
Plan your adventure by heading to australiascoralcoast.com, and make sure you check out @australiascoralcoast on socials for all the can't-miss places.

MARGARET RIVER REGION

Where wine meets nature

FOODIES | NATURE LOVERS

Known as one of Western Australia's great wine regions, Margaret River is so much more than just vineyards and cellar doors. This little peninsula, prominently sticking out of South-West WA is home to incredible natural landscapes, beautiful secluded beaches, great surf breaks, iconic attractions and an abundance of outstanding food and wine experiences.

Encompassing the surrounding towns of Busselton, Yallingup and Bunbury, the Margaret River region is dotted with unique experiences and attractions. From the longest jetty in the Southern Hemisphere, to caves, giant hedge mazes and a peaceful beach where stingrays like to swim up to you and say hello, the Margaret River region really has it all.

Margaret River will have you falling in love the minute you arrive and scrambling to extend your weekend stay to experience more. It's laid-back and carefree, with epic surfing during the daytime and live music at the pubs in the evenings. What more could you ask for!

BEST PHOTO SPOTS

There are just so many stunning photo spots to choose from in the Margaret River region, but some of the best include Injidup Nature Spa, Sugarloaf Rock, Hamelin Beach, Busselton Jetty and Black Diamond Lake, all completely unique and remarkable spots that bring to life the dynamic region.

CAN'T MISS

In the morning:

Learn to surf with **Margaret River Surf School** and catch a few waves at one of WA's best surf breaks. Choose from group or private surf lessons, which are both normally held at Redgate Beach. If you prefer just to watch, head to Surfers Point to get amongst the action while still staying dry. This is also a great place to spot dolphins right from the shore, so keep your eyes peeled.

The iconic **Busselton Jetty** is the longest timber-piled jetty in the Southern Hemisphere, and extends for 1.8 kilometres into the ocean. Known for its four iconic blue boat houses that sit just off the beach, the jetty also has an underwater observatory and a jetty train that will take you all the way to the end. Keep an eye out for whales and dolphins swimming along as you go.

Head down to **Hamelin Bay** to watch the cheeky stingrays that like to swim in the shallows of the beach. Regularly spotted throughout the day, the stingrays are often looking for a few fish scraps from the fishers as they return from their fishing trips. If you stand very still, they're likely to glide right past you as they continue on their way.

Explore life underground with a visit to **Lake Cave**, a crystal chamber where you enter through a sinkhole in the karri forest and are greeted with a massive 'suspended table' that hangs from the cave ceiling and almost touches the water of the underground lake. It's a super unique spot that really needs to be seen to be fully understood.

PLAN YOUR TRIP FOR

Completely immerse yourself in Margaret River by planning your visit during **Western Australia Gourmet Escape**, in November each year. An indulgent celebration, the festival is a showcase of WA's fine wines, craft beers and local produce, held in the most spectacular locations. The Gourmet Beach BBQ is always one of the highlights, with delicious wine and fine dining right on the beach.

Busselton Jetty

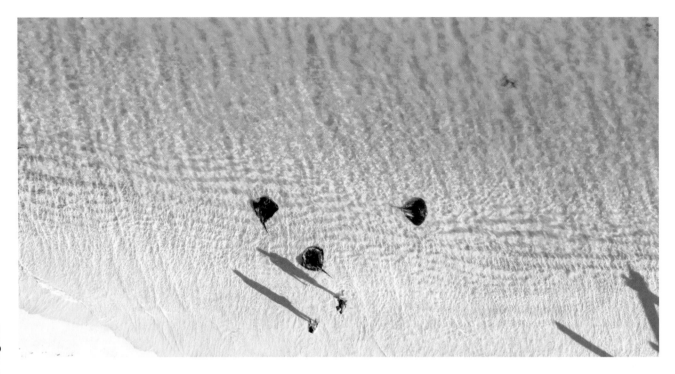

In the afternoon:

Hop around the cellar doors of **Margaret River** and taste your way through some of WA's best wines. More than 120 wineries can be found dotted across the region, with many of them offering vineyard tours, tours to meet the winemakers, barrel-room tastings and even the chance to blend your own bottle of wine. Some of the top choices include **Voyager Estate**, **Vasse Felix**, and **Cullen Wines**.

Head inland a little to **Black Diamond Lake**, just out of the mining town of Collie. A favourite swimming hole in the region, on a sunny day the water in the lake is the brightest azure blue colour, sparkling in the sunshine and inviting you for a swim. It's a great spot for swimming, stand-up paddleboarding, and kayaking, as well as a barbecue lunch with friends.

Cool off with a swim in the rockpools near **Sugarloaf Rock**. This huge granite rock stands tall from the depths of the ocean, and is a sight all of its own. Make your way carefully down the rocks to the little rockpool at the bottom for a swim in the calm, clear water.

Drive along Caves Road to the **Boranup Karri Forest**, with trees that stand more than 60 metres tall and plenty of lookouts along the way. This unique forest is so peaceful and photogenic, one of the prettiest scenic drives in the South-West.

Walk some of the **Cape to Cape Trail**, a 135-kilometre-long hiking trail from Cape Naturaliste in the north to Cape Leeuwin in the south. The trail is a great place to spot dolphins and whales (June to Dec) from the shore, as well as blooming with wildflowers when they are in season. Choose a small part of the trail to wander or embark on a full-day hike to explore more of this epic coastline.

Get lost at **Amaze'n Margaret River** in the half hectare hedge maze that will keep you running in circles for hours. A great place for pretty photos, there's 5 hectares of beautiful gardens here to explore, as well as an 18-hole mini golf course.

In the evening:

Take a sunset dip at **Injidup Nature Spa**, Australia's most perfect little swimming hole, with a nature waterfall that crashes through the rocks and into the pool when the waves roll in. It's best to visit at high tide, when the waves are largest to check out the waterfall effect in full force. Climb over the rocks at the end of Wyadup Road to find this spot. Another great sunset spot is **Indijup Beach** right next door, where the rocky coastline of the beach glows in the brightest deep red colour. While it's beautiful to visit at any time of the day, there is something so special about the glow at sunset.

Early mornings with the stingrays at Hamelin Bay
Opposite Sunset at Injidup Nature Spa

Where
The Margaret River Region is in the South-West corner of Western Australia.

Getting here
From Perth, it's a quick 3-hour drive to get to Margaret River, passing through Bunbury and Busselton along the coast, or follow the South Western Highway inland to see a little more of the countryside along the way. Jetstar has started offering direct flights from Melbourne to Busselton-Margaret River Airport (BQB) three times a week. South West Coast Lines also offers daily coach services from Perth's Elizabeth Quay bus station and Perth airport to Margaret River, Dunsborough, Busselton, Manjimup, Collie and Bunbury.

Getting around
Make sure you rent a car to really explore as much of the Margaret River region as you can, with so many incredible spots to check out along the coastline, as well as a little further inland. A rental car gives you the freedom and flexibility to create your own itinerary and get around to all those can't-miss spots along the way.

When to go
Head to Margaret River during the summertime (Nov to April) to take advantage of the warmer weather, giving you the best conditions to explore the incredible coastline and sip on wines in the many outdoor gardens. Winter (Jun to Aug) is a great time for whale-watching, with humpback whales migrating along the coastline, while spring (Sept to Nov) is wildflower season when whole paddocks bloom to life in waves of vibrant pretty colours.

Main towns
The main towns of Margaret River, Yallingup, Bunbury and Busselton make up the coastline of the Margaret River region. Each town has great accommodation options, as well as restaurants, bars, shops and cafes to hop across during your visit, and essentials such as supermarkets, pharmacies and camping grounds.

Get planning
Explore more of the Margaret River region and plan your visit at margaretriver.com, and be sure to check out @margaretriver on socials for all the can't-miss spots.

SOUTH-WEST

Explore the rugged coastline

NATURE LOVERS

Hugging the whole southern coastline of Western Australia, from Esperance in the east to Margaret River in the west, the area of South-West WA is an incredibly dynamic part of the country. With more than a thousand kilometres of coastline, 24 national parks, incredible beaches, amazing swimming spots, gourmet food and wine, caves and natural wonders to explore, there's something new and exciting around every corner of this region.

The rugged coastline makes for some of the best beaches in WA, with tiny sheltered bays surrounded by huge granite rocks, and spectacular views that need to be seen with your own eyes. You can often find that you have some of the prettiest places all to yourself, with deserted beaches to explore, quiet rockpools to snorkel, and hiking trails where you don't pass another soul.

Known as Kinjarling, which means 'the place of rain' to the local Menang Noongar people, Albany is the hub of this part of South-West WA. It is the oldest colonial settlement in Western Australia, dating back to 1826, with the port of Albany the first landing place for European settlers in WA. Base yourself in Albany to be right in the heart of the action, as well as close to some of the best beaches, museums, restaurants and national parks along the southern coastline. Although it might seem like a remote destination, Albany is only an hour's flight or a 4-hour drive from Perth, making it a great weekend destination.

PLAN YOUR TRIP FOR

Visit South-West WA towards the end of March for the **Taste Great Southern**, a festival celebrating award-winning wine, delicious fresh produce, amazing flavours and gourmet food. There's a music festival, long lunches, community markets and plenty of free events spanning roughly 11 days, with events spread out over Albany, Denmark, Mount Barker, Kojonup and Katanning.

The Gap Lookout at Torndirrup National Park
Opposite Two Peoples Bay Nature Reserve

CAN'T MISS

In the morning:

Start your morning with a hike to **Bluff Knoll**, one of the tallest peaks in Western Australia standing at 1095 metres above sea level. Found in Stirling National Park, it's a 3 kilometre hike to get to the top, which can be quite tough in sections, but the views from the top are worth it as you can look out over the valley and the forests. A great spot for a sunrise first thing in the morning.

Explore **Two Peoples Bay Nature Reserve**, home to some of the most beautiful beaches in the South-West. Little Beach is always a top favourite, famous for its perfectly circular rock with a half-moon rock underneath that sits right in the middle of the shore. Then follow the rocks around to Waterfall Beach, hidden away and often completely deserted.

Head to the **Natural Bridge** and **The Gap** in **Torndirrup National Park**, where you can stand on a viewing platform out over the cliffs and watch the waves crash into the rocky gully below that has been naturally created by the Southern Ocean. The landscapes out here are just incredible and easy to explore, with walking trails and lookout spots taking you to all the best bits.

Wander around the treetops at the **Valley of the Giants Treetop Walk** in **Walpole-Nornalup National Park**. Suspended 40 metres in the air, this 600-metre-long walk gives you exceptional views over the forest and makes you feel like you're up in the clouds.

Learn more about the Noongar Aboriginal culture on a tour with **Poornarti Aboriginal Tours**. From healing ceremonies, to connecting with the land and learning about this ancient culture, there are all kinds of tours to choose from.

BEST PHOTO SPOTS

Head to Little Beach at Two Peoples Bay and Elephant Rocks for some of the best beaches and photo opportunities in the area. Both of these beaches are secluded and absolutely stunning, with huge granite boulders surrounding them, protecting them from the ocean.

In the afternoon:
Spend an afternoon at Williams Bay National Park to see the iconic **Elephant Rocks**. This tiny little beach is covered in huge granite boulders that surround the beach and look like they have just fallen from the sky onto the sand, and the boulders literally look like a herd of elephants lumbering out to sea. The water here is a bright shimmering turquoise, with sandy white shores, and it's just such a beautiful little beach to explore. **Greens Pool** just around the corner is another great stop, with a big calm rockpool protected by boulders, giving you some great swimming and snorkelling conditions.

Head inland to the **Granite Skywalk**, with a suspended walkway taking you up Castle Rock, a huge granite outcrop in the middle of nowhere. More than 1100 million years old in the heart of **Porongurup National Park**, you will experience views for miles in this incredibly unique spot. Nearby you can also visit the ancient tingle forest, home to the **Giant Tingle Tree**.

Pop into the **Great Southern Distilling Company** to taste test some of its award-winning whisky, or go behind the scenes with a distillery tour and learn about how they use Albany's pure air and pristine waters to develop their signature whiskys.

Visit some of the excellent museums in Albany, home to the **National Anzac Centre**, a moving tribute to the Australian and New Zealand forces who served in World War I, and the **Albany Whale Museum**, which shares the stories of the South-West's whaling history.

In the evening:
Check out the sunset views from the **Padre White Lookout** in Albany Heritage Park, with views all the way to Middleton Beach and over the town. It's particularly pretty during sunset, when the sun is dropping down and the whole town is glowing.

DAYTRIPS
Take a daytrip off the coast of Bremer Bay with **Whale Watch Western Australia** to spot orca whales in the wild. Orca season (Jan to March) is when you can spot huge pods of orca whales that swim around the Bremer Canyon. The cruise goes deep into the ocean canyons so it can be quite rough throughout the day (definitely one for seasickness tablets even if you've never been seasick before), but they have guaranteed sightings and it's so magical to see these beautiful orcas swimming around together.

Where
South-West WA encompasses the whole southern coastline of Western Australia.

Getting here
Land right in the middle of South-West WA at Albany Airport (ALH), which has easy one-hour, 10-minute direct flights from Perth with REX Airlines several times each day. By car it's about a 4-hour, 50-minute drive from Perth to Albany, via the Albany Highway.

When to go
Take advantage of the warmer weather and visit in summer (Dec to Feb) so that you can hop around all the different beaches and beautiful swimming spots the South-West has to offer. It can get a little chilly and windy along the coast no matter what time of the year, but in summer you're likely to find you have the most consistent warm weather for exploring.

Where to stay
Albany is a great place to base yourself. It's centrally located along the south coast, giving you plenty of options to check out the sites to the east and the west. There is a wide range of accommodation, including hotels, holiday homes and caravan parks, as well as lots of campsites and free camps in the national parks along the beaches.

Need to know
There are lots of national parks, so make sure you know where they are and if you need a National Parks Pass for your visit. If you're planning to visit a few of them it's a good idea to get a multi-day pass that covers everything, instead of paying for parks individually. Some of the most popular national parks you might visit include Stirling Range National Park, Valley of the Giants, Two Peoples Bay Nature Reserve and Torndirrup National Park.

Get planning
Head online to australiassouthwest.com to plan your next adventure to the great South-West region and check out @australias_southwest, @discoveralbanywa and @visitalbanywa for all the best spots along the way.

Opposite Elephant Rocks in William Bay National Park, Denmark

BROOME

Where the outback meets the sea

ADVENTURERS

Considered one of the most luxe places to holiday in Oz, Broome is such a unique little town. Sitting high along the coastline in north-west Australia, Broome is one of the most beautiful places to witness the bright red soil of the Aussie outback, lying right alongside the vibrant turquoise water of the ocean and Roebuck Bay. The town is known as Rubibi in the language of the Traditional Owners, the Yawuru people.

Broome has created a name for itself as the ultimate bucket-list destination. It's remoteness and distance from capital cities, particularly along the East Coast, make it a little more of an expensive getaway, and one that everyone seems to be saving for a special occasion. But with overseas travel currently off the cards for a while, more and more people are turning to their Aussie wishlists when they need a getaway.

Lying at the base of the Kimberleys, Broome is a great place for a weekend getaway, or the beginning of an epic adventure into the Aussie outback and wilderness. Surrounded by tropical waters and white sandy beaches, you can combine adventuring and exploring in the morning, and relaxing by the pool with a cocktail in the afternoon.

BEST PHOTO SPOTS
You can't beat a sunset shot at Cable Beach with the camel trains slowly wandering by. The most famous photo for anyone visiting Broome.

PLAN YOUR TRIP FOR
Immerse yourself in the extremely unique Broome culture at **Shinju Matsuri – the Festival of the Pearl**. Held over two weeks at the end of August and beginning of September, it's a festival to mark the end of the pearl harvest season, with all kinds of exciting events, plenty of both Japanese and Aboriginal flavours and touches, and a celebration that brings the whole community together.

Sunset over Broome
Opposite Camel train along Cable Beach

CAN'T MISS
In the morning:
Check out **Streeter's Jetty** at high tide to really appreciate the beauty of Dampier Creek. It's a favourite photo spot, sitting on the peaceful little jetty surrounded by mangroves and bright blue water. It's also a popular fishing spot for the locals.

Head to **Roebuck Bay**, one of the most beautiful natural attractions in Broome, where the red soil from the outback literally bleeds right into the bright water of the ocean. It's absolutely a can't miss during your visit, a place unlike anywhere else in Australia and offers some of the best photo opportunities in the region. Another great spot to see is **James Price Point**, where the dramatic red cliffs provide an incredible backdrop to the secluded little beaches along the coastline.

Keep an eye out for the rare **snubfin dolphins** that are native to the northern coastline of Australia. Roebuck Bay is home to around 150 of these unusual dolphins, which often pop out of the water to say hello. You can get a little closer on a Snubfin Dolphin Cruise with **Broome Whale Watching**, where you're also likely to spot turtles and dugongs.

Further north, **Cape Leveque** on the Dampier Peninsula has some of the most unique and incredible beaches, where the rocky red cliffs literally lead right to the water. It's about a 2-hour, 30-minute drive from Broome, but well worth the amazing landscapes.

In the afternoon:
For one of the most amazing experiences in the region, book a tour of the very unique **Horizontal Falls** with **Horizontal Falls Seaplane Adventures**, with half- and full-day tour options. You'll get the chance to fly over Cape Leveque and the islands of the Buccaneer Archipelago in a seaplane, before a thrilling fast boat ride right through the waterfalls of the Kimberley.

At **Gantheaume Point** you can see the footprints of dinosaurs that formed in the reef rock over 125 million years ago. The footprints are only visible at low tide, but there are plaster casts of the dinosaur tracks embedded in the top of the cliff, so you can still see some if the tide is high.

Eat your way through the afternoon in Broome, with plenty of incredible al fresco dining options, so you can soak in the food and the atmosphere all at once. Head to **18 Degrees** for a fantastic cocktail menu and mouthwatering share plates, **Zanders** for spectacular views over Cable Beach, **Matso's Broome Brewery** to try their hard lemon, melon or berry, or **The Bay Club** for all the beach club vibes overlooking Roebuck Bay.

Learn more about Broome's fascinating pearling history with a visit to **Cygnet Bay Pearl Farm**, which has been operating here for almost 80 years. Take a **Pearl Farm Discovery Tour** to learn more about how they cultivate some of the most sought-after and beautiful pearls in the world, or jump on their **Sea Safari Tour** to see exactly where the pearls come from and a little sneak peek of the Kimberley coastline. And of course, stop by the gift shop to purchase a special pearl of your own.

In the evening:
Head to the famous **Cable Beach** to watch the camels strolling past at sunset. A favourite beach in WA, Cable Beach is more than 22 kilometres long, with calm warm water and soft white sand. You can drive all along Cable Beach, so pack the car with everything you need for a sunset barbecue or picnic and find a spot all to yourself to witness one of Broome's famous spectacular sunsets. Or if you want to be part of the action, book yourself a camel ride and enjoy a slow leisurely stroll along the beach as the sun sets.

DAYTRIPS

Get a sneak peek of the incredible **Kimberley** with a daytrip north to explore some of this dynamic region. There are so many incredible places and it's absolutely impossible that you would be able to even scratch the surface with a daytrip, but rent a car and choose a spot close by to get a little taste of the great north. Some of the closest places to explore in the Kimberley include the town of Derby (2-hour, 15-minute drive), Windjana Gorge National Park (4-hour, 15-minute drive) and Dalmanyi, also known as Bell Gorge (5-hour, 40-minute drive).

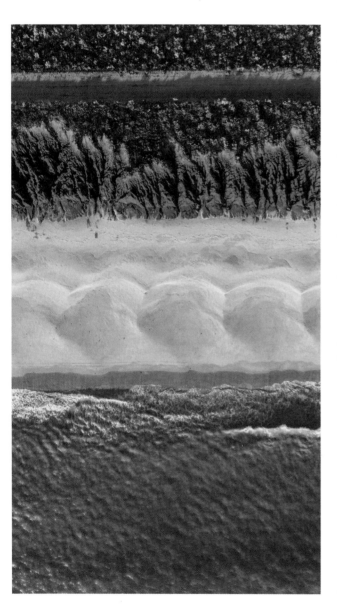

Where
Broome is in north-west Western Australia.

Getting here
Book a flight directly into Broome Airport (BME) all year round, with multiple flights per day between Broome and Perth on Qantas and Virgin. There are also regular direct flights between Broome and Melbourne, Sydney and Darwin during the dry season (approximately June to Sept) with Qantas, although the flight schedule does change each year.

Getting around
Rent a car when you arrive in Broome so that you can explore a little further and get out to some of the dynamic and unique landscapes that lie on the outskirts of Broome. Being the gateway to the Kimberley, there are so many incredible places to see only a few hours out of town.

When to go
With a wet and a dry season, Broome is best visited in the dry season (late April to early Oct), when you'll be treated to clear blue skies and nice warm temperatures each day. Make sure to avoid the monsoon season (Jan to March), when you're likely to have lots of rain, flooding and possible cyclones.

Where to stay
There are plenty of great beach resorts to stay at dotted around Broome, as well as several caravan parks to choose from if you're road tripping, and also secluded eco-friendly glamping options. To beat the heat in the afternoon, it's always a good idea to book somewhere with a pool - you'll want a fresh dip after a sweaty morning of exploring.

Get planning
Plan your Broome getaway at visitbroome.com.au and australiasnorthwest.com/explore/broome-dampier-peninsula, and check out @australiasnorthwest, @visitbroome and @thebroomebible on socials for all the best spots.

James Price Point at sunset

KALGOORLIE & THE GOLDEN OUTBACK

The real 'wild, wild west'

OFF-THE-BEATEN TRACK

Kalgoorlie is a very interesting and unique little place. You could say that it's Australia's version of the 'wild, wild west'. Some of the streets are still home to historic buildings, dating back to the late 1800s, when gold was just starting to be discovered here. It's a place where some of the oldest brothels in the country still operate on the main street, directly across the road from the post office in plain sight, and there are boards outside the pubs with the names of the 'skimpies' (pretty much bikini bartenders) that will be working that night. Locals head to the outback pubs on dirt buggies, taking the backroads and showing up covered in mud. A mining 'super pit' operates literally at the end of the main street, pulling out millions of dollars in gold each week, and runs 24 hours a day.

The gateway to some of the most remote parts of the Western Australian outback, Kalgoorlie is home to some fascinating attractions. The ultimate destination for an off-the-beaten track weekend, with charm and character you won't find anywhere else, it's sure to keep you interested and entertained, with its many unique quirks and strange traditions. It's a crazy and hectic and wonderful place all at once.

BEST PHOTO SPOTS

Head to the lookout at **Mount Charlotte Reservoir** for the best views over the city of Kalgoorlie. From here you can see all the way from the super pit to the main streets of town, and it's definitely best viewed at sunset to take advantage of that golden hour.

Exploring Lake Ballard

CAN'T MISS

In the morning:

Road trip out to **Lake Ballard**, a huge dry lake in the middle of the outback, with pinky red soil and parts of the lake that are so dry the earth is literally cracking open. Lake Ballard is home to one of the most remote art exhibitions in the world; there are 51 creepy statues scattered across the lake that are meant to represent residents of Menzies, the closest town to Lake Ballard.

Take a walk down **Boulder Historical Street**, the beautiful preserved main street of Boulder that hasn't changed since its heyday during the gold rush 100 years ago. The buildings have so much character and detail, it's a really lovely step back in time. To learn more about the city and its history stop into the Boulder Town Hall, or jump on the Kalgoorlie-Boulder Tram, which will give you a guided tour of the landmarks in the area.

Visit the **Museum of the Goldfields**, which shares stories of the city's mining heritage, the history of the goldfield days, and the local history of the Wangkatha people. The museum features WA's biggest collection of gold bars and nuggets, and takes you back in time to see how prospectors found this precious gold, before the super pit was in Kalgoorlie.

Have a swing on the world's longest golf course, the **Nullarbor Links**. Stretching all the way across the Nullarbor Plain, for more than 1365 kilometres across the remote outback, the Nullarbor Links golf course has stops at all kinds of roadhouses and random places across the outback. And hole number 18 can be found in Kalgoorlie.

In the afternoon:

Home to the only legal **two-up game** in Australia, every Sunday the locals gather to join in or watch the two-up competition and, let me tell you, they do not take it lightly. Huge bets are made on the game, which is essentially heads or tails with two coins, and there is some seriously big money moving around here. It's still played in the original corrugated-iron shed and bush ring on Sunday afternoons, starting at about 1.30pm.

Check out the infamous **Kalgoorlie Super Pit**, the largest open-pit gold mine in Australia and one of the largest in the whole world. It's 3.5 kilometres long, 1.5 kilometres wide and more than 600 metres deep, where 15 million tons of rock is moved each year to find about 800,000 ounces of gold. There's a viewing platform, or you can jump on a tour to go inside the pit and learn more about gold mining.

Stop into **Broad Arrow Tavern** for lunch, a favourite for both locals and visitors where you can sign your name on the walls of the pub. There's not a clean piece of wall in the place, with signatures and messages scribbled across the

walls, doors and even on the ceiling! They're famous for their absolutely huge burgers that will keep you full for hours.

Boulder's unique microbrewery, **Beaten Track Brewery** brings its own unique craft beer to the goldfields. The brewery offers beers, ciders, burgers and barbecue.

In the evening:

Eat your way around the city, with heaps of modern restaurants and bars popping up all the time. While the classic old-school pubs are still around, lots more hipster options have been popping up in recent years, with beer gardens covered in fairy lights all over the place. Some of the favourites for dinner include **Cecilia's On Hay**, **Prime West Grill**, **Restaurant 259** at the York Hotel and **Blue Monkey Restaurant**.

DAYTRIPS

You can see more of the Western Australian outback with a road trip along the Golden Quest Discovery Trail. Home to all kinds of random gems, the highlights of this will take you to a real-life ghost town in Gwalia, Australia's most remote art exhibition at Lake Bellard, a lake that swirls pinks and purples, and a collection of random outback pubs, like the one at Kookynie with its famous outback horse that hangs out the front. It's a part of the country that few choose to explore, but it is definitely an interesting and unique corner of Australia.

Where
Kalgoorlie is 596 kilometres east of Perth, and is one of the closest towns to the end of the Nullarbor Plain.

Getting here
You can fly from Perth to Kalgoorlie-Boulder Airport (KGI) on a direct flight with either Qantas or Virgin Australia. If you would prefer to travel by road, the drive from Perth takes about 6-hours, 30-minutes (593 kilometres) via the Great Eastern Highway through the Wheatbelt region of the Golden Outback.

When to go
Kalgoorlie is in an interesting weather position, with scorching hot summers and cold chilly winters. For the most comfortable weather, visit during spring and autumn, especially if you're planning to road trip a bit further into the outback. During winter, make sure you bring lots of layers for unexpectedly cold mornings and nights.

Need to know
Be careful of road trains when you're driving around this part of the outback, particularly if you explore a little more of the Golden Quest Discovery Trail. You're likely to see some of the biggest trucks you've ever seen, with multiple huge, long trailers that will literally make your car shake as they pass. Give them plenty of room and never pull out in front of a road train!

Get planning
To plan your visit to Kalgoorlie, head to kalgoorlietourism.com and westernaustralia.com/en/Destination/Kalgoorlie for all the best things to do and places to stay, and check out @cityofkalgoorlieboulder and @kalgoorliebouldervisitorcentre for all the best spots along the way.

Top Looking out over the town of Kalgoorlie
Bottom Kalgoorlie Super Pit
Opposite Two-up Sundays in Kalgoorlie

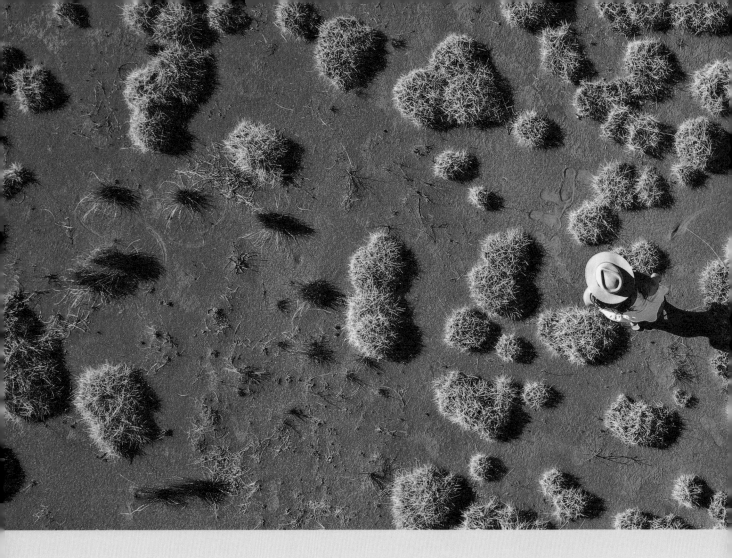

Can't-miss place
Uluṟu-Kata Tjuṯa National Park
(*see* p.146)

Top experience
An island getaway at Tiwi Island Retreat
(*see* p.168)

Important dates
Plan your trip to the NT to coincide with
some of the Territory's best festivals
and important dates:

- Territory Day (1 July)
- Darwin Festival (Aug)
- Garma Festival (Aug)
- Parrtjima - A Festival in Light (Sept)

Time zone
The Northern Territory follows the
Central Australian Time Zone (GMT
+9.30) throughout the whole year.

Stay connected & get featured
Follow @ntaustralia for all the hidden
secrets and best places to visit in the
NT, and have your travels featured by
using hashtag #ntaustralia.

Helpful websites
- For the Top End
  tourismtopend.com.au
- For Central Australia
  discovercentralaustralia.com
- Road reports, conditions and closures
  roadreport.nt.gov.au
- Entering Aboriginal Lands
  nic.org.au
- Drone permit for the NT
  nt.gov.au/leisure/parks-reserves/
  rules-and-permits
- National Parks information
  nt.gov.au/leisure/parks-reserves

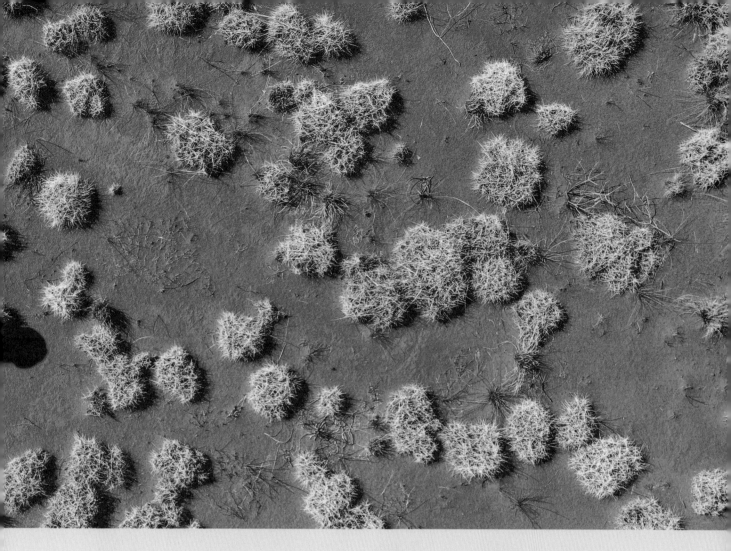

Northern Territory

There's something special about the Northern Territory (NT). Rugged and remote, with beautiful landscapes and a history that dates back tens of thousands of years, there are so many hidden treasures to discover. It's the perfect place to immerse yourself in First Nations culture, incredible bucket-list experiences and breathtaking outback landscapes that have formed over millions of years.

The NT is vast and enormous, with plenty of space to explore and to be free. From the expansive Red Centre in the south, to the unique vibes of the Top End, it's a barren desert and a tropical oasis all at once. There are remote outback drives (*see* p.154), natural hot springs in the middle of the desert (*see* p.157), a plethora of waterholes and gorges to hop through in the Red Centre (*see* p.154) and incredible First People's history in Kakadu (*see* p.162).

They say the Territory is the answer, and there's never been a better time for you to take a weekend getaway to the NT, so get out here and explore. It's all just waiting for you.

DARWIN

The Traditional Owners are the Larrakia people

ADVENTURERS

Darwin might be the smallest city in the country, but that doesn't mean it should be underestimated. It has gone above and beyond to create some really great experiences, and is so jam-packed full of things to do and see you could easily keep yourself entertained here for days. With a long history of tragedy, from World War II to Cyclone Tracy in 1974, Darwin has rebuilt itself more than once, and the city you find today is a wonderful blend of its history and future.

As the gateway to the Top End, Darwin is the perfect place to start if you're coming to explore Kakadu National Park (3-hour drive), Litchfield National Park (1.5-hour drive) or heading further south to Katherine (3-hour drive). The Top End is home to about 100,000 crocodiles, and many of them live up in the waters around Darwin. Chances are if you're looking at a body of water in Darwin, there is a croc in it. There are some amazing crocodile experiences to be had in and around Darwin – from crocodile cruises to a 'cage of death' – and it's definitely the best place in Australia to get up close and personal with this prehistoric predator.

Whether it's your first or your tenth visit to this vibrant little city, there is always something new to explore and discover. And if Darwin isn't on your bucket-list yet, now's the time to add it!

PLAN YOUR TRIP FOR

There's nothing better than a winter festival in 32°C tropics, right? Set under twinkling lights, the **Darwin Festival** is held in August annually, and is a great time to immerse yourself in the spirit of the city with live music, cultural performances, street food, events and celebrations. It is usually spread over two or three weeks, so there's lots of weekend options to choose from!

CAN'T MISS

Catch the sun setting over the ocean in Darwin, as the whole sky glows a brilliant shade of orange while it descends under the horizon. **Gunn Point**, about half an hour out of Darwin, is the perfect spot for a romantic sunset.

Jump aboard one of the **jumping crocodile cruises** on the Adelaide River, to get up close and personal with some giant crocodiles.

Grab some friends together to see the **local street art** on a self-guided walking tour around the city. Head to West Lane and Austin Lane to find the street art, and download the free Darwin Street Art Festival app to make the art come to life.

If you're in Darwin on a Sunday, head to the **Mindil Sunset Markets** (from 4pm to 9pm during the dry season), which is full of food stalls with cuisines from all over the world. Grab a plate and then head over the sand dune to Mindil Beach to eat your dinner as you watch the sunset.

Catch a monster barra on a **deep-sea fishing charter** departing from Darwin. For the super adventurous, you could even try heli-fishing. Yep that's right, fishing out of a helicopter.

Take a dip at **Berry Springs**, only about half an hour south of Darwin. This is the best place if you're looking for a swim in a waterhole, although check ahead as it may be closed in the wet season (Oct to April).

Cruise around Darwin Harbour at sunset. There are lots of different options for a sunset on the harbour, from dinner onboard a luxury catamaran, to drinks on an isolated sandbar in the middle of the water.

Swim in the **Cage of Death at Crocosaurus Cove**, the only place in Australia where you can actually get inside the water with a monster crocodile.

Watch a movie at the **Deck Chair Cinema**. Playing movies at 7.30pm each night, it's such a Top End way to enjoy the cinema. Dinner is served from 6pm on the outdoor terrace, with a different local business catering throughout the week.

Learn more about Darwin's military history. After more than 300 bombs were dropped on Darwin in 1942, the city was pretty much flattened. Immerse yourself in this complex history by visiting the **Darwin Military Museum**, the **oil storage tunnels** or the **Aviation Museum**.

Visit **MAGNT Darwin** (Museum & Art Gallery of the Northern Territory) for an insight into Darwin's history through European colonisation, World War II and Cyclone Tracy. There are also some beautiful exhibits of Aboriginal artwork, as well as Sweetheart, the infamous saltwater crocodile.

Darwin

DAYTRIPS

Take a daytrip to **Litchfield National Park** to waterfall hop through the park and spend the day jumping in all the fresh waterholes. Make sure to visit Florence Falls, Bluey's Rockhole and Wangi Falls for some of the best swimming spots, which you can often have all to yourself if you visit early in the morning. Bring your own lunch for plenty of great picnic spots, or you can grab some food at the cafe at Wangi Falls. Best visited during the dry season, as the wet season (Oct to April) can often see monsoon flooding and crocodiles sneaking into swimming holes.

Where
Darwin is right at the top of the Northern Territory and is the heart of the Top End.

Getting here
There are direct flights to Darwin Airport (DRW) from all major capital cities around Australia daily, as well as from Alice Springs, Cairns and Broome. The airport is only a short 15-minute drive from the heart of the city and costs about $20 by taxi.

Getting around
Hire a rental car for the weekend if you're planning to explore anywhere out of the city. There are car rentals available at the airport and in the city from a number of different providers. For a fun and easy way to get around the city, you can pick up an electric scooter. There's a free app to download to rent them, and if it's your first time you can refer whoever you're travelling with for a $5 credit. Grab one when you see it and then park it on the street and leave it wherever you're done - so simple and easy to use.

When to go
Visit Darwin during the dry season (May to Oct) for the best experience. During this time temperatures sit around a steady 32°C, with mostly sunny days. The humidity is also a lot lower during the dry season, ideal for getting out and exploring.

Where to stay
Base yourself near the Waterfront Precinct to be within walking distance of many of the city's best areas and attractions. The waterfront has lots of great restaurants and bars, as well as an inland beach with an ocean pool that keeps the crocs out and is safe to swim in. It's only a short walk to the mall and Mitchell Street in the heart of the city.

Need to know
It's important to know that as with all waters in the NT's Top End, there could be crocodiles in the waters around Darwin. They are checked regularly by the rangers in the parks, but it is always important to be croc-wise when you are swimming and keep an eye out for anything suspicious.

Get planning
Head to northernterritory.com/darwin-and-surrounds or tourismtopend.com.au to help you plan your itinerary.

Top Darwin street art found in West Lane
Bottom Florence Falls in Litchfield National Park
Previous The vast desert of the Red Centre

ULURU

The 'spiritual heart of Australia'

CULTURE BUFFS | NATURE LOVERS

Considered the 'spiritual heart of Australia' there is something indescribable about Uluru. There's no doubt this is a magical place, one that truly needs to be felt to be understood. Rising seemingly out of nowhere and surrounded by the barren desert of the Red Centre, Uluru is a place of cultural significance and profound meaning to the Traditional Owners, the Yankunytjatjara and Pitjantjatjara people, called the Anangu people, and would be revered by any Australian who has the opportunity to experience it.

Uluru itself is simply breathtaking. It looks different from every angle and throughout the day, depending on where the sun is shining from. It changes colours across a palette of reds and oranges, glowing brightest just before the sun sets in the evening. You could spend your whole day just driving or walking around the rock, and still feel like you are continuing to see it from a new perspective.

Uluru-Kata Tjuta National Park expands across more than 327,414 acres of Australia's Red Centre and is also home to Kata Tjuta, a marvel of the outback all on its own. Made up of 36 unique domes, Kata Tjuta is thought to be about 500 million years old and is actually taller than Uluru at its highest point.

With the opening of the new airport, only a short way from the main town of Yulara, and regular direct flights between most major cities around Australia, there has never been an easier time to plan a weekend at Uluru.

BEST PHOTO SPOTS

You can't miss getting a photo of Uluru at sunset. Head to the sunset platform at least an hour before the sun sets to see the colours of the rock change and glow as the sun drops below the horizon behind you. But take note of the 'no photo' signs around the base of Uluru. These signs indicate significant cultural views of the rock that are not allowed to be photographed, and instead are best appreciated in person.

Sunset scenic flight over
Uluru-Kata Tjuta National Park

Uluru

CAN'T MISS

Whilst the absolute highlight of your visit will no doubt be seeing Uluṟu for yourself, there is actually so much more to explore, with many great experiences that encompass the rock. Start your experience by visiting the **Uluṟu Cultural Centre** within Uluṟu-Kata Tjuṯa National Park, to learn more about the park and its history. The rangers here can let you know more about the different tours and experiences that are on offer and give you some great ideas about how to spend your day.

In the morning

Start your visit by watching the sun come up over the outback at the **sunrise platform**. Follow the signs as you drive around the rock that say Talinguru Nyakunytjaku.

Right after the sunrise is a great time to complete the **base walk**, which will take you on a 10.6 kilometre walk all around the base of the rock. Along the way you can find rock art paintings, a waterhole and an endless number of great photo opportunities. In the summer months, you should start as early as possible and complete the walk by 11am to avoid heat exhaustion and dehydration during the hottest parts of the day. Alternatively, you can rent a bicycle to explore the trail, or jump on a guided segway tour to explore the base. Head to the Uluṟu Cultural Centre to find out more.

Drive out further into the park to visit **Kata Tjuṯa**, a collection of giant domes that actually stand taller in size than Uluṟu. There are a couple of different hikes that can be taken around Kata Tjuṯa, with the longest and most beautiful known as Valley of the Winds. Kata Tjuṯa also has a great sunrise viewing platform for another day, with views all the way across to Uluṟu.

In the afternoon

Join a traditional dot painting workshop and learn from the local Aṉangu people how to create your own piece. Throughout the workshop they'll share creation time stories, culture and traditions. There's a morning and an afternoon session each day which go for around an hour and a half on the lawn of the Yulara Town Square.
Book online (maruku.com.au).

Ride a camel through the outback, with the perfect back drop of Uluṟu in the distance. You can visit **Uluṟu Camel Tours Farm** for free, which is a great opportunity to get up close and personal with some of their 80+ camels and learn more about wild camels in the outback. Make sure you head around to their Funny Farm before you leave, to meet their entertaining assortment of wild goats, ducks, llamas, pigs, emus and their baby camel, who was just so cute and fluffy.

Ayers Rock Resort also offers an amazing program of **free activities about the culture of the local Aṉangu people**. There are lots of different activities to join, but some of our favourites were joining a storytelling circle for a Bush Yarn to learn about some of the traditional hunting items used in the area; taking a Guided Garden Walk to find out more about the plants of the Western Desert and the ways in which they were and are used by the local communities; and learning how to make some delicious shortbread in a Bush Tucker demonstration. The activities operate daily and don't require a booking - just look at the timetable in the main square and show up when you feel like it!

If you're visiting during the warmer months, the afternoon is also a great time to grab a drink, go for a swim in the resort pools, or just have a rest in the shade before heading out again to explore as the sun goes down.

In the evening:

Head to the **sunset viewing platform** to watch the natural light show that's on at the end of each day. As the sun goes down behind you, the rock changes colour from brown to orange and a striking deep red. Bring a picnic blanket and a bottle of wine to enjoy as you watch.

Take a sunset **scenic flight** over Uluṟu and Kata Tjuṯa to experience these incredible landmarks from a whole new perspective. You can either go on a scenic flight or a helicopter flight, and flying at sunset has the whole park lit up in a beautiful pop of colour. This is definitely a splurge, but also an absolute highlight of any Uluṟu itinerary.

Spend an evening at the iconic **Field of Light**, an incredible art installation created by Bruce Munro that is made up of more than 50,000 bulbs, changing colours and glowing in the darkness. Make the most of your experience by booking the Star Pass experience, where you can watch the Field of Light come to life atop a sand dune as the sun sets behind you. Before heading down to the installation, you can enjoy Australian-inspired canapes and sparkling champagne, watching the bulbs shimmer to life as the darkness falls.

At the top of many bucket-lists is the **Sounds of Silence dinner** which offers a delicious menu of bush tucker-inspired foods, under the stars of Uluṟu. There's a didgeridoo performance, a guided tour of the night sky, Australian beer and wine and the most unique dining experience, under a blanket of stars and silence for miles around.

Where
Uluṟu is in Central Australia in the Northern Territory (NT).

Getting here
Ayers Rock Airport (AYQ) is located just a 12-minute drive away from Yulara and the Ayers Rock Resort (*see* Where to stay), making it super easy to plan a weekend getaway to Uluṟu. A complimentary shuttle bus can pick you up from the airport and take you to any of the hotels within Ayers Rock Resort.

Getting around
Rent a car from the airport to give yourself the freedom and flexibility to explore Uluṟu-Kata Tjuṯa National Park at your own pace. Otherwise you can buy a ticket for the **Uluṟu Hop On Hop Off Bus**, with one-, two- or three-day passes available, that runs between Yulara and the national park, with stops at Uluṟu, Kata Tjuṯa and the Uluṟu Cultural Centre.

When to go
Visit Uluṟu during the winter months (May to Sept), when the weather is cooler during the day, making it easier and safer to embark on the different walks around Uluṟu-Kata Tjuṯa National Park. You'll still find that you have mostly sunny days and warm weather during the day, but temperatures can drop quite a bit at night so bring some warm clothes as well.

Main towns
Yulara is the only town near Uluṟu, and is mostly made up by Ayers Rock Resort. The town centre is right in the heart of the resort and offers a post office, IGA supermarket, restaurant, cafe, a couple of gift stores and the visitors centre. There's also a petrol station near the campground.

Where to stay
Ayers Rock Resort is made up of several accommodation options, with something to suit different budgets and types of travellers. Within the resort you can find everything from ultra-luxury accommodation, to self-contained apartments, campgrounds and hostel options. There's a number of different restaurants, galleries and spas scattered through the hotels of the resort, and as a guest you have access to visit any of them - no matter what property they sit on. The campgrounds here are our favourite place to stay if you have a caravan or camper, with great amenities, a pool to cool down in the afternoons, and surrounded by the desert. There's a lookout right in the middle of the campground too, which gives you views of Uluṟu in the distance.

Need to know

You will need to purchase a pass to enter Uluṟu-Kata Tjuṯa National Park. A 3-day pass costs $25 per person, or if you're going to be visiting for longer you can grab an annual pass for only $32.50 per person. Tickets can be purchased from the ticket booth at the entrance to the park when you arrive. The park is open at different times across the year, generally opening an hour before sunrise and closing an hour after sunset. The park is closed overnight and there is absolutely no camping allowed within the park.

Get planning

For more information on accommodation and experiences, head to ayersrockresort.com.au, and for all the inspo you need for your visit, follow @exploreuluru and tag #exploreuluru in photos of your visit to be featured.

Left Wandering the base walk of Uluṟu
Right Camels at Uluṟu Camel Tours
Opposite The Field of Light coming to life

ALICE SPRINGS

The city in the desert

NATURE LOVERS | CULTURE BUFFS

Right in the centre of Australia, in the middle of a vast desert outback, is the small city of Alice Springs. Alice has long been considered the gateway to Central Australia's amazing Red Centre region, the first stop on an epic outback adventure. Surrounded by the mountains of the MacDonnell Ranges on either side of the city, with a gap that allows the traffic to flow through the middle, Alice Springs is so much more than meets the eye.

For a long time, Alice Springs thrived on the fact that it was home to the only airport in Central Australia. You needed to pass through Alice if you were planning a trip to visit Uluṟu-Kata Tjuṯa National Park (*see* p.146). However, since the opening of Ayers Rock Airport in 2013, tourism has been a little on the decline in Alice Springs, with many visitors choosing to fly directly to Uluru and avoid the 6-hour drive through the desert.

But Alice Springs shouldn't be missed on any Red Centre itinerary. It holds so much natural, untouched beauty, with some of the Red Centre's best gaps and gorges only a short drive away. It's also home to some unique attractions, like the Kangaroo Sanctuary and the Alice Springs Desert Park. It's a booming city in the middle of the desert that's perfect for a weekend getaway.

PLAN YOUR TRIP FOR
Experience thousands of years of culture in a single weekend at **Parrtjima – A Festival In Light**. In April each year the outback comes to life at Parrtjima, the only authentic First People's light life festival and a one-of-a-kind experience, using the newest technology to illuminate the 300-million-year-old landscapes of the MacDonnell Ranges. A weekend not to be missed, with performances, art displays, light shows and interactive workshops, music and food to experience.

Baby kangaroo at the Kangaroo Sanctuary

CAN'T MISS

Top highlight:

Known as **Tjoritja** to the local Aranda people, and also West MacDonnell National Park, Tjoritja stretches from Alice Springs all the way across the famous Larapinta Trail. Estimated to be more than 340 million years old, the ranges formed when two tectonic plates collided, causing rocks deep beneath the Earth's surface to thrust upwards towards the sky. Tjoritja has so many great spots to visit, with waterholes surrounded by the towering cliffs of the ranges, scenic hiking trails, beautiful waterholes, lookouts that offer incredible views and all kinds of different landscapes. Some of the top spots to check out include Simpsons Gap, Angkerle Atwatye (Standley Chasm), Ellery Creek Big Hole, Kwartatuma (Ormiston Gorge), the Ochre Pits, Glen Helen Gorge and Redbank Gorge. Read about the Red Centre Way (*see* p.154) for more details.

In the morning:

Pick up some local goodies at the **Todd Mall Markets** each Sunday from around 9am until 1pm, with souvenirs, gifts and local produce on offer.

Embark on a mountain-bike adventure through the rock terrain around Alice Springs with **Outback Cycling**. A guided ride will give you a great insight into a bit of Alice Springs's history, while you tackle some of its trickiest bike trails.

Hike a part of the iconic **Larapinta Walking Trail** that travels for 230 kilometres along Tjoritja. It is made up of 12 individual trails, connecting all the different gorges, waterholes, lookouts and places to see within Tjoritja. Some of the easier walking trails that can be tackled in a morning include Jay Creek to Angkerle Atwatye (Standley Chasm, 13.6 kilometres, about 5.5 hours one way), and Kwartatuma (Ormiston Gorge) to Finke River (9 kilometres, 4 hours one way).

In the afternoon:

Head to **Anzac Hill** for views across the whole city, as well as the iconic gap and the MacDonnell Ranges on either side.

The **Alice Springs Telegraph Station Historical Reserve** is the birthplace of the Alice Springs township. Established in 1871, the Telegraph Station would send messages between Darwin and Adelaide on the Overland Telegraph Line. It has such an interesting history, also connecting Australia to England through the undersea telegraph network.

Visit the **Yubu Napa Gallery** to see some of the artwork by local First Nations artists. Some of the artists actually create their pieces inside the gallery, so if you're lucky you might even get to see someone creating a beautiful piece during your visit. They also have a great shop with all kinds of locally made gifts.

Learn more about the vast desert environment, native animals and plants at **Alice Springs Desert Park**. It has all kinds of exhibits that depict life in the desert, as well as a captivating bird show each afternoon.

In the evening:

Take a tour of the **Kangaroo Sanctuary**, home to some of the most adorable joeys and toughest red kangaroos you have ever seen. You can cuddle a joey as you wander around the sanctuary, and learn about how they rescue and rehabilitate these cute little roos. Tours run in the evenings a few days per week when the kangaroos are waking up and most active. Call in advance and book your spot to avoid missing out.

DAYTRIPS

If you have a spare afternoon, head about 4 hours north of Alice Springs to **Karlu Karlu**, also known as the Devils Marbles. Described as the fossilised eggs of the Rainbow Serpent by the Warmungu people, and dating back millions of years, these huge rocks lie over a huge space of land, some of them standing up to 6 metres in height. Follow the Mayijangu Walk from the carpark to the Nyanjlkl Lookout for views across the marbles.

Alice Springs

Where

Alice Springs is right in the heart of Central Australia in the NT.

Getting here

There are regular flights to Alice Springs Airport (ASP) flying direct with Qantas from most major cities around Australia, with Virgin also offering direct flights from Darwin and Adelaide. If you're planning to drive, Alice Springs is pretty much 16 hours drive away from the closest major cities, with Darwin sitting 1498 kilometres north and Adelaide 1539 kilometres south.

Getting around

Rent a car from the airport when you arrive to get out and explore all the best parts of Alice Springs and the surrounding national parks.

When to go

Head to Alice Springs during the middle of the year (April to Oct), when the temperatures are a little bit cooler in the day. You will find mostly sunny days all year round in Alice, with the winter months offering better conditions for hiking and exploring.

Where to stay

For a luxury stay head straight to **Lasseters**, Alice's only casino complex with rooms decorated with Aboriginal art and beautiful views over the McDonnell Ranges. There are also many comfortable and affordable hotels in the area, including **DoubleTree by Hilton** and **Desert Palms**.

If you're travelling by caravan or campervan, book into the **Big4 MacDonnell Range Holiday Park**. The park is big and spacious, with all sorts of fun activities for guests, including local live music on Wednesdays, cheese and wine night on Fridays, didgeridoo shows on Saturdays, and pancake breakfasts on Sundays.

Need to know

Alice Springs has strict alcohol restrictions in place that can be quite a shock to first-time visitors. Always take your ID, no matter how old you are, as they will need to scan it to complete your purchase. There may be police outside bottle shops asking where you're going to consume your purchase, and trading hours are quite limited.

Get planning

For everything you need to plan your visit to Alice Springs, head to discovercentralaustralia.com. Follow @visitcentralaus on social media and hashtag #RedCentreNT to be featured.

Angkerle Atwatye (Standley Chasm) in Tjoritja
(West MacDonnell National Park)
Opposite Karlu Karlu (Devils Marbles)

RED CENTRE WAY

Explore the vastness of the red desert

ADVENTURERS | OFF-THE-BEATEN TRACK

This part of Australia is unlike any other. You can drive for hours and not see another car. You can have the most beautiful waterholes all to yourself for a whole afternoon. You can stand in the middle of the highway and see nothing but red dirt in every direction, all the way to the horizon. There's no better way to get to know the heart of Australia than by driving along this iconic route and stopping at as many of the lookouts, gorges, waterholes and landmarks as you can.

The Red Centre Way is an absolutely epic road trip, taking you through the very best of Central Australia. Depending on how much time you have, you could do this drive in a couple of days or a couple of weeks, making as little or as many stops as you have time for along the way.

If you're planning a trip to the Red Centre, make sure you do extensive research on where to find fuel, food, water and phone reception if you need it. Amenities and services are few and far between, so it's definitely a trip that requires a little more planning. But to pump you up for your journey, let's jump straight into some of the best stops and places to see for your weekend.

BEST PHOTO SPOTS

Tjoritja is absolutely full of picture-perfect photo spots that embody the Red Centre, including Kwartatuma (Ormiston Gorge), Angkerle Atwatye (Standley Chasm) and Ellery Creek Big Hole.

CAN'T MISS

You can tackle the Red Centre Way from either direction, but for the best experience start in Alice Springs (*see* p.150) and head west.

The **MacDonnell Ranges** are the first stop along the way when you leave from Alice Springs. Home to so many gorges, gaps, chasms, swimming holes and hiking trails, there are endless places to explore in Tjoritja (West MacDonnell National Park). Make the most of your trip by stopping at:

- **Simpsons Gap** is a prominent gap dividing the ranges, with a small waterhole in the middle.
- **Angkerle Atwatye (Standley Chasm)** is a tall chasm in the middle of a gorge, with rock walls that change in colour from a deep red to a bright orange depending on the time of day you visit.
- A favourite spot along the way, **Ellery Creek Big Hole** is where you can find one of the permanent waterholes in Tjoritja, which is a perfect place for a dip if you can brave the freezing water temperature.
- At **Ochre Pits**, the colourful walls of the pit are still mined by the Arrernte people for red, yellow, orange and white ochre used in traditional ceremonies and decorations.
- **Kwartatuma (Ormiston Gorge)** is an absolute highlight. There is a small waterhole here, surrounded by incredible scenery, with red rocky mountains around the gorge. Don't miss the short walk up to Ghost Gum Lookout for spectacular views over the whole area.
- Another beautiful gorge is **Glen Helen Gorge**, home to many Arrernte Dreamtime stories, including the well-known Rainbow Serpent. You can also find fuel and a small convenience store here.
- **Redbank Gorge** is a tougher gorge to get to, after a 1.5 kilometre walk over a very rocky pathway. But Redbank is unlike any other gorge along the way, with striking red walls that surround a small waterhole.

From Tjoritja (West MacDonnell National Park), you find yourself on the **Mereenie Loop**, an unsealed dirt road that connects the ranges with Kings Canyon. It's 154 kilometres long (about an hour and 45-minute drive) through some of the most rugged outback terrain you're likely to come across on your journey. Keep an eye out for wild camels and dingoes, as they are both regularly spotted in this part of Central Australia.

Opposite Driving the Mereenie Loop

Stop at **Morris Point Lookout** (also known as Ginty's), almost at the end of the Mereenie Loop for impressive views over the outback.

The next stop along your journey is **Kings Canyon**. An epic highlight along the Red Centre Way, Kings Canyon is found in Watarrka National Park and stands 270 metres high. Within the canyon you can find all kinds of unique environments, from stark tall canyon walls, to desert gardens filled with palm trees and ferns. For the ultimate experience, set out early in the morning on the **Kings Canyon Rim Walk**. The 6 kilometre walk takes about 3 to 4 hours to complete and gives you the best views all around the canyon. It's important to note that for safety reasons the walk closes at 9am on days which are forecast to be hotter than 35°C.

Kings Creek Station is 36 kilometres down the road from the canyon, and is a working cattle and camel station that also offers camping and accommodation, as well as helicopter rides, camel rides and quad bike tours. There's a fuel station here, and a small shop that offers basic supplies.

Finally you'll find yourself at **Uluṟu** (*see* p.146), the 'spiritual heart of Australia' that absolutely needs to be on everyone's bucket-list. Uluṟu-Kata Tjuṯa National Park is of course home to Uluṟu itself, as well as the impressive formations of Kata Tjuṯa, and is a place that needs to be seen and experienced to be fully understood.

And there you have it, you've conquered the legendary Red Centre Way! It is such an amazing piece of land to explore, and really gives you an insight into just how vast and incredible this great country is.

From Uluṟu you can take the shortcut back to Alice Springs, which takes about 4 hours and 40 minutes via the Lasseter Highway and Stuart Highway. It's completely sealed all the way, making it a much quicker drive. There are some great roadhouses to drop into, including **Erlunda Roadhouse**, which is home to dozens of emus, and **Stuarts Well Roadhouse**, which is right next to a camel farm. Both are great stops if you didn't spot much wildlife along the way.

Where
The Red Centre Way connects Alice Springs and Uluṟu via the Mereenie Loop.

Getting here
Fly into Alice Springs Airport (ASP) to start your journey.

Getting around
Not all rental cars are able to be taken on dirt roads, so make sure you look at four-wheel drive rentals that do not have limitations on unsealed roads before you book. **Camplify** offers lots of great options to rent troopies, campervans and motorhomes, and you can also search by the option to take them off road.

When to go
Visit the Red Centre during the winter months (May to Oct), for more comfortable temperatures and access to more hiking trails and activities. You will still find the days are sunny and nice and warm, but you will avoid the extreme heat that comes with summer in the desert.

Where to stay
For the best experience of the Red Centre Way, plan to stay in a few different spots along the way. There are many campgrounds and free camping spots that can be found in Tjoritja. Download the WikiCamps App to find them.

Kings Canyon has campgrounds and accommodation at both **Kings Creek Station** and **Kings Canyon Resort**, which also offers outback glamping tents.

Most roadhouses along the main highways offer camping and accommodation options.

And of course, at Yulara (*see* p.146) you can find all kinds of accommodation, including a campground, hotels, hostels, self-contained apartments and luxury glamping.

Need to know
If you're driving the Red Centre Way, you need to make sure you have enough fuel and also know exactly where the next fuel stops are so you don't run into trouble. There are huge remote distances between petrol stations, with limited phone reception most of the time and few cars passing by, so you don't want to run out of fuel anywhere along these roads.

Fuel stops along the Red Centre Way can be found at: Glen Helen Gorge, Kings Canyon Resort, Kings Creek Station, Curtain Springs Inn and Yulara.

Phone reception can be found at Neil Hargrave Lookout and Hermannsburg for Telstra, and Kings Canyon Resort for Optus.

Get planning
To help plan your road trip along the Red Centre Way check out northernterritory.com, discovercentralaustralia.com and traveloutbackaustralia.com for lots of planning tips, advice and of course, great places to stop on your journey.

Left Ormiston Gorge in Tjoritja (West MacDonnell National Park)
Right Camels found in the outback

KATHERINE

The gateway to the Never Never

NATURE LOVERS

Sitting on the fringe of the Never Never is Katherine. About a 3-hour drive south of Darwin, Katherine is the Northern Territory's third-largest city, although it really has more of a country town feel. The Katherine region extends from the Gulf of Carpentaria, near the Queensland border in the east, across the country towards the Kimberley in the west.

If you do a little digging, Katherine is really home to so many of the NT's natural wonders. One of the main drawcards of the Katherine region is Nitmiluk Gorge found in Nitmiluk National Park. Also known as Katherine Gorge, Nitmiluk is made up of 13 different gorges, which wind their way around impressive rock walls, where you can find Jawoyn artwork that dates back tens of thousands of years. And if you look carefully, you might even spot a sun-dried crocodile – frozen on the banks of the gorge.

From a bush-tucker dinner under the stars, to waterfalls, hiking trails and natural thermal hot springs with the most beautiful clear water, Katherine will keep you busy for the whole weekend. Make sure to bring your camera – you're going to want to capture this.

BEST PHOTO SPOTS

Nitmiluk Gorge simply cannot be beaten in the Katherine region. Whether you see it from hiking above or canoeing right through the middle, it's absolutely the most beautiful place to visit in Katherine.

DAYTRIPS

Take a drive down to **Mataranka**, about an hour south of Katherine, which is home to some absolutely amazing natural hot springs that can be found within Elsey National Park. The natural pool of **Bitter Springs** and the manmade **Mataranka Thermal Pool** both share the same superbly warm and crystal-clear water, giving you a full natural spa experience. It is such a highlight, you definitely won't regret making the drive.

Wandering around Nitmiluk Gorge

CAN'T MISS

In the morning:

Without a doubt, one of the biggest highlights of your visit to Katherine will be going to **Nitmiluk Gorge**. Jump on the **Malappar Traveller** canoe trip to see it. The tour goes for about 5 hours, which includes a boat ride into and out of the main gorges. It's definitely the most beautiful way to experience the gorges, and it's so peaceful and relaxing as you have your own time and space to experience this natural wonder. Make sure you bring your own lunch, as well as your swimming gear and a towel as you are able to swim in the second and third gorges. Alternatively, if you don't want to canoe, you can also experience Nitmiluk Gorge via a scenic cruise or overhead helicopter flight.

If you don't want to get wet you can also explore **Nitmiluk National Park** on a number of different hikes around the park, which range in their levels of difficulty and distance. Start your day at the **Nitmiluk Visitors Centre** as early as possible and always check the daily temperatures and hike conditions before you depart. Many of the hikes are closed in days of extreme heat to prevent possible heat exhaustion.

In the afternoon:

Take a dip in **Katherine Hot Springs**, right in the heart of the town. It's the best way to cool down on a hot day, with clear water filling a few different pools, giving everyone the chance to spread out. It is the ideal way to escape the high temperatures of the Top End.

Learn more about the Warlpiri culture from the Katherine region with a visit to **Top Didj Cultural Experience** where you can chat to and learn from Top End Dalabon artist Manuel Pamkal. Learn about the different Aboriginal painting styles, weapons and spear-throwing techniques, and how the Traditional Owners lived off the land around Katherine. You will also get the chance to interact with some of the local wildlife, as there are always baby wallabies around who love a cuddle.

Experience what farm life is like in outback NT at the **Katherine Outback Experience**. Led by musician Tom Curtain, the show is a live demonstration of life on the farm, as they break in horses, sing country songs standing on horseback and train more than a dozen dogs all at once. There are also often puppies who have been born on the farm to have a cuddle with before you go.

Only about 45 minutes north of Katherine, **Edith Falls** has plunge pools, rockpools and waterfalls, and is a lovely place to take a dip on a hot day. Follow the 1.2 kilometre walking trail to the upper pools of the falls, where you can often find you have the waterfall and surrounding pools all to yourself.

In the evening:

Have dinner under the stars at **Marksie's Stockman's Camp** for Tucker Night. This is a true bush experience, with everyone seated around the campfire, and Marksie serving stews and dampers flavoured with all kinds of native bush fruits, foods and herbs. Their season only runs during the dry season (July to Oct), and it's a good idea to book in advance so you don't miss out.

Where
In the Top End of the Northern Territory, Katherine is 320 kilometres south of Darwin.

Getting here
Darwin Airport (DRW) is the closest passenger airport to Katherine. The drive from Darwin to Katherine takes about three and a half hours via the Stuart Highway, through the towns of Pine Creek and Adelaide River.

Getting around
Rent a car from Darwin airport and head out to Katherine. Having your own car will allow you to explore a little further, getting out to Nitmiluk National Park and the hot springs in Mataranka.

When to go
Katherine is best visited during the winter time (June to Oct). During this time temperatures are a little bit lower, which means more of the walks, activities and attractions in the region are open to visitors.

June to August is the most popular time to visit Katherine, so make sure you book accommodation and activities in advance if you're planning a visit during this time.

Where to stay
You can either choose to stay right in the heart of Katherine, or at Nitmiluk Gorge, approximately a 45-minute drive away. Nitmiluk Gorge has all kinds of accommodation available, including powered and unpowered campsites, cabins and a luxury lodge.

Need to know
It's important to know that as with all waters in the NT's Top End, there could be crocodiles in the waters around Katherine. They are checked regularly by the rangers in the parks, but it is always important to be croc-wise when you are swimming and keep an eye out for anything suspicious.

Get planning
To plan your visit to the Katherine region, head to visitkatherine.com.au, or check out @visitkatherine on Instagram.

Aerial view of Bitter Springs
Opposite Exploring Nitmiluk Gorge by canoe

Top End Safari Camp

UNIQUE WEEKEND

You can experience the very best of the Top End in just one weekend with a stay at Top End Safari Camp. Just over an hour from Darwin, you get to spend the whole afternoon on unique NT adventures, from helicopter rides to airboating across the flood plains, before a sleepover in the cutest little bell tents around. An epic creation from Matt Wright, known for his National Geographic series Outback Wrangler, *Top End Safari Camp is a special place in the Northern Territory.*

Encompassing some of the best things to do in the Top End, our stay at the safari camp gave us a little taste of the way of life up here.

The overnight camp starts just after midday, for an afternoon packed with activities. The adventures begin when you meet Otis, a huge saltwater crocodile who likes to hang out right near the shore. He's not shy, so make sure you don't get too close to the water. Take a nice peaceful cruise down the wetlands, keeping an eye out for birds and wildlife along the banks while enjoying a cheese plate onboard. Get an aerial perspective with a helicopter flight over the flood plains, fields of cathedral termite mounds and, if you're lucky, maybe even a buffalo or two. Jump aboard a thrilling airboat ride, where you can count crocodiles on the bank and in the water, as you slide across the waters of the wetlands.

Back at the camp, you can cool down with a quick dip in the unique rain tank plunge pool or your own personal outdoor open-top shower and before you know it, it's dinner time. Get ready for a homecooked, gourmet barbecue dinner, eaten under the stars as you swap stories with other travellers. The evening ends around the campfire, roasting marshmallows and toasting s'mores, spotting stars and constellations in the sky, before you head back to your bell tent for the night.

IMPORTANT INFO

The Top End Safari Camp operates during the dry season (April to Oct). The tour starts at 1.30pm when you arrive and ends at around 10am the following morning.

Your night at the Top End Safari Camp includes all experiences, an afternoon cheese board, barbecue dinner under the stars, overnight stay and a delicious cooked breakfast in the morning.

Make sure you pack sunscreen, a hat, lots of insect repellent and some warm clothes for overnight.

To find out more, head to topendsafaricamp.com.au.

KAKADU

Home to the oldest living culture on Earth

NATURE LOVERS | CULTURE BUFFS

Kakadu National Park is one of the big bucket-list places when you come to the Top End. It's an iconic Australian experience and a unique place to explore, with wetlands sprawling across the park, waterfalls and rock holes to swim in, ancient Aboriginal rock art sites that date back tens of thousands of years, and more crocodiles than you will ever know.

It's also a UNESCO World Heritage area, gaining the title for its cultural and natural heritage, as well as being one of the world's greatest nature reserves. Kakadu is also the largest national park in Australia, covering almost 20,000 square kilometres. Some of the Top End's most famous locations can be found within Kakadu National Park, including some of the filming locations from the movie *Crocodile Dundee*.

Kakadu National Park has a rich history, and has been home to the Bininj and Mungguy people for more than 50,000 years. It has preserved some of the oldest artworks on the planet, telling the story of the oldest living culture on Earth. The Traditional Owners of Kakadu work together with Parks Australia to help preserve the environment, while also sharing this beautiful place with visitors from around the world.

It's important to know that as with all waters in the NT's Top End, there could be crocodiles at literally any of the swimming holes or waterways in Kakadu National Park. They are checked regularly by the rangers in the park, but it is always important to be croc-wise when you are swimming and keep an eye out for anything suspicious.

BEST PHOTO SPOTS
Make the steep climb up to the **Gunlom Infinity Pool** around sunset, for beautiful pink skies, stunning views over the Arnhem Land escarpment and unreal photo opportunities.

Sunset at Nawurlandja Lookout

CAN'T MISS

In the morning:

Start your visit at the **Bowali Visitors Centre**, just a 5-minute drive down the road from Jabiru. Built to look like an Aboriginal rock shelter, the building is impressive all on its own. Staff can help with any info you need about Kakadu, as well as road conditions and recent croc sightings.

One of the best ways to learn more about the wetlands that encapsulate Kakadu is to jump on a **Yellow Water Cruise**. Taking you out on the Yellow Water Billabong, you can spot crocodiles, buffalo and wild horses on the floodplains, as well as many species of unique birdlife. Hop on a sunrise or sunset cruise to see the wildlife of the wetlands at their most active.

Maguk Waterhole (Barramundi Gorge) is another popular swimming spot in southern Kakadu, found at the end of a 1.5 kilometre nature hike through the beautiful surrounding rainforest. There's a small waterfall at Maguk that runs most of the year, so it's a great spot to visit if some of the main waterfalls have dried up for the season.

In the afternoon:

For one of the most beautiful rock holes that you will often find you have all to yourself, **Moline (Ikoymarrwa) Rock Hole** is the place to go. With a small swimming hole and a waterfall that runs year-round, surrounded by tall rocky walls that make up some of the oldest rock formations in the world, Moline is absolutely stunning. It's regularly checked by rangers but, of course, always keep an eye out for crocodiles.

Australia's most breathtaking natural infinity pool can be found at the top of **Gunlom Falls**. With extensive views over Kakadu National Park and the Arnhem Land escarpment, it's the place for a sunset swim right on the edge of the waterfall. At the bottom of the waterfall you can also find Gunlom Billabong, a great place to cool down and take a dip, but make sure you heed crocodile warnings.

Visit early in the dry season to see the amazing **Barrkmalam (Jim Jim Falls)** flowing at full force, with a beautiful waterhole plummeting down into a plunge pool at the bottom. Surrounded by high cliffs, you'll find the most perfect little sandy beach oasis, and a great place for an afternoon picnic.

Head to the famous **Cahills Crossing** when the tide changes, a known place to see crocodiles fishing for barramundi that are sent over the causeway. Cahills Crossing connects Kakadu to Arnhem Land, and while crocodiles can be spotted here at almost any time of the day, they are the most active when the tide changes. This is not a place for swimming.

In the evening:

Nawurlandja Rock offers one of the best sunset spots, overlooking the beautiful Burrungkuy (Nourlangie) Rock, which lights up in all different shades of red and orange as the sun sets. It's a short but steep climb up the rock to get there, so give yourself some extra time before the sun sets to grab the ideal spot.

At **Ubirr Rock Art Site** in the northern part of Kakadu, you can see some of the most detailed and well-preserved Bininj/Mungguy rock art in the NT, and learn more about the creation stories it depicts. This is another great spot to watch the sun go down.

Top Crocodiles roaming Kakadu
Bottom Ubirr rock art site at sunset
Opposite Sunrise over Yellow Water Billabong

Where
Kakadu National Park is in the Top End of the Northern Territory, between Darwin and Arnhem Land.

Getting here
From Darwin, it's about a 2-hour and 45-minute drive to Kakadu National Park, down the Arnhem Highway. You can also get to Kakadu from Katherine (about a 3-hour drive), by turning right at Pine Creek onto the Kakadu Highway.

Getting around
Rent a car from Darwin to explore all the best spots around Kakadu National Park. All the roads getting to and in Kakadu are sealed, so you won't need a four-wheel drive to get there, however many of the tracks to get to waterfalls, rock holes and lookouts do require one.

When to go
Visit Kakadu National Park during the dry season (May to Sept) when you will find that most of the waterholes are open and you'll have lovely sunny weather every day. Visit a little earlier in the season if you can (perhaps before the middle of July), as this is when some of the most dramatic waterfalls are still flowing, like Barrkmalam (Jim Jim Falls) and Gungkurdul (Twin Falls) that completely dry up later in the year.

Main towns
Jabiru is the main town in Kakadu National Park. It is where you can find the supermarket, petrol station, newsagency and a couple of other small shops.

Where to stay
The **Mecure Kakadu Crocodile Hotel** is one of the most famous hotels in the NT, built in the shape of a huge crocodile. You can even notice the shape of it from the ground, with eyes looking at you as you approach. Located in Jabiru, it's a great place to stay for hotel-style accommodation.

Cooinda Lodge is the other place to stay, which is a little more centrally located in Kakadu. Cooinda has a huge campground, as well as lodge-style accommodation, cabins and even glamping tents. It puts you roughly in the middle of Cahills Crossing in the north of Kakadu, and Gunlom Falls in the south, as well as right next to the Yellow Water Billabong.

Need to know
You will need to purchase a park pass to enter Kakadu National Park. An adult pass generally costs $40 and is valid for 7 days, but can be extended to 14 days at no extra cost. Park passes are free for Northern Territory residents, and there are discounts for children and families. There are also discounts if you're visiting during the tropical summer (Nov to May). Permits can be purchased from parksaustralia.gov.au/kakadu.

Get planning
For everything you need to know about Kakadu National Park, including accommodation options, booking activities and special offers, head to kakadutourism.com, or check out @kakadutourism on Instagram for all the best spots.

TIWI ISLANDS

The 'island of smiles'

OFF-THE-BEATEN TRACK

Affectionately known as the 'island of smiles' the Tiwi Islands are an incredibly unique place in the diverse Northern Territory. Lying just off the coast of Dawin in the Arafura Sea, and surrounded by the crocodiles that inhabit the oceans in the Top End, the Tiwi Islands is the NT's very own island paradise.

The Tiwi Islands are made up of two main islands, Bathurst Island and Melville Island, which are known as Ratuwati Yinjara (Two Islands) to the Traditional Owners, as well as a whole handful of small uninhabited islands. Bathurst and Melville Islands are home to about 3000 Tiwi people, separated by the Apsley Straight. The Tiwi people have a very different history to the mainland Aboriginal people, considering themselves uniquely Tiwi.

There are two main ways to visit the Tiwi Islands that each offer completely unique and memorable experiences.

Tiwi Island Retreat's resident crocodile, Claudia
Opposite Aerial view over Tiwi Islands

HOW TO VISIT THE TIWI ISLANDS
Tiwi by Design with SeaLink NT
SeaLink NT offers a couple of different Tiwi Island tours, but for the most insightful cultural experience book onto the Tiwi by Design tour. After arriving at Wurrumiyanga, the morning begins with a traditional smoking ceremony, where a small group of local artists and dancers bless the group visiting for the day as well as share some of their own totem dances and Dreamtime stories.

You then get to stop by Tiwi by Design, the art studio and small gallery that is home to work by dozens of local Tiwi Islanders, before creating your own screenprinted T-shirt, tea towel or canvas. The talented artists that work at Tiwi by Design teach you how to screenprint, helping you create a special piece to take home with you. They have all kinds of different stencils to use, with crocodiles, turtles, stingrays, fish and even Tiwi Island prints.

The tour then takes you on a short walk around the town, sharing some of the highlights of Wurrumiyanga. The walk takes you to the Patakijiyali Museum and the historical church that was also featured in the movie *Top End Wedding*. One of the highlights is definitely the chance to have a chat with some of the local Tiwi people, who are so open to sharing their traditions and way of life, as well as some of their unique travel stories.

The Tiwi Islands are mad about their AFL, with 14 teams between the two islands and three Norm Smith Medalists making it big in the AFL. If you're around the Top End in March, check out SeaLink NT's Tiwi Football Grand Final and Annual Art Sale tour. It's a massive event on the Tiwi Islands and an extremely special and unique way to get amongst the Tiwi spirit.

Getting to Wurruminyanga
SeaLink NT offers a ferry service between Cullen Bay and Wurrumiyanga on Bathurst Island. The ferry takes about 2.5 hours each way, departing Darwin at 8am and returning from Wurrumiyanga at 3.15pm.

Get planning
To book your visit, head to sealinknt.com.au, or check out @sealinknt for trip insights.

Tiwi Island Retreat

Find island paradise on Bathurst Island with a visit to Tiwi Island Retreat. A creation of Matt Wright, the famous Outback Wrangler from *National Geographic*, Tiwi Island Retreat is a place to disconnect, unwind and immerse yourself in nature. It's the kind of place where you will be barefoot the whole time, the food is absolutely delicious, and you can spend the whole weekend outside enjoying the beautiful surroundings. We can't speak highly enough about our visit at Tiwi Island Retreat - it was absolutely incredible.

There is a small menu to choose from, depending on availability and what has been caught by the fishing charters throughout the day. Camp host Siggy makes all the meals herself and they are absolutely delicious. You could easily head here just for the food - it was amazing.

Despite its remote location, there is always something to do at Tiwi Island Retreat. Head out on a deep-sea fishing charter and try to catch yourself a massive barramundi for dinner, take a beach buggy ride to a secret spot on the island where you can enjoy a cheese plate and some drinks, or even just go for a quick boat ride with the hosts to check the crab pots. If you're going anywhere near the water though make sure you keep an eye out for Claudia, the resident crocodile who swims up and down watching the shore. When the water looks this good, Claudia is the pertinent reminder that you can't swim here. But the Tiwi Island Retreat has you covered, with a stunning pool that runs alongside the beach.

It was one of the most relaxing weekends we had on the road, such a great place for a little bit of rest and rejuvenation before we made the long drive from Darwin to Cairns.

Getting to Tiwi Island Retreat

To visit Tiwi Island Retreat or any of the other remote accommodations around the Tiwi Islands, you might need to charter a plane to get there. There are quite a few airlines that offer charter flights from Darwin (just search online for Tiwi Island charter flights), which generally start at around $550 for a one-way flight. It's a short 30-minute flight from Darwin Airport to Port Hurd near Tiwi Island Retreat.

Get planning

Head to tiwiislandretreat.com.au to book your stay and for the latest deals and promotions, and check out @tiwiislandretreat on Instagram to really fall in love with this beautiful location.

Where
The Tiwi Islands lie north of Darwin, 80 kilometres off the coast of the Northern Territory.

When to go
The Tiwi Islands have a wet and dry season like the rest of the Top End, with the dry season being the preferred time to visit (May to Oct). Check with either SeaLink NT or Tiwi Island Retreat for up-to-date travel options.

Need to know
If you are planning an independent visit to the Tiwi Islands, you will need to apply for a permit from the Tiwi Land Council (tiwilandcouncil.com). If you choose to visit Tiwi Island on a day tour with SeaLink NT or to visit the Tiwi Island Retreat, you will not need to obtain a permit as it is already covered in your booking. The Tiwi Land Council requires a minimum of 30 working days to process permit applications, so apply well before you want to visit. There are a couple of different types of permits, depending on whether you want to stay in the communities (free of charge and valid for 3 months) or travel outside of the communities ($100 fee and valid for 3 months).

For a great glimpse into the Tiwi Islands and Wurrumiyanga area, as well as some of the cultural traditions of the Tiwi people, watch the movie *Top End Wedding*.

It's also important to know that as with all waters in the NT's Top End, there could be crocodiles in the waters around the Tiwi Islands. They are checked regularly by the rangers in the parks, but it is always important to be croc-wise when you are swimming and keep an eye out for anything suspicious.

Screenprinting with Tiwi by Design
Opposite A relaxing stay at Tiwi Island Retreat

EAST ARNHEM LAND

The most untouched part of Australia

ADVENTURERS | OFF-THE-BEATEN TRACK

Arnhem Land might just be one of the last true wild and untamed destinations that you can find in Australia. You can travel for hours without seeing another car, have a family of buffalo wander across the road right in front of you, or find that you have some of the most beautiful beaches in Australia all to yourself.

Sprawling across just under 100,000 square kilometres of land, Arnhem Land is bigger than many countries around the world. It is home to around 16,000 people, with about 12,000 of them being Yolngu people, the Traditional Owners of the land. Arnhem Land is Aboriginal Land, with dozens of small communities across it, as well as nearby communities that dot the coastline.

Visiting East Arnhem Land requires a lot of pre-planning, with multiple permits (*see* p.173) required to visit. The permit system acts as a form of written permission to enter Aboriginal Lands by the Northern Land Council (NLC). The NLC only lets a certain number of people visit East Arnhem Land at a time, to conserve the environment and so the Traditional Owners know who is travelling through their land at any one time. It's a good idea to completely plan out your trip in advance, including anywhere you hope to stay, to avoid missing out when you arrive.

If you're planning to drive you're definitely going to need longer than just one weekend for this one, but you can also fly into East Arnhem Land if you only have a weekend to spare.

CAN'T MISS

Arnhem Land is bursting with beautiful untouched places to visit. Some of them are free and easy to get to, while others require special permission or jumping on a day tour with Traditional Owners.

In the morning:
Head to the **Buku-Larrnggay Mulka Arts Centre** in Yirrkala for a complete immersion into artwork from local artists across Arnhem Land. Throughout the gallery and shop there are so many beautiful pieces, with delicate details sharing creation stories through each piece.

Learn more about the Yolngu people with a tour of their homelands with **Lirrwi Tourism**. Offering the most immersive cultural experience, you get the chance to interact with locals, learn more about their land, culture and traditions and take part in activities like spear-fishing or crab-hunting. This tour will also take you to some of the most beautiful places around **Bawaka**, including the famous **Lonely Beach** that can only be accessed on the tour.

In the afternoon:
See where the red dirt meets the turquoise ocean at **Garanhan** (Macassan Beach). There are some great fishing spots along the rocky shoreline here, and even a cute rope swing to chill out on as you watch the waves roll in. It's surrounded by a few other beaches, including **Barinura** (Little Bondi Beach), **Numuy** (Turtle Beach) and **Binydjarrna** (Daliwuy Bay), so you can hop between them throughout the day.

Considered one of Australia's most beautiful beaches, **Wanuwuy** (Cape Arnhem) is a can't-miss beach during your visit. It's important to note that it's closed for about six weeks across August and September due to turtles nesting on the beach, so keep that in mind when you're planning your visit.

In the evening:
Watch the sunset from **the Gove Boat Club** while you have dinner and drinks outside. It's a beautiful spot, with huge meals, cheap drinks and palm trees lining the shore. If you're camping, the Gove Boat Club is also the best place to stay, with grassy sites, hot showers and phone reception.

Opposite Where the desert meets the ocean

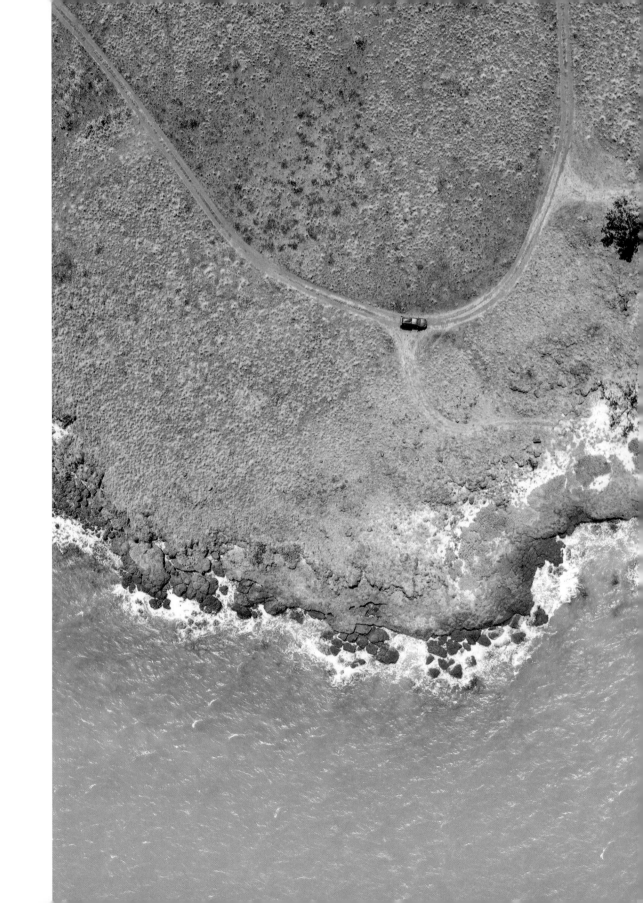

DAYTRIPS

Enjoy the Arnhem version of island life, with a stay at the boutique accommodation on either **Groote Eylandt** or **Bremer Island**. Both are very unique islands in their own way; they offer all different kinds of cultural experiences, fishing opportunities and lovely settings to relax and soak in this remote corner of Australia.

Top Sunset at Gove Boat Club
Bottom Exploring the beaches of East Arnhem Land

Where
Arnhem Land encompasses almost half of the Top End of the Northern Territory, covering everywhere from Port Roper on the Gulf of Carpentaria, around the coast to the East Alligator River, where it connects to Kakadu National Park via Cahills Crossing.

Getting here
The drive from Katherine to Nhulunbuy takes about 8 hours (729 kilometres), or if you're coming directly from Darwin it's about an 11-hour drive (1043 kilometres). The drive into Nhulunbuy is almost entirely on dirt roads, with the conditions of the road changing along the way. It's long and dusty, with corrugations in several different places, and very few places to stop along the way. Make sure you let down your tyre pressure before you hit the dirt to make your drive a little more comfortable. Stop at the **Mainoru Outback Store** for some snacks and a bathroom break if you need to, or you can stay in their accommodation if you need to break the trip up a bit.

You can also fly into Nhulunbuy via Gove Airport (GOV) directly from Darwin or Cairns, with both Qantas and Air North. The airport is close to town and there's a taxi service that can take you into the heart of Nhulunbuy.

Getting around
Rent a four-wheel drive for your stay so you can get around to all the different places to visit - many of them are found out of town.

When to go
Visit during the dry season (May to Oct). This is when you will find the majority of the roads around East Arnhem Land are open, and cultural tours and experiences are operating. Many roads are closed between November and May due to monsoon season, with even the main road closing depending on the conditions.

Main towns
The biggest town in Arnhem Land is Nhulunbuy, sitting on the Gove Peninsula. It is one of the most isolated towns in the world, with a 729-kilometre drive from Katherine to get there. Despite being so remote it's actually the sixth-largest town in the NT, and you can find a petrol station, two supermarkets, a hospital, several accommodation options, car rental and a couple of pubs.

Where to stay
There are a few hotels around Nhulunbuy, but if you're planning on camping head to the **Gove Boat Club** - The most reasonably priced campgrounds that offer bathrooms and hot showers, with views overlooking the peninsula.

Need to know
Permits are required before you enter Arnhem Land, and note that they can take time to be approved.

Northern Land Council: Apply for a permit to travel by road through Aboriginal Lands along the main Central Arnhem Road. The permit is free of charge, but can take up to two weeks to be approved. Apply online: (nlc.org.au/apply-for-permit).

Dhimurru Aboriginal Corporation: To visit any of the recreational areas around East Arnhem Land, you will need to apply for a Dhimurru Visitor Access Permit. This one can be applied for via its online booking system and is approved instantly. Permits start from $33.50 per adult for a three-day access pass, with 14-day, one-month and annual permits also available. Camping permits will need to be applied for on top of the recreational permit. Apply online: (dhimurru.com.au).

East Arnhem Liquor Permit: To purchase takeaway alcohol from any bottle shops or the pub, you will need to apply for an individual liquor permit in advance. This applies to Aboriginal dry areas, including Nhulunbuy, Yirrkala, Ski Beach, Galupa and Gunyangara. Apply online: (nt.gov.au/law/alcohol/permits).

It's also important to know that as with all waters in the NT's Top End, there could be crocodiles in the waters around East Arnhem Land. They are checked regularly by the rangers in the parks, but it is always important to be croc-wise when you are swimming and keep an eye out for anything suspicious.

Get planning
Dhimurru Aboriginal Corporation website (dhimurru.com.au) has the most information to help you plan your visit to East Arnhem Land, and is definitely the best place to start. To find out more about where to stay and things to do, head online to: eastarnhemland.com.au.

Can't-miss place
The Whitsundays (*see* p.202)

Top experience
Helicopter ride over the Great Barrier Reef (*see* p.198)

National Parks Pass
Most national parks in Queensland are free to visit for the day, but have fees for camping overnight. Head to parks.des.qld.gov.au to check if you need a camping permit for your next adventure. Vehicle access permits are always required for K'gari (Fraser Island), Green Island, Mulgumpin (Moreton Island), Bribie Island, Inskip Peninsula, Cooloola and Minjerribah (North Stradbroke Island) recreation areas. They can easily be purchased online or at various places around the islands.

Important dates
Check out some of Queensland's festivals and events to make the most out of your visit:

- Queensland Day (6 June)
- Taste Bundaberg (June)
- Laura Quinkan Dance Festival (July)
- Great Barrier Reef Festival (Aug)
- Brisbane Festival (Sept)

Time zone
Queensland follows the Australian Eastern Standard Time Zone (GMT +10) throughout the whole year.

Stay connected & get featured
Follow @queensland for all the inspiration and best places to visit, and have your Queensland photos featured by using hashtags #thisisqueensland.

Helpful websites
- Queensland National Parks
  parks.des.qld.gov.au
- Road conditions and closures
  racq.com.au/cars-and-driving/safety-on-the-road/road-conditions
- Restrictions for travelling in remote communities
  datsip.qld.gov.au

Queensland

They don't call it the Sunshine State for nothing, do they! Queensland has the weather that all of Australia is envious of, with around eight to nine hours of sunshine a day across most of the state. As a kid who grew up in Melbourne, this place absolutely feels like a dream to me.

There is so much diversity to explore in the second-biggest state of Australia – from the hinterland in the south, to the incredible Wet Tropics in the north, and a coastline that lies alongside the desert of the outback on one side and the world's largest coral reef ecosystem on the other. Queensland is also home to five of Australia's 11 UNESCO World Heritage–listed sites, including the Great Barrier Reef, K'gari (Fraser Island), the Wet Tropics, Gondwana Rainforest and Riversleigh Fossil Mammal Site.

Whether you're visiting for a weekend or longer, you'll fall in love with Queensland. Island destinations include Hamilton Island (*see* p.208) and Yunbenun (Magnetic Island, *see* p.188), and you can explore the Great Barrier Reef from Tropical North Queensland (*see* p.195) or the Bundaberg region (*see* p.191), as well as visit the incredible outback (*see* p.214). The sunny state will have you planning your next trip back before you've even left.

BRISBANE

The Turrbal and Jagera peoples are the Traditional
Owners of Meanjin, the location known as Brisbane

FOODIES | CULTURE BUFFS

Welcome to Brisbane, where the sun shines for an average
of 283 days per year and the temperature is always pretty
constant. Affectionately known as Bris-Vegas, there's no
shortage of great rooftop bars, alfresco dining options and
cute cafes to visit, with new hot spots opening all the time,
and always another Instagrammable cocktail to be found.

Australia's third-largest city is a little more cosmopolitan
than its southern neighbours, with a sleek modern look and
buildings built entirely out of windows. Most of the city can be
explored by scooter, making it super easy for you to zip along
the river, stopping at shops, cafes and cocktail bars along the
way. It's a great weekend destination.

PLAN YOUR TRIP FOR

The **Brisbane Festival** is in September and is one of the
biggest events on the Queensland calendar, when the whole
city comes to life with street concerts, suburban symphonies,
huge outdoor installations and epic light and laser shows.
There's something for everyone with hundreds of performances
and events going on across the city, so check the dates before
you book your visit.

Fairy light trees can be found near the Goodwill Bridge
Opposite Views from Kangaroo Point Lookout
Previous Radical Bay on Magnetic Island

CAN'T MISS

Check out the views over the city from **Kangaroo Point
Lookout**. It's also a great spot to bring a picnic and watch
the sun go down.

Jump on a ferry and cruise along the **Brisbane River**, easily
one of the best ways to soak up all the city views.

Grab a colourful cocktail at one of the city's many rooftop
bars. Some of our favourites include **The Terrace at
Emporium Hotel**, **Fiume at the Fantauzzo**, **Eagle's Nest**,
The Boundary Hotel and **WET Deck at W Brisbane**.

Hang out in **Fortitude Valley**, known as the trendy inner-city
spot. With an abundance of cool clubs and bars, unique
fashion boutiques, vibrant street art and hidden cafes, as
well as Brisbane's Chinatown, it's a great place if you're
looking for some fun.

Head to the **Goodwill Bridge** around dusk to see the
huge magical fig trees shimmer to life with millions of tiny
fairy lights.

Cool down at **Streets Beach**, Australia's only inner-city,
manmade beach with a sparkling lagoon surrounded by
white sandy beaches and overlooking the Brisbane River.

Shop up a storm at **The Collective Markets** at Stanley
Street Plaza each weekend (Fri 5-9pm, Sat 10am-9pm, Sun
9am-4pm), with all kinds of souvenirs and lots of local street
food to try.

Head to the lookout at the top of **Mount Coot-tha**, which
offers 360-degree views over Brisbane, all the way to the
coast and is particularly pretty at sunset.

Cuddle a koala at the **Lone Pine Koala Sanctuary**, the
biggest koala sanctuary in the world.

Visit **Australia Zoo**, home to the world-famous crocodile
hunter Steve Irwin and his legacy. It's about an hour's drive
north of Brisbane. There are plenty of croc demonstrations,
as well as animals from all around the world.

The **Gallery of Modern Art (GOMA)** is the largest modern
art gallery in the country and offers free admission to exhibits
by huge international artists.

The **Queensland Museum** on Southbank is also free with
lots of interesting exhibits.

Brisbane

DAYTRIPS

Mulgumpin (Moreton Island): Snorkel amongst the reefs that have formed in the **Tangalooma Shipwrecks**, a collection of 15 huge ships that have all been sunk together just off the coast of Mulgumpin (Moreton Island), a little north of Brisbane. You can jump on a daytrip from Brisbane, where they'll take you to the ferry and on a guided tour around the island, or stay the night at **Tangalooma Island Resort**.

A favourite holidaymaker spot on the Sunshine Coast, head north to **Noosa** to spend a great day at the beach and explore the expansive Noosa Heads National Park. Follow the walking trail past Tea Tree Bay and Granite Bay, to find the inviting fairy pools and take a dip before you head back. Hastings Street offers a selection of surf shops, fashion boutiques, cafes and restaurants. Before you leave, make sure you stock up on goodies at the **Noosa Chocolate Factory** in Noosaville for the drive home.

Start your day early with a hike in the **Glass House Mountains** for some of the best sunrise views in the area. There are 13 mountains which can be explored by hiking, climbing, riding or even on horseback.

Where
Brisbane is in the south-eastern pocket of Queensland.

Getting here
There are direct flights to Brisbane Airport (BNE) from all major airports around the country.

From the airport you can catch the Airtrain which runs from both the domestic and international terminals to Central station. It takes just 20 minutes from the city to the airport, with services running every 15-30 minutes.

Getting around
Brisbane is quite an easy city to get around. Grab yourself a scooter to easily navigate the city. You will see orange scooters all over the place - all you need to do is download and register for the app, scan the QR code on the scooter and you're on your way.

There is also the free CityHopper ferry, which operates between Sydney Street and the North Quay terminals, giving you an easy way to go between the city centre and Southbank. And on the road, the City Loop and Spring Hill Loop bus lines provide a free way to easily get around the city.

When to go
Southern Queensland is in a sweet spot of year-round subtropical weather, which makes Brisbane a great place to visit at any time of the year. The summertime can be a little wet and rainy, with temperatures that remain pretty consistent throughout the whole year. Winter is a great time for whale-watching, outdoor festivals and live music.

Where to stay
Book yourself accommodation close to Southbank along the Brisbane River to be within walking distance of lots of great bars and restaurants, close to the river lagoon beachfront and right in the heart of the action.

Kangaroo Point also offers great views over the river and the city, with many affordable accommodation options.

Get planning
To plan your visit, head to visitbrisbane.com.au or check out @visitbrisbane for all the inspo you'll need and up-to-date events.

MINJERRIBAH (NORTH STRADBROKE ISLAND)

Brisbane's closest island getaway

NATURE LOVERS

Known as Minjerribah to its Traditional Owners, the Quandamooka people, and affectionately known as Straddie, Minjerribah (North Stradbroke Island) is the closest island from Brisbane for a quick island getaway, less than an hour and a half away from the city. It's great for daytrips and weekends, with plenty of beach driving, freshwater lakes, sunshine and wildlife to spot around the island.

Straddie has a very laid-back vibe, getting you into the holiday spirit from the minute you step foot on the island. The sunrises and sunsets are bright and beautiful, the beaches are clear and perfect for swimming and surfing, and there are plenty of cute little cafes and restaurants to keep you trying something new around the island for every meal.

There are three little towns around the island, with Point Lookout claiming to be one of the best land-based whale-watching sites in the world. No matter where you decide to base yourself, you're never far from a great beach or somewhere offering a bite to eat. Everything is very chilled out on Straddie, so it's easy to plan your days around the sunshine or a great surf break.

PLAN YOUR TRIP FOR

Visit during late May through to early November for whale-watching season. During this time, hundreds of pods of humpback whales swim past the island during their annual migration. You can often spot little baby calves swimming along too, as they play together and jump out of the water. They're easy to spot from the island, so you don't even need to head out into the ocean to find them.

CAN'T MISS

In the morning:

The Gorge Walk is the most popular thing to do on the island. The walk is only 1-kilometre long and is quite easy to follow along the dedicated boardwalks. Along the way you're likely to spot turtles swimming in the gorge, and maybe even a koala or kangaroo along the trail.

Head to **South Gorge** to take a dip, right next to the Gorge Walk. It's such a unique little beach, surrounded by the rocky walls of the gorge with big waves rolling in from the ocean.

The **Brown Lake** gets its name and colour from the tea trees that surround it. This is a sacred place for the local Quandamooka women of the island. The water is actually lovely and warm and feels so nice and soothing on your skin. Around the corner there's also a Blue Lake, although this isn't for swimming in - due to its spiritual significance.

Join a guided walk along the historical **Goompi Trail** which is led by a local Quandamooka guide, sharing stories about their traditional hunting methods, bush-tucker recipes, medicines and traditional ochres. The walk takes around an hour along the foreshore of Dunwich.

Head to some of the **local art galleries** to view all kinds of beautiful works of art created on the island. The main ones can be found in Dunwich, including **Made on Minjerribah**, **Island Arts Creative** and **Salt Water Murris**.

In the afternoon:

Spend the afternoon rockpool hopping along the shore at **Deadmans Beach**. Check the tide times to visit during low tide when most of the rockpools are accessible and out of the water. Head towards the right side of the beach to find several little rockpools deep enough for you to jump in for a swim. On the beach behind the rockpools you can also find a giant sandhill that you can climb up, giving you incredible views across the beach and the island.

Take a drive along **Main Beach**, where you can fish, surf and swim or park up along the sand for a great beach day. It's easy to find a spot all to yourself where you can set up a picnic or head straight into the ocean for a dip. There's also a patrolled section of Main Beach, which is the safest place to swim on the island when the lifeguards are watching.

Another favourite is **Cylinder Beach**, located right in front of the beach camping sites. As well as having a great surf beach, Cylinder Beach also has a nice lagoon running along the sand, lovely for a lazy swim and soak in the water.

Jump on a **kayaking tour with Straddie Adventures** from Dunwich. It offers local tours around the island with a cultural twist and they are highly recommended.

In the evening:

Watch the sunset from **Amity Point**. There's a small jetty you can walk along, as well as a grassy park for a local fish and chip dinner. You can often spot dolphins swimming by Amity Point if you're lucky, as well as koalas in the trees. There's also a small ocean pool near the jetty, offering a calmer place to swim.

Have dinner at the **food trucks on Cylinder Beach**. You can usually find **Straddie Wood Fire Pizza** there on Friday and Saturday nights from 5pm, and **Sunshine Street Food** from Thursday to Sunday nights with great Mexican food!

DAYTRIPS

Straddie is also home to the **Manta Bommie**, known as one of the best dive sites in Australia, where you can swim with turtles, reef sharks and friendly manta rays. Only accessible on diving trips, book yourself a day tour out to the bommie to explore the colourful marine life and underwater world. Head to the Manta Lodge in Adder Point to book a scuba-diving tour and to find out more about the diving sites around the island.

Driving along Main Beach
Opposite Sunset walk along Amity Point Jetty

Where
Minjerribah (North Stradbroke Island) is just off the coast of Brisbane in South-east Queensland.

Getting here
SeaLink South East Queensland offers a vehicle and passenger ferry between Straddie and Cleveland, just out of Brisbane. It takes about 45 minutes to travel from the mainland to Straddie, with regular ferries running every hour to 90 minutes. Tickets start from $83 one-way for a standard car, or $92.50 one-way for a four-wheel drive or large car, with passenger fares costing just $17 per adult for a return trip.

When to go
Southern Queensland has pretty good weather all year round, so there's really no bad time to visit Minjerribah (North Stradbroke Island). Between late May and early November whales can be spotted from the land, as they pass by during their migration.

Main towns
There are three main towns on Straddie: Dunwich, Amity Point and Point Lookout. Dunwich is the gateway to the island, where the ferry arrives from the mainland, and is also where you can find the main supermarket, shops and fuel station. Amity Point and Point Lookout are both a bit smaller, with a handful of cafes and places to eat, but more known for their scenery and beaches.

Where to stay
Experience the best of island life by camping on the beach during your stay on Straddie. Beach camping is available at both **Main Beach** and **Flinders Beach**, although you will need a four-wheel drive to access them, as well as a vehicle access permit (*see* below). These are also great options if you're travelling with pets, as dogs are welcome at both camp areas. Camping fees do apply and can be booked and paid for at Adder Rock.

Alternatively, you can find all types of accommodation on the island, including hotels, cabins, campgrounds, holiday houses and even glamping tents at Adder Rock and Amity Point. With the island being so small it doesn't really matter where you choose to base yourself, as you're always only a short distance away from anything on the island.

Need to know
If you're bringing your car over to the island and plan to drive on the beach, you will need to purchase a vehicle access permit from Minjerribah Camping. Permits cost $53.65 per vehicle for up to one month and can either be purchased online or at the Adder Rock Camping Ground when you arrive. You will need to collect the physical sticker from the Adder Rock office and display the permit on your dashboard whenever you're driving along the beach or in restricted bushland.

Get planning
Head to stradbrokeisland.com and sealinkseq.com.au to help you plan your visit, or check out @northstraddieisland on social media for all the can't-miss spots.

Amity Point

THE GOLD COAST

The best thrill rides in the country

FOODIES

Affectionately known as 'the GC', the Gold Coast is one of Australia's most popular holiday spots for tourists and locals alike. With some of the best beaches in Southern Queensland, a booming foodie scene and home to the best theme parks and thrill rides in the country, it's easy to see why so many people choose to spend their holidays in the Gold Coast each year.

Although it hasn't quite shaken its reputation for being a party destination, the Gold Coast has been levelling up in recent years, with cute cafes and rooftop bars popping up all over the city, as well as First Nations experiences that immerse you in the local culture and traditions, and treetop walks that give you a taste of the rainforest. There's an endless number of ways to spend your weekend in the Gold Coast, with a new spot to visit every day of your trip.

Sitting in the perfect position to avoid any extreme weather, the Gold Coast is sunny all year round, with temperatures in the mid 20s to low 30s (Celsius) through every season. Keep an eye out for dolphins swimming along the beaches – it's so exciting when you spot them from the shore.

Aerial view of Tallebudgera Creek

Get into nature with a visit to **Lamington National Park**. Only a short drive from the Gold Coast, Lamington is home to beautiful lookouts and views, cascading waterfalls and all kinds of wildlife. Head to **O'Reilly's Rainforest Retreat** to take a walk around the treetops or relax and rejuvenate at its Lost World Spa.

Visit during October and November to experience **whale-watching season**, when huge pods of humpback whales swim south on their annual migration. There are plenty of great whale-watching tours you can jump on to get you up close to the action.

Burleigh Heads is a culturally significant area for the local Yugambeh people, having once been a feasting ground for First Nations people travellers passing through the region. Pay a visit to **Jellurgal Aboriginal Cultural Centre** focused on Aboriginal history and culture on the Gold Coast.

CAN'T MISS
In the morning:
Why not start your day in the most extreme way - by **skydiving** over the Gold Coast! You can't beat the view from above, with beaches as far as the eye can see and the glittering city buildings standing tall along the shoreline.

Head to **Surfers Paradise Beach** for a dip in the ocean or a surfing lesson at one of Australia's favourite beaches. It became an iconic beach in 1965, when the famous Meter Maids started strolling up and down the beachfront in shimmery gold bikinis and a sash, adding coins to expired parking metres and saving beachgoers from a parking fine. They have hilariously become an iconic fixture at Surfers Paradise Beach and don't mind stopping for a selfie and a chat.

In the afternoon:
Known for its sprawling beaches, try and hop across as many of the local beaches as you can during your weekend. Some of the top spots include **Rainbow Bay**, **Burleigh Heads** and **Currumbin Beach**, which is far enough away to offer epic views of the Gold Coast skyline. Another one of our personal favourites is **Tallebudgera Creek**, which is actually a river that runs through the city to the ocean, with some of the brightest blue river water you've ever seen.

For lunch, there is plenty of choice - from farm-to-table restaurants to fusion cuisines, wineries and distilleries and local cheesemakers to taste test from. A top favourite is **Canungra Valley Vineyards** where you can have an 'alpaca picnic', with local wine and cheese, followed by a walk with some of the cutest alpacas you've ever seen, with a beautiful tropical landscape around you.

Shop up a storm at some of Australia's best markets, including the **Carrara Markets**, which are Australia's biggest permanent weekend markets (Sat-Sun 7am-3pm), with more than 300 stalls that sell everything from homewares and fashion to fresh produce. The **Miami Marketta** on Broadbeach comes alive on Wednesdays, Fridays and Saturdays from 5pm with street food from around the world, main stages that host local artists and onsite bars serving specialty cocktails.

Get up close and personal with some of Australia's native wildlife animals at **Currumbin Wildlife Sanctuary** that offers all sorts of wildlife experiences, including taking a selfie with a kangaroo, cuddling a koala or even feeding a crocodile.

In the evening:
Check out the best views over the Gold Coast at the top of the **SkyPoint Observation Tower**. The observation deck is 77-floors high, and is the only beachside observation tower in Australia, offering views over the ocean as well as the intricate river system that circles the Gold Coast. It's a great spot to visit as the sun is setting for a pretty pink and orange skyline.

Immerse yourself in the local Aboriginal culture at **The Evening Experience** at **Spirits of the Red Sand**. It's a live theatre and dinner experience, complete with a three-course dinner complemented by song and dance, followed by a meet and greet at the end of the night. Sharing powerful stories from the Dreamtime, it's a great way to connect with 60,000 years of culture from the Yugambeh and Kombumerri people from around the Gold Coast.

Take a **sunset cruise** along the Gold Coast waterways with wine and a nibbles plate with fruit, cheese and seafood as the sky turns the prettiest pink and orange colours during the sunset.

DAYTRIPS

Get your adrenaline pumping with a day at one of Australia's best theme parks. The Gold Coast is where you go if you're looking for heart-stopping thrill rides, the biggest and best water parks, show bags, parades, wildlife experiences and real-life movie characters. Head to **Dreamworld** or **Warner Bros**. **Movie World** for thrill rides that will take your breath away; **Wet'n'Wild** or **White Water World** for epic waterslides to cool off in; or **Sea World** on Main Beach to meet Australia's only polar bear and swim with the dolphins. There are multi-park passes available, both online and at the gate, to give you a discounted rate if you're planning to hop across a few of them.

BEST PHOTO SPOTS

Hike up to the top of **Mt Tamborine** for incredible views across the hinterland and lots of great photo opportunities. Take a picnic and a woven rug at sunset for the ultimate shot.

Where

The Gold Coast sits right on the most south-eastern point of Queensland, along the border with NSW.

Getting here

Fly into Gold Coast Airport (OOL), with regular flights from most major cities around Australia. Pick up a rental car from the airport and then it's only a short 15-minute drive into the heart of the Gold Coast.

Alternatively, you can often find more choices in flight times if you fly into Brisbane Airport (BNE). The Airtrain connects Brisbane Airport and the Gold Coast in 60 minutes, running every 15-30 minutes with stops at Surfers Paradise and Broadbeach.

Getting around

The G-link Tram easily connects the whole Gold Coast together, running between Helensvale and Broadbeach South. A tram arrives roughly every 10-15 minutes, so you never have to wait very long, and you can buy a ticket at the station. Tickets cost $4.90 for any trip, so it is cheap and easy to get around the Gold Coast.

When to go

The Gold Coast is the ideal year-round destination, with 300 days of sunshine a year and warm temperatures all year around. There's never a bad time to visit.

Where to stay

Caville Avenue is the main street in the Gold Coast, with most of the resorts and hotels being located in the surrounding streets. Stay in this area to be within close walking distance to the action, with lots of great accommodation options. Most hotels are only a short walking distance from the beach and the main street, with the tram connecting you to anywhere else you want to go.

Need to know

It's important to note that the last week of November and first two weeks of December are generally when 'schoolies' is happening in the Gold Coast. During this time, thousands of school leavers head to the Gold Coast for their first taste of freedom, so unless you want to get caught up in that mayhem it's generally a good time of the year to avoid.

Get planning

Head to destinationgoldcoast.com to find out everything you can do on the Gold Coast and check out @destinationgoldcoast on Insta for all the inspo.

Koala at Currumbin Wildlife Sanctuary
Opposite The Gold Coast skyline along the beach

K'GARI (FRASER ISLAND)

K'gari – truly paradise

ADVENTURERS | NATURE LOVERS

Known as K'gari (pronounced *gurri*) to the local Butchulla people, K'gari means paradise and comes from the Butchulla Dreamtime creation story. K'gari (Fraser Island) might just be the most unique island in all of Australia, also the largest sand island in the whole world, and is the only place on Earth where a luscious rainforest grows right out of the sand, with trees reaching more than 200 metres tall.

K'gari is 123 kilometres long and 22 kilometres wide. It takes around 45 minutes to cross the island from one side to the other by car, and it can take a good couple of hours and good tide conditions to get all the way to the tip of the island, as almost all of the roads and tracks are purely made up of sand, so you'll definitely need a four-wheel drive to explore. The island has more than half of the world's perched lakes, where depressions in the dunes are permanently filled with rainwater.

Safe to say, K'gari is a pretty incomparable environment and a great place to spend the weekend exploring.

CAN'T MISS

In the morning:
One of the most beautiful lakes in Australia, **Lake McKenzie** is a sight that needs to be seen with your own eyes to appreciate how special it is. This incredible freshwater lake has some of the clearest bright turquoise water close to the shore, before it drops off into a deep blue only a few metres from the bright white sand. Visit early in the morning if you want to avoid the crowds.

Lake Wabby is another great lake to stop at for a swim. It's the deepest lake on the island at the edge of Hammerstone Sandblow.

Take a drive down the iconic beach highway of **Seventy-Five Mile Beach**. Stretching for 75 miles, it actually takes hours to drive the whole length of the beach, and you will need to check the tide times if you are hoping to get to the tip, as some spots are impassable if the tide is too high.

Our favourite spot on K'Gari, Lake McKenzie

Stop to see the *Maheno* **Shipwreck** right in the middle of Seventy-File Mile Beach. The *Maheno* was originally a Trans-Tasman luxury liner and a World War I ship hospital that was washed onto the shores in 1935 when it was being towed to Japan. The sand blows across the wreck and comes in and out with the tides, so visit at low tide if you're hoping to see more of the shipwreck exposed.

The **Pinnacle Cliffs** are just a little north of the *Maheno* shipwreck. These impressive cliffs stand tall along the beach and are a swirling mix of red, orange, yellow and white sandstone, making them a picturesque backdrop to any beach day.

In the afternoon:

Jump on the **West Coast Explorer Tour** to explore more of the wild and largely untouched western side of the island. Departing from 12pm each day from Kingfisher Bay Jetty, the tour goes for about three hours and explores some of the prettiest places between Fraser Island and Hervey Bay. During the tour you get to stop at a remote sand caye for a swim, birdwatch on the nearby island and maybe even spot turtles, dolphins and dugongs swimming.

Try and catch a monster fish right off the shore of the beach. The island is known for its exceptional **fishing**, with whiting, dart, bream, mackerel, trevally, tuna and flathead regularly being caught off the beach, depending on the season of course. The jetty near Kingfisher Bay Resort is another great fishing spot, although you might be competing with a lot of other fishers here.

Eli Creek is a cool freshwater creek that comes out of the rainforest and runs all the way down to the ocean. There is a pretty boardwalk that runs alongside the creek, and if you

jump in at the end of the boardwalk you can float back down to your car or the ocean. Bring your own floaties for this one - it's so relaxing.

Another amazing swimming spot to check out is the **Champagne Pools** right at the northern end of Seventy-Five Mile Beach. These inviting rockpools are full of calm crystal-clear water and are a great place to cool off. You can see great views over the Champagne Pools from the boardwalk before you even get there, it's such a pretty spot.

Visit during the winter months to jump on a **whale-watching tour**, where you can spot humpback whales along the coastline as part of their annual migration. It's a great place with regular sightings and tours to see these gentle giants up close.

In the evening:

Watch the sun go down on the **Sea Explorer Sunset Cruise** jet boat. Taking off just as the sun begins to set, there are drinks onboard, good music and incredible natural scenery that changes colours with the sunset. You can often see dingoes running along the beach as the sun goes down too. After the sun sets, get ready for a quick thrill ride on the jet boat before returning to the jetty.

Treat yourself to a nice dinner and a cocktail at the **Sand & Wood Restaurant** in the Kingfisher Bay Resort. It has an incredible menu, covering all dietary requirements, from seafood towers and steaks to vegetarian dishes. End the evening with their signature bounty chocolada cocktail. It's a can't miss and so delicious.

Keep an eye out for **dingoes** running along the beach around the island. The island is home to the most pure strain of dingoes remaining along the East Coast of Australia, and they can often be spotted running along the beach and in the sand dunes. You can also join a ranger for a guided night walk to find out more about the dingoes and other wildlife. It's always good to remember though that dingoes are wild animals, so always keep your distance if you spot one and make sure to pack away all your food if you're camping so they don't have a feast on your snacks during the night.

DAYTRIPS

If you don't have your own four-wheel drive vehicle you can still experience the island on the **Fraser Explorer Tours**. The guided four-wheel drive tours will take you from the mainland across to the island, and then show you around to all the best spots. They have multi-day and overnight tours depending on how long you want to visit for, and they depart from either Rainbow Beach or Hervey Bay.

K'gari (Fraser Island)

BEST PHOTO SPOTS

There's no better place to capture the essence of the island than **Lake McKenzie**. It's impossible to take a bad shot of this beautiful lake, with the different colours of the water visible at all times of the day.

Where

Just off the coast of Southern Queensland, K'gari can be found a short distance from both Hervey Bay and Rainbow Beach on the mainland.

Getting here

There are two ferries that connect K'gari to the mainland. The Kingfisher Bay Ferry Service departs from River Heads near Hervey Bay four times per day, arriving at the small jetty at Kingfisher Bay Resort. The trip takes about 50 minutes and is the best choice if you're staying at the resort. If you're planning to beach camp on the island, the **Manta Ray Fraser Island Barge** drops you straight onto Seventy-Five Mile Beach after a short 10-minute barge trip from Inskip Point. It's important to note that Inskip Point is notorious for people getting bogged on both sides of the barge, so make sure you're prepared for the conditions if you choose this option. There's a lot of videos on YouTube about people getting bogged, if you want to check them out.

Getting around

You will need your own four-wheel drive vehicle if you want to explore on your own. With most of the island made of sand, four-wheel drives are the only way to get around the island without getting stuck. If you're not bringing a car to the island, jump on a **Fraser Island Explorer Tour** to head out in their iconic blue four-wheel drive bus to see all the best sights.

When to go

K'gari is a great destination to visit at any time throughout the year, with sunny weather most of the time. The temperature generally varies from low to high 20s (Celsius) throughout the year, with cooler nights during the middle of the year. Winter (June to Aug) is whale season, when you can often spot humpback whales passing along the beach during their annual migration.

Where to stay

The main resort is **Kingfisher Bay Resort**, located on the western side of the island. It offers nice big rooms, four swimming pools, three restaurants and super comfy beds. The small town of the resort is a great place to base yourself as you explore the island. Around the resort you can find the Island Day Spa and the Sunset Bar on the beach near the jetty, which is a great place to grab a cocktail as the sun goes down.

If you're looking to stay a little closer to the main beach, **Eurong Beach Resort** on the eastern side of the island is the other resort option. Only a few steps away from Seventy-Five Mile Beach, Eurong has accommodation options for every budget, with hotel rooms and two-bedroom apartments to choose from. You can also camp right on the beach in Great Sandy National Park. To camp on K'gari you will need a vehicle access permit, as well as a booking for your camp area, which can be booked up to 6 months in advance at: parks.des.qld.gov.au/parks/kgari-fraser/camping.

Need to know

Before driving on K'gari you will need to purchase a vehicle access permit from Queensland National Parks (qpws.usedirect.com/qpws). The permit costs $53.65 per car for visiting for one month or less, and should be displayed on your dashboard at all times during your visit.

Get planning

Start planning your visit at visitfrasercoast.com. Check out kingfisherbay.com for their 'What's On' guide, to find out all the activities, experiences and events that are on during your stay.

Colour changes at Lake McKenzie
Opposite Driving along Seventy-Five Mile Beach

YUNBENUN (MAGNETIC ISLAND)

An island getaway off the coast of Townsville

ADVENTURERS | NATURE LOVERS

If you're looking for a good place to kick back, unwind and completely embrace the island life, Yunbenun (Magnetic Island), just a short ferry ride off the coast of Townsville, is absolutely the place to do it. Despite its small size, Maggie, as it is affectionately called, is overflowing with hilly hiking trails, pretty beaches, stunning lookouts, an abundance of native wildlife, and those cute little Barbie-style cars that can only be found on the island.

Sitting just 8 kilometres off the coast of Townsville, Maggie is home to 23 beautiful beaches and bays. Two-thirds of the island is protected national park, and it is also part of the UNESCO World Heritage–listed Great Barrier Reef Marine Park. In fact, it's the only self-contained island in the Great Barrier Reef Marine Park. Maggie is also home to northern Australia's largest colony of wild koalas, which can often be spotted in the trees along many of the walking trails around the island.

Boasting an average of 320 days of sunshine per year, you're almost guaranteed to have a warm sunny day on your visit to the island, so you can fully embrace island life. Whether you're heading to Maggie on a daytrip from Townsville or you're spending a full weekend, this sleepy little island is sure to be a highlight of your travels.

BEST PHOTO SPOTS

There are lots of different lookouts and hikes across Maggie that offer incredible photo opportunities. Some of the best include Arthur Bay Lookout, Hawkings Point Lookout and the Forts Walk. Try and get to a couple of them at sunrise, sunset or the golden hour to see views in the prettiest colours.

CAN'T MISS

In the morning:

Jump on the **Maggie Discovery Tour with Aquascene** to really experience the best of Maggie from the eyes of the locals. On the tour you get the chance to try a bit of catch and release fishing to see some of the colourful reef fish, snorkel in the Great Barrier Reef that lies around the island, and check out some of the parts of Maggie that you can't access from the mainland. Run by Adam, a local who has lived on Maggie for his whole life, you also gain a great insight to life on the island and the interesting history.

Check out **Arthur Bay Lookout**, which offers one of the best views on the island. Found along Radical Bay Road, about 700 metres from the Forts Walk carpark, follow the small sign that points to the lookout and enjoy some beautiful views over picturesque Arthur Bay.

One of the most popular walks on the island is the **Forts Walk**, which runs between Arcadia and Horseshoe Bay. As well as offering beautiful views over the island, the Forts Walk is also home to lots of World War II history, and is one of the best places on the island to spot wild koalas sleeping in the trees. It's a 5-kilometre return walk, and it's a good idea to start early in the day to avoid the heat.

Meet the cute little rock wallabies that hang out amongst the boulder rocks at **Geoffrey Bay**. The spot is known as Bremner Point in Arcadia, but if you look it up on Google Maps it literally says 'rock wallabies' at the right location, so you won't have any issues finding them.

In the afternoon:

Rent an **open-roof 'Barbie' car** to get around the island. These little cars are so cute and bright, and give you the ultimate island look as you cruise around with the wind in your hair. The cars are low to the ground, with pretty much no sides. Book in advance, as they often completely book out.

Take a dip at **Radical Bay**, one of the best spots for swimming on the island. From Horseshoe Bay you can follow the 1.5 kilometre walking trail to get to Radical Bay, where you can often have this stunning palm tree-lined beach all to yourself.

Bungalow Bay Koala Village in Horseshoe Bay is a small wildlife park where you can get up close and personal and make friends with all kinds of Australian wildlife. Book one of their guided tours with a ranger at 10am, 12pm or 2.30pm, where there are plenty of wildlife encounter opportunities and stories about their life on the island. It's also one of the only places where you can cuddle up to a wombat.

Snorkel the **self-guided snorkelling trails** in Nelly Bay and Geoffrey Bay that take you to some of the fringing reefs in Arthur Bay and Florence Bay. You can often spot sea turtles swimming along the reef, as well as all kinds of colourful reef fish.

If you're visiting during the winter months, check out the **Butterfly Walk** right next to Bungalow Bay. Each year thousands of blue tiger butterflies migrate to Maggie, and walking through the bushland as they flutter around and above you is such a unique experience.

In the evening:
Hike to the top of **Hawkings Point** for panoramic views over both Picnic Bay and Nelly Bay from the top of a huge boulder rock. It stands tall out of the native bushland, and on a clear day you can even see as far as Townsville. It's a great sunset spot.

Check out the quiet beachfront and have dinner at **Picnic Bay**. Whilst it used to be the heart of the island, Picnic Bay is a pretty quiet spot now, after the main jetty moved down to Nelly Bay. There are plenty of places to eat in Picnic Bay, though.

DAYTRIPS
If you have some extra time, you can always head back to the mainland for a day or an afternoon to explore more of **Townsville**. It might seem funny to take a daytrip from an island back to the mainland, but that seems to be the better way to do things here.

Head to trendy hot spot **The Ville** where you can grab a great lunch at the **Quarterdeck Restaurant**, serving everything from wood-fired pizza and burgers, to specialty cocktails and sharing platters. Check out the views from **Castle Hill** and **Mount Sonder** - the latter is particularly beautiful at sunset. Or head to **Reef HQ**, the world's largest living coral reef and aquarium, to get a glimpse of the Great Barrier Reef without even getting wet.

Views from Arthur Bay Lookout

Where

Yunbenun (Magnetic Island) is just 8 kilometres off the coast of Townsville in northern Queensland.

Getting here

It takes just 20 minutes to get from Townsville to Yunbenun (Magnetic Island) or vice versa on SeaLink QLD's passenger ferry service. SeaLink operates 18 daily services to Maggie, so you can actually just turn up and buy a ticket at the ferry terminal whenever you want to go across to the island. There is a little discount if you pre-purchase them online though, where an adult ticket will cost $30 for a return trip.

Getting around

Pick up a rental car when you arrive to make the most of your weekend on the island. Since it's only 10 to 15 minutes from one side of the island to the other, everything is really in close driving range. As of 2020 you can no longer drive down Radical Bay Road or out to West Point, due to the terrible road conditions. Hire cars are no longer allowed there, so it's best to stick to hiking over to Radical Bay.

When to go

Yunbenun is truly a year-round destination, with mostly warm sunny days and very little rain throughout the year. The average temperature is between 27 and 29°C year-round. To dodge the worst of the crowds, try to avoid the Australian school holidays (which vary between states).

Main towns

Nelly Bay is the largest town on the island, which is where you can find the ferry terminal, an IGA supermarket, the biggest hotels, car rental companies and even an aquarium. You can also find tiny little towns in Arcadia, Horseshoe Bay, Nelly Bay, Picnic Bay and Florence Bay.

Where to stay

Across Yunbenun, you can find all kinds of accommodation, from luxury hotels to hostels and campgrounds. One of our favourites is **Bungalow Bay Koala Village** where you can stay in a very cute little triangle bungalow. Some of the bungalows have their own ensuite, while others use a shared bathroom. It's in a great location, only a short walk from Horseshoe Bay and the beach, and is kind of a mix between a caravan park and a hostel.

Get planning

To plan your visit to Yunbenun head online to thisismagneticisland.com.au or townsvillenorthqueensland.com.au, or you can check out @thisismagneticisland and @townsvillenorthqueensland on Instagram for all the best spots.

Bungalow Bay Koala Village

BUNDABERG REGION

Gateway to the Southern Great Barrier Reef

NATURE LOVERS

There's so much to love about Bundaberg. Only a four-hour drive north of Brisbane, Bundaberg is a dynamic region, with a history of sugar cane trade and some of the most beautiful parts of the Southern Great Barrier Reef (*see* p.198) found only a short way off the shore. Bundaberg boasts that it is the town the turtles call home, with incredible reef sites found right off the beach that turtles love to visit throughout the year.

Affectionately known as the sugar cane city, Bundaberg is home to one of the most iconic and historic distilleries in the country, Bundaberg Rum. Bundaberg offers a completely different experience to anywhere else along the coast of Queensland, with the vibe of an overgrown country town full of heritage colonial buildings, and a crazy amount of community spirit that you just don't feel in the cities. Make sure you also take the time on your weekend away to head a little further north to the coastal towns of Agnes Waters and 1770, which will make you feel a million miles away from the city.

PLAN YOUR TRIP FOR

Visit during the **Taste Bundaberg Festival** to immerse yourself in the community and the history of this sugar cane town. Held over 10 days in June each year, the festival is a showcase of authentic Bundabergian food and drink experiences, from the farmer, distiller, brewer, grazier and fisher; to the restauranteur, food stall owner, chef and caterer; through to the table.

Lady Musgrave Island

CAN'T MISS

In the morning:

Jump onboard the **Bundy Belle**, for a two-and-a-half hour cruise along the Burnett River and see Bundaberg from a different perspective. Learn about the history of the town and see some of the biggest highlights and attractions around Bundaberg.

Take a **self-guided walking tour** of the town to see some of the beautiful heritage colonial buildings. They are scattered all around the city and really make you feel like you have stepped back in time. Make sure you pop into the **Bundaberg Botanic Gardens** for the sub-tropical garden environment with more than 10,000 plants and a working sugar cane train.

Check out the beaches of **Agnes Waters**, in particular the less-well-known **Chinaman's Beach**, which looks like a beach straight out of a guidebook. Jump in the water for a swim or throw in a line and see if you catch anything - it's a great place for a relaxing afternoon. After the beach head to the **Paperbark Forest Boardwalk**, a short walk amongst the tall paperbark trees, it's like a forest out of a fairytale.

Head to the **Discovery Coast Markets** on the second and fourth Sunday of every month at the SES Grounds between Agnes Waters and the town of 1770. The market is always buzzing with people, where you can buy all kinds of gifts, clothing and fresh produce - or even take a ride on a camel.

In the afternoon:

Take a tour of the iconic **Bundaberg Rum Distillery**, which has been producing their world-famous rum since 1888. Taking pride in the fact that all the ingredients that go into the rum are home grown and locally sourced, Bundaberg Rum has won awards around the world, including the World's Best Rum in international competitions several times. It offers a great distillery experience that takes you through the Bundaberg Museum and the history of the rum, before showing you around the distillery where the drinks are made. At the end, of course, there is a delicious taste test, where you can choose any of their products to try. Make sure you try their salted caramel liqueur - it's incredible.

If you're looking for something just as famous but non-alcoholic, head to the **Bundaberg Barrel**, home to another famous beverage, Bundaberg Ginger Beer. Take a walking tour around the barrel, sharing the history of the drink and how it's made, before heading to the Tasting Bar and testing a sample of their 19 flavours.

BEST PHOTO SPOTS

You can't leave Bundaberg without an iconic photo with the huge bottle of rum outside the Bundaberg Rum Distillery.

Bundaberg region

Eat your way across Bundaberg, with local produce taking charge here and cafes and restaurants all trying to find their own unique feel and signature dishes. Bundaberg even likes to call itself the 'food bowl'! Some of the favourites include the **Windmill at Bargara**, **Vinters Secret Vineyard Cellar Door**, **Bert's Restaurant** and **Grunske's By The River Seafood Market and Restaurant**.

Jump on a **LARC! Tour**, a family run business that takes you out in a bright pink ex-military cargo amphibious vessel that drives across the land and then floats along the water as you explore the best of Agnes Water and 1770. Before we got to the Bundaberg region, everyone recommended that we go on this tour and it didn't disappoint. Highly entertaining and a great way to see more of this unique coastline.

In the evening:
Jump on a **Mon Repos Turtle Encounter** night tour, to see turtles coming to nest on the beach. Led by an experienced guide, from November to January you are able to watch the turtles come out from the ocean, dig themselves a nest and lay their eggs. Then about six to eight weeks later, from January to March, you can come and watch the hatchlings emerge from their nests and make their way across the beach to the ocean. The tour is highly popular, so it's important to book in advance, or put your name on the waiting list if bookings have closed. January is a great time to visit, when you can often see both the nesting females and the tiny hatchlings starting to emerge.

DAYTRIPS
Explore the best of the Southern Great Barrier Reef by jumping on the **Lady Musgrave Experience**. The lagoon around Lady Musgrave Island is one of the most colourful and abundant parts of the Great Barrier Reef we had the opportunity to snorkel in. There is an incredible amount of marine life here, with thousands of colourful fish, plenty of green sea turtles, reef sharks and manta rays often spotted during the tour. The Lady Musgrave Experience gives you plenty of snorkelling time, as well as a glass-bottom boat tour and a guided walk around the island itself. One of our favourite snorkelling experiences on the reef.

Opposite top Turtle swimming in the Great Barrier Reef
Opposite middle Bundaberg Rum Distillery
Opposite bottom The Paperbark Forest in Agnes Water

Where
Bundaberg is on the East Coast of Queensland.

Getting here
You can fly directly into Bundaberg Airport (BDB) from Brisbane in only 45 minutes, with connecting flights from the rest of the country. Bundaberg is an easy drive from Brisbane, sitting just four hours north on the Bruce Highway.

Alternatively, you can take the Tilt Train which takes about four and a half hours, departing from Brisbane at 11am daily except Wednesday, with an additional service at 4.55pm on certain days.

When to go
During the summer months (Oct to April) is the best time to visit the Bundaberg region, when the weather is a little warmer and you have no excuse not to get in the water. For all the turtle encounters you can think of, visit between November and March, with January being a great time to come for both nesting and hatchling experiences.

Where to stay
Bundaberg offers lots of accommodation options, with hotels, hostels and campgrounds all within a short distance of the city.

Alternatively, stay at **Bargara** (less than 15 minutes from the heart of the city), where you can find beachfront resorts, lots of Airbnbs, and cute places to eat right along the beach, while also being super close to the action.

Head to **Agnes Waters** and **1770** for more of a laidback beach town-vibe.

If you're solely coming to experience the Southern Great Barrier Reef, then you can also stay on **Lady Elliot Island**, a small coral caye at the southern tip of the island with an eco-resort. Wake up here in the morning and the reef is only a few steps away from your door, giving you ultimate amounts of time to spend in the water. It's an incredible island, with eco-friendly tents, cabins or units to choose from, with rates that include breakfast and dinner, snorkelling equipment, glass-bottom boat tours and a range of guided tours and activities.

Need to know
If you're only in the early stages of planning your visit to the Bundaberg region, it's a good idea to put your name on the waiting list for the turtle encounters. They are super popular and often booked out days and weeks in advance, so it's worth planning your trip around the dates you are able to grab for the encounters.

Get planning
Plan your visit at bundabergregion.org or head to their socials at @visitbundaberg and @southerngreatbarrierreef.

TROPICAL NORTH QUEENSLAND

Home to the oldest rainforests on Earth

NATURE LOVERS | ADVENTURERS

Made up of some of the oldest rainforests on Earth, Tropical North Queensland is an epic region to explore, full of waterfalls, rolling green hills and beaches right at the foot of the rainforest. Stretching from Mission Beach in the south, all the way to Cape York in the north, the rainforests that make up the Wet Tropics World Heritage Area here are thought to be six to 10 times older than the Amazon, dating back more than 100 million years.

If you're from the southern states, Tropical North Queensland is the ideal weekend getaway in the middle of the year, when the weather is warm and sunny and you can swap your winter coat for your bathers and thongs (flip-flops) and soak up that heat and humidity. It's the perfect place to immerse yourself in nature, whether it be snorkelling the reefs, or hiking through the rainforests in search of your very own private rockpool with a view over the mountains.

You can visit in as little as a weekend, or spend weeks exploring all the little nooks and crannies that Tropical North Queensland has to offer. There's always another waterfall to find, reef to snorkel, lookout to hike to, and rainforest to explore. Each of the different locations offer completely different experiences. To start your planning process, choose your base destination depending on what you're coming to experience – and go from there.

Four Mile Beach, Port Douglas

CAN'T MISS

Whether you're coming for the reef or the rainforest, there are sites to be visited all along the coast of Tropical North Queensland. A bit of planning is a great idea for a weekend here, to ensure you have enough time to fit everything in and you don't miss out on any of the highlights.

In the morning:

Start your day in **Palm Cove**, catching the sunrise from the palm tree-lined beach. A pretty quiet little beach town, there are plenty of great cafes to stop at for breakfast after you've grabbed the perfect shot.

If you're feeling a little more energetic, another great sunrise spot is **Windin Falls** in **Wooroonooran National Park**. It takes about 90 minutes to hike each way (and I'll be honest, there's a steep incline), but views over the Wet Tropics World Heritage Area are unparalleled from up here, and there's a small waterhole at the top to cool off in before you start your trek back down.

Head to the **Port Douglas Sunday Markets**, on every Sunday from early morning until around 2pm. The markets are very popular in the community, with all kinds of unique and creative stalls and some really beautiful pieces to be found here, so give yourself plenty of time to shop around.

Experience a piece of the UNESCO World Heritage-listed Daintree Rainforest with a visit to **Mossman Gorge**. This peaceful spot is home to a crystal-clear river, full of huge boulders and surrounded by the rainforest. The water is absolutely freezing here, so get ready for the cold if you're planning to go for a dip. You take a bus from the gorge's Visitor Information Centre and then the gorge is only a short walk from the entrance to the park.

Visit **Kuranda**, the village in the rainforest that sits high above Cairns. For the best experience, take the famous **Skyrail** cable car up to Kuranda, where you can visit the **Kuranda Original Markets**, **Koala Gardens** and **Butterfly Sanctuary**, as well as grab a bite to eat. Once you've finished exploring, catch the **Scenic Heritage Railway** back down to Cairns, getting a great glimpse of the rainforest and waterfalls tumbling through the mountains as you travel back down.

In the afternoon:

Spend an afternoon exploring the waterfall trail of the Atherton Tablelands. Set amongst a picturesque landscape of rolling green hills, there are some absolutely beautiful waterfalls to be found in the depths of the Tablelands. Some of the highlights include **Millaa Millaa Falls**, **Zillie Falls**, **Elinjaa Falls** and **Pepina Falls**, which are all quite close together and easy to hop across in one afternoon. There are also lots of cute tea houses and dairies offering cheese plates with wine and a view to stop at when you're feeling a bit peckish.

Head to the beautiful **Four Mile Beach** in Port Douglas for an afternoon swim or picnic under the palm trees. You can always find a spot all to yourself here, so it's a great place for a beach afternoon.

Get your crocodile fix with a visit to **Hartleys Crocodile Adventures**. As well as being a wildlife park, it is also a real working crocodile farm, where you can learn about the crocodile industry or jump on a wetlands cruise through the Hartleys Lagoon to meet some of their jumping crocodiles. It's definitely one of the best places for a crocodile encounter on the East Coast.

Take a drive to **Babinda Boulders**, one of our favourite spots that seems to be a little quieter than others. You can take a chilly swim in the clear river that runs through here, or follow the walk up to the lookout for the best perspective. There is also a small free campground here, with a bathroom and shower and beautiful peacocks roaming around.

Cruise along the **Captain Cook Highway** that connects Cairns and Port Douglas and is one of Australia's most scenic drives, with beautiful greenery from the rainforests on one side and the Coral Sea on the other.

In the evening:

Rex Smeal Park in Port Douglas is a great place for a sunset picnic, with the whole park often glowing a beautiful golden colour as the sun goes down. There are palm trees lining the park that really give you that tropical holiday feel.

Head to the **Iron Bar** on the main street of Port Douglas, an iconic hot spot that has been racing cane toads for almost 20 years. Every night is a party at the cane toad races, so bring a group of friends and get ready to have some fun. Cane toad races are on every night from 8pm, but come down early and grab yourself a meal before the chaos happens.

Have dinner at **Dundee's @ Cairns Aquarium**, where one whole wall of the restaurant is completely made up of a tank that is connected to the aquarium. You can watch the fish and even a few little sharks swimming around while you have dinner. The menu has been curated with flavours of Australia that includes options like oysters, crocodile spring rolls, octopus salad, kangaroo loin and an epic Great Barrier Reef seafood platter.

DAYTRIPS

Take a trip over to **Fitzroy Island**, only a short ferry ride off the coast of Cairns. This little island is a great spot for snorkelling with sea turtles right off the shore, as well as being home to the stunning Nudey Beach. The Fitzroy Flyer goes between Fitzroy Island and Cairns a couple of times a day, so you can either visit for a daytrip or half a day, or stay a bit longer and check into the Island Resort. Make sure to stop in at **Foxy's Bar** to grab a cocktail while you're there - definitely our favourite lunch views in Tropical North Queensland. For more about Fitzroy Island, *see* p.200.

No trip to this region would be complete without a visit to the incredible **Great Barrier Reef**. There are daily daytrips out to the reef from both Cairns and Port Douglas, heading to lots of different reef sites, nearby sand cayes and islands. Hopping on a daytrip to explore more of the outer Great Barrier Reef offers a whole different experience, great for scuba divers and those wanting to explore a little further.

Head north to explore **Cape Tribulation**, the only place in the world where two UNESCO World Heritage Sites meet. The Daintree Rainforest meets the Great Barrier Reef, and Cape Tribulation is a beautiful beach and a great place to immerse yourself in the rainforest.

The coastline of Port Douglas
Opposite Millaa Millaa Falls in the Atherton Tablelands

BEST PHOTO SPOTS

Head to Palm Cove at sunrise for the ultimate tropical photo, with the sun rising over the ocean and a beach lined with palm trees. The lawns of **Thala Beach Reserve** are also where you will find those iconic rows of straight palm trees that seemingly go on for miles. You can spot them from the Captain Cook Highway as you're heading into Port Douglas and there's space to pull over on the side of the road.

Where

Tropical North Queensland covers much of northern Queensland, extending from Mission Beach in the south all the way to Cooktown and beyond in the north.

Getting here

Cairns Airport (CNS) is the main airport hub in Tropical North Queensland, with direct flights connecting every major city around the country to Cairns.

From Cairns Airport, you can get a rental car to head out and explore the many different parts of Tropical North Queensland.

When to go

Tropical North Queensland has two distinct seasons - a wet and a dry season. During the winter (May to Oct) you will get the best weather, with warm days and nights and very little rainfall; while the summer period (Nov to April) offers hot days with very high humidity and rainfall almost daily.

Where to stay

To stay right in the heart of the action, Cairns is a great place to base yourself. The biggest city in Tropical North Queensland, Cairns is full of great markets, restaurants and beachfront resorts, while also giving you access to explore much more of the region. The marina in Cairns is the gateway to the Great Barrier Reef and the surrounding islands, and it's only a short drive to the Atherton Tablelands, Kuranda and the Daintree Rainforest.

If you're looking for more of a beach escape and a laid-back holiday, head about 45 minutes north to Port Douglas. It's such a cute town, full of stunning tropical resorts and towering palm trees, and this is personally our favourite place to stay whenever we're in the region.

Get planning

Plan your adventure at tropicalnorthqueensland.org.au or check out @tropicalnorthqueensland on social media for all the inspo and best places to check out.

THE GREAT BARRIER REEF

The world's most incredible coral reef

ADVENTURERS | NATURE LOVERS

The Great Barrier Reef is undoubtedly one of Australia's greatest natural attractions and a destination that should definitely be on everyone's bucket-list. As well as being one of the country's most iconic and beautiful locations, it is also the world's largest living organism and coral reef system – and it can even be seen from space. Covering more than 344,400 square kilometres, the reef stretches from the northern tip of Cape York, all the way down to Bundaberg in the south. Made up of 3000 coral reefs, 600 islands and 300 coral cayes, it is home to nearly 5000 different marine species and a third of the world's coral. It is truly one of the great wonders of the world.

The Great Barrier Reef is also the only place on Earth where two UNESCO World Heritage Sites meet. If you head into the Daintree Rainforest you can visit Cape Tribulation, where the reef meets the coastline of the Wet Tropics, the oldest rainforest in the world. You can go snorkelling right off the shore at Cape Tribulation, completely immersing yourself in the Great Barrier Reef and life under the sea, before heading straight back into the jungle tropics on the land.

You can explore the reef in so many different ways. There is literally an endless list of experiences, with half-day, full-day and multi-day tours available. If you haven't been before, there is no bad place to start, but the Great Barrier Reef definitely needs to be seen on your next trip to Queensland.

TOP DESTINATIONS ALONG THE REEF

Since the reef covers such a large area, there are several different places where you can base yourself for your weekend away. It's a good idea to do a little bit of research to see what each place has to offer before booking your adventure.

Cairns and **Port Douglas** in Tropical North Queensland both offer great snorkelling day tours, with fast ferries taking you out to small remote islands, reefs, cayes and bommies that make up the Great Barrier Reef. It's particularly good if you're heading to the outer Great Barrier Reef, with every tour going to great places for scuba-diving and snorkelling. A few of the nearby islands offer excellent snorkelling conditions, with regular tours visiting Lowe Isles from Port Douglas and Green Island from Cairns (*see* p.195).

Airlie Beach and **The Whitsundays** are full of islands that offer premium snorkelling and diving sites. From Airlie Beach (*see* p.202), you can visit iconic sites like Heart Reef, Reef World and Hardy Reef on a daytrip, or base yourself on one of the islands of the Whitsundays to explore more of the reef right off the beach. This part of the reef is also one of the prettiest to witness from above, so it's a great place for a scenic flight.

Whilst often overlooked by its northern neighbours, the **Southern Great Barrier Reef** has some phenomenal places to visit, with daily sightings of turtles, rays and reef sharks, as well as all kinds of bright colourful fish. Stretching from Yeppoon to Bundaberg on the mainland, the Southern Great Barrier Reef also offers a range of resort islands, including Pumpkin Island, Great Keppel Island, Heron Island, Wilson Island and Lady Elliot Island. One of the best ways to experience the Southern Great Barrier Reef is on a daytrip to Lady Musgrave Island (*see* p.200).

Opposite top Turtle swimming near Fitzroy Island
Opposite bottom Snorkelling on the reef with Dreamtime Dive & Snorkel

CAN'T MISS

Make the most of your visit to the Great Barrier Reef with some of these unique bucket-list experiences:

Have a sleepover on the Great Barrier Reef at **Reef World**. About three hours from Airlie Beach, Reef World is a pontoon sitting right alongside Hardy Reef, offering some of the most unique accommodation and snorkelling on the reef. If you choose to stay overnight, you can either sleep in a swag-style reef bed, or in one of their ultra-exclusive underwater hotel rooms, where you can watch the marine life swim past your full-length windows all night long. During your time on the pontoon there's lots of activities to keep you busy, including diving lessons, guided snorkelling tours, heli-scenic flights and tours in a semi-submarine. Go onto the Cruise Whitsundays website to find out more about visiting Reef World.

Perhaps the most iconic landmark within the Great Barrier Reef, a **scenic flight over Heart Reef** offers some of the best views of the whole reef. This small heart-shaped reef, floating within the larger Hardy Reef is positioned alone in a little clearing, perfectly visible from the sky. Scenic flights depart from both Hamilton Island and Airlie Beach in either a helicopter, small plane or seaplane, and will also offer you unparalleled views over Whitehaven Beach, Hill Inlet and the Great Barrier Reef. For more about Heart Reef, *see* p.209.

Head to **Fitzroy Island** either for a day or weekend trip, where the reef hugs the beach and you can go snorkelling right off the shore. Fitzroy Island acts as an important feeding ground for turtles along the reef, so it's a great place to spot them only a few metres into the water. Rent a stand-up paddleboard or a kayak from the beach to explore more of the island, with turtles often seen popping up for air around the shallow water. For more about Fitzroy Island, *see* p.197.

For one of the most unique and best snorkelling experiences on the reef, **Dreamtime Dive & Snorkel** offers the only cultural reef experience in Queensland. The tour leaves from Cairns and is led by **Indigenous Sea Rangers** and takes you to three spots in the Outer Great Barrier Reef. Throughout the day, the Sea Rangers also share Dreamtime stories from the area from the Gimuy Walubara Yidinji, Gunggandji, Mandingalbay and Yirrhanydji people, who are the Traditional Owners of this area. It's such a unique way to experience the reef and we couldn't recommend it highly enough.

To explore some of the Southern Great Barrier Reef, the **Lady Musgrave Island Experience** offers some of the most colourful snorkelling on the whole reef. Leaving from Bundaberg, the tour takes you out to the tiny and remote Lady Musgrave Island, where the reefs are some of the most impressive in the region. The tour includes a glass-bottom boat tour, and a guided walk around the small island, as well as plenty of snorkelling time. Turtles seem to like to hang around in groups out here, with lots of their cleaning stations found amongst the coral, so if you spot one keep an eye out for their friends hanging around close by.

If you're hoping to witness baby turtle hatchlings, **Heron Island** is the place to go. Heron Island is a significant nesting location for Green Turtles and Loggerhead Turtles who come to lay their eggs on the beaches of the island each year. Nesting season happens between November and March, and hatchlings begin to emerge from early January, making their courageous journey from the beach to the ocean for the first time. It's such a special moment to witness, and one that you will never forget.

Where
The Great Barrier Reef covers a huge area, sprawling 2600 kilometres from Cape York to Bundaberg along the east coast of Queensland.

Getting here
Since the Great Barrier Reef covers such a huge area in Queensland, your airport destination will be dependent on your holiday choice. For Cairns, Port Douglas and Tropical North Queensland, book a flight to Cairns Airport (CNS). Fly to Whitsunday Coast Airport (PPP) also known as Proserpine for Airlie Beach and any of the Whitsunday Islands. Or jump on a flight to Bundaberg Airport (BDB) for connections to much of the Southern Great Barrier Reef.

When to go
Visiting during the dry season (May to Oct) offers the best conditions for swimming and snorkelling around the reef. Days are mostly sunny, which often means clearer conditions in the water and higher visibility, great for snorkelling and seeing more of the reef. Stinger season (Nov to May) is when the Irukndji and Box Jellyfish like to come out to play. Stinger suits are often required during this time and mandatory on many of the snorkelling tours around all areas of the Great Barrier Reef to protect you from stings.

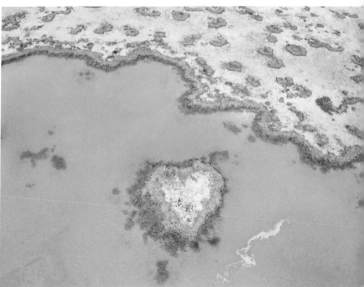

Where to stay
Your options are endless, from Cairns or Port Douglas in the north to one of the Whitsunday islands or Bundaberg in the south.

Get planning
To find out more about all the different places and experiences along the Great Barrier Reef, head to queensland.com and choose 'Great Barrier Reef' from its list of places to go, or check out @gbrmarinepark and @southerngreatbarrierreef on Instagram for daily life on the reef.

Top Early morning glow at Reef World
Bottom The iconic Heart Reef
Opposite Sleepover at Reef World with Cruise Whitsundays

THE WHITSUNDAYS

Home to the most beautiful beach in the world

NATURE LOVERS

The Whitsundays is one of the most beautiful regions in all of Australia. Home to more than 74 remote islands, floating in the brightest blue water full of incredible marine life, the Whitsundays are made up of a combination of resort islands and small beach towns on the main coast. Bringing together some of Australia's most sought-after bucket-list destinations and experiences, the Whitsundays is home to Whitehaven Beach, regularly crowned as one of the best beaches in the world; ideal holiday islands such as Hamilton (*see* p.209), Hayman and Daydream Island; as well as being a great place to explore the Great Barrier Reef.

Whether you choose to base yourself on the mainland or on one of the resort islands, most of the fun can be had off the coast, checking out the best of the islands and spending your days in the water. There are so many spectacular places to visit around the Whitsundays, with secluded beaches, island cruises and snorkelling spots to explore at every turn.

After Tropical Cyclone Debbie devastatingly ripped through the Whitsundays in 2017, flattening many of the resorts and causing significant damage to the reef and the islands, the region has bounced back, rebuilding and reopening, ready to offer you the ultimate weekend getaway.

BEST PHOTO SPOTS
The views over Whitehaven Beach from the **Hill Inlet Lookout** cannot be beaten. With the sand and water swirling together in a mixture of white and blue hues, this view is something very special.

PLAN YOUR TRIP FOR
The **Great Barrier Reef Festival** is considered one of the biggest parties in the north and has been getting bigger and better every year. Held in Airlie Beach in August, there's live music, fireworks, parades, performances, carnival rides, food and markets, to celebrate this incredible region.

A scenic flight over Hill Inlet at low tide

WAYS TO EXPLORE THE WHITSUNDAYS

There are all different ways you can explore the Whitsunday Islands, from resort islands to overnight cruises, and daytrips around the islands from the mainland. The best way to start planning your trip is by deciding where you want to base yourself, and which islands you would like to visit. You can choose between:

The gateway to the Whitsundays on the mainland is **Airlie Beach**. What once used to be a bit of a backpacker town has grown to a beachside haven and is a great place to base yourself, with palm tree-lined beaches, outdoor restaurants and beachfront markets on Saturday mornings. There are heaps of different day tours out to the islands that depart from Airlie Beach, the best place to start is by checking out the Cruise Whitsundays website (cruisewhitsundays.com).

The largest and most popular of the resort islands, **Hamilton Island** is one of Australia's favourite holiday destinations, and a great place to base yourself or even visit for the day. The island vibe starts the minute you set foot on the island, with golf buggies zipping around, the main pool bar serving colourful cocktails every afternoon, and palm trees everywhere you turn. It's definitely a highlight of any visit to the Whitsundays, with island and sunset cruises taking you out to explore the Whitsundays region daily. For more about Hamilton Island, *see* p.209.

The biggest of the islands is **Whitsunday Island**, home to the famous and iconic **Whitehaven Beach**, stretching all the way along the eastern side of the island for more than 7 kilometres. Whitehaven Beach has insanely brilliant white sand, made up of 98.9 per cent silica, which is some of the purest in the world. Jump on a Whitehaven Beach daytrip from wherever you're staying to experience the best of Whitsunday Island, including **Hill Inlet** and **Betty's Beach**.

Reopening after it was completely flattened by Tropical Cyclone Debbie, **Daydream Island** is back and better than ever. The closest to the mainland, this island is completely taken up by the resort, offering a perfect location to unwind and chill out, surrounded by the beautiful views of the Whitsundays. Daydream Island is also home to the only living coral lagoon in Australia, which wraps around the resort for 200 metres and includes a walk-through underwater observatory. It's an incredible way to view the marine life of the Great Barrier Reef, right off the shores of the beach.

Made up of just one exclusive luxury resort, the **Intercontinental Hayman Island** is definitely a splurge for a very special occasion. Only accessible by boat or helicopter, **Hayman Island** is the ultimate in island luxury, with 5-star restaurants, expansive guest rooms and suites, and an incredible infinity pool that is going to be hard to get yourself out of. **Blue Pearl Bay** off the island is also a great place for snorkelling, with regular turtle sightings around the reef.

There are several other large islands that are scattered around the Whitsundays, which can be easily accessed on a day cruise. There are lots of different companies that offer all kinds of group and private tours, so you can create your own itinerary tours and awesome fun days out on the water. Some of our favourite islands that are a little more remote include **Shaw Island** and **Hook Island**.

directly with the InterContinental Resort. To explore at your own pace and visit some of the more remote islands, hire a bareboat charter (see p.206) for a few extra days to explore wherever the wind takes you.

When to go
The Whitsundays generally has great weather all year round, with temperatures averaging 29 to 30°C in the summer months and 22 to 23°C in the winter months. A tropical wet season occurs during January and March, when days can be hot and humid with tropical showers, while August to October is often considered the windy time of the year.

Need to know
Marine stingers are found in the waters of tropical Queensland all year round, but November to May is the main stinger season, when the Irukndji and Box Jellyfish like to come out to play. It is recommended to wear stinger suits in the water during this time, as jellyfish are prevalent in the waters along most of the beaches, as well as out on the reef.

Get planning
Head to thewhitsundays.com.au to plan your trip and check out @whitsundaysqld, @cruisewhitsundays and @hamiltonisland on social media for all the best spots to visit.

Where
The Whitsundays are located on Queensland's central coast in north-eastern Australia.

Getting here
Whitsundays Coast Airport, known as Proserpine Airport (PPP), is the main airport on the mainland for the Whitsundays region. It is easily accessible, only about 20 minutes out of Airlie Beach.

If you choose to drive, Airlie Beach is 1120 kilometres north of Brisbane and 630 kilometres south of Cairns.

From Airlie Beach, Cruise Whitsundays offers island transfers to Hamilton Island and Daydream Island from the Port of Airlie.

Alternatively, if you're planning to base yourself on Hamilton Island you can fly directly into Hamilton Island Airport (HTI), from Brisbane, Sydney, Melbourne and Adelaide.

Getting around
Cruise Whitsundays offers island transfers between Airlie Beach on the mainland and the main resort islands of Hamilton Island and Daydream Island. To get to Hayman Island you can organise transfers either by boat or helicopter

Betty's Beach
Opposite Hill Inlet Lookout

Bareboating in the Whitsundays

This is definitely the most incredible way to explore the Whitsunday Islands. Bareboating is where you can skipper yourself on a powerboat, sailing yacht or catamaran, with the freedom to create your own itinerary and explore wherever you want. Gather a group of friends or family together and take off on the experience of a lifetime. The Whitsundays is actually one of the only places in the world where you can charter your own yacht without a boat licence, so it's truly a very unique experience.

After picking your boat up in Airlie Beach, you will be given a 3-hour lesson on everything you need to know about the boat, the sea and sailing around the islands – and then you're off on your own! You have constant communication with the base if you need it and there are daily weather reports and check-ins for you, making you feel safe out on the sea.

The freedom of sailing around the Whitsundays is indescribable. Plan your days around the wind forecast, hopping across different islands, jumping in for a swim whenever you get too warm, snorkelling around the reefs, and finding ideal little beaches for a lunchtime barbecue. You will get to see more of the Whitsundays than you ever expected, with a greater understanding of the art of sailing and exploring than you ever thought you would.

At night you simply pull into an anchorage or mooring around the islands and enjoy the night on the boat. Some of our favourite places to stop overnight include Tongue Bay at Hill Inlet, Chalkie's Beach at Whitehaven Beach, Macona Inlet and Stonehaven Anchorage on Hook Island, and Blue Pearl Bay on Hayman Island.

IMPORTANT INFO

Head to rentayacht.com.au to find absolutely everything you need to rent a bareboat charter for the first time, including the different yachts to choose from, preparation advice, planning guides, recommended anchorages, snorkelling sites, islands to visit, weather in the Whitsundays and more.

Before you board your boat, make sure you stock up with enough groceries and drinks to get you through your trip so you don't have to come back to the shore for more supplies. Bring sunscreen and a hat to protect you from the sun, as well as a jumper or light jacket to put on when you're moving between islands, because the wind can really get quite chilly.

There is generally mobile phone reception on the eastern sides of the islands, closest to the mainland, so if you want to get online or give anyone a call, choose a mooring or anchorage on this side. We were even able to stream Netflix at some of our overnight spots on the eastern side of Hook Island and Whitsunday Island.

HAMILTON ISLAND

Gateway to the Whitsundays

NATURE LOVERS

Right in the heart of the Whitsundays (*see* p.202), located alongside some of the most beautiful beaches and waterways in the whole country, is where you will find Hamilton Island. With near-perfect weather throughout most of the year, hotel rooms that overlook palm tree-lined beaches, and golf carts scooting all over the island, it really is the ultimate island getaway.

After only a few hours on the island you'll feel like you're a local. The island is small and easy to navigate, with the main streets found around the marina and most of the resorts and hotels sitting along the main beach. It's a place that feels like everyone is on holidays, the sun is always shining and there are water activities to keep you going for days.

There's really no better place to base yourself in the Whitsundays than at Hamilton Island. Daytrips from Hamilton Island can take you from the island to some of Australia's most iconic attractions, including Whitehaven Beach, the Great Barrier Reef and Heart Reef.

There are plenty of great places to eat around the island, so you can choose from a different cuisine every night, with new and exciting options popping up all the time.

Hamilton Island

BEST PHOTO SPOTS

If you choose to stay at the **Whitsunday Apartments** or **ReefView Hotel**, the views from your balcony are sure to be one of your favourite during your stay. Overlooking the main beach and out to the islands, lined with palm trees and with cockatoos flying around, there's a reason all rooms face the water on Hamilton Island.

CAN'T MISS

Top experience:

Take a daytrip out to **Whitehaven Beach**, where the famous white sand is made up of 98.9 per cent silica, the water is crystal clear and always a lovely temperature. It is regularly voted one of the best beaches in the whole world and is an absolute highlight of the Whitsundays. Book yourself on the **Whitehaven Beach & Hill Inlet Chill and Grill tour** with **Cruise Whitsundays** for the best experience on offer, with a full day of exploring the best spots as well as a gourmet lunch on the beach. This tour gives you the most time to explore Whitehaven Beach, with plenty of time for swimming, hiking, sunbathing and, of course, taking a thousand photos.

In the morning:

Hike up to the **Passage Peak Lookout** and watch the sunrise over the islands. It's considered the best place on the island to see the sunrise, although you will need to wake up a little earlier to get up there before the sun begins to rise. The round-trip takes you along a 5.3 kilometre incline trail, up to 200 metres above sea level before you get to the peak and it can be a little tough in different spots. It's a good idea to take a torch if you're heading up while it's still dark.

Book a **helicopter ride over Heart Reef and the Great Barrier Reef** to see some of the best views in the Whitsundays. Departing from Hamilton Island airport, a scenic helicopter ride takes about an hour, flying you over Whitehaven Beach, Hill Inlet, Hardy Reef and the iconic Heart Reef. Organise your flight for when the tide is low and plenty of the sand is visible for the best views of the white and blue swirl at Hill Inlet. For an even more unforgettable and incredible way to experience the reef, jump on **Hamilton Island Air's Journey to the Heart Tour**, where your helicopter will land on the exclusive private Heart Reef pontoon helipad, and you can go swimming among some of the most active marine life on the Great Barrier Reef. For more about Heart Reef, *see* p.200.

In the afternoon:

Explore more of the island by **renting a golf buggy**. Not only are they the best way to get around, they make you feel like you're living the ultimate island life and are so much fun.

Head to **Catseye Beach** to spend time in the water, with paddleboards, kayaks, snorkelling equipment,

catamarans and windsurfers all available to rent from the **Hamilton Island Beach Sports Hut** (daily 8.30am to 5pm). Paddleboards and kayaks are complimentary for guests staying at the Reef View Hotel, Palm Bungalows, Beach Club, Hamilton Island Holiday Homes and Qualia.

Grab a cocktail or a beer at the main pool. As part of the public resort centre, the main pool can be used by anyone, and it's a great place for a dip and a drink on a warm summer day. The swim-up bar in the pool is open from 12pm to 4pm each day and offers some of Hamilton Island's delicious signature cocktails. Find your island vibe with a blue margarita - they're so delicious.

Play a round of **golf on Dent Island**, one of the most unique golf courses in the world. The golf course takes up the whole island, and offers beautiful ocean views from almost every hole. If you're not really into golf you can also head over to Dent Island for lunch at the **Clubhouse Restaurant**, which is highly recommended by anyone who grabs a meal there.

In the evening:

Watch the **sunset from One Tree Hill**. Only a short buggy ride from the marina or the resorts, One Tree Hill is a great place to grab a cocktail, bring a picnic and watch the sun go down over the neighbouring Whitsunday Islands, with 360-degree views over the water and stunning panoramic photo opportunities everywhere you turn.

Have dinner at a different spot every night, with so many great choices and different types of cuisine to try across the island. The **Marina Tavern** is an excellent go-to pub, with a great vibe and outdoor beer garden, serving huge pub-style meals. **Sails** alongside the resort pool is a great place for lunch (both eat in and take-away options) when you need a break from swimming in the pool.

Catseye Beach
Opposite Cruising around Hamilton Island at sunset

Where
Off the coast of Airlie Beach, Hamilton Island is part of the Whitsunday Islands.

Getting here
Hamilton Island has its own domestic airport (HTI), which has regular direct flights to and from Brisbane, Sydney, Melbourne and Adelaide and connecting flights from everywhere else. Alternatively, if you're coming from Airlie Beach you can jump on an island transfer ferry with Cruise Whitsundays, which will drop you off right at the Hamilton Island Marina. The ferry ride takes about an hour from the mainland, and is also a great option if you have a flight that lands at Proserpine Airport (PPP).

Getting around
You can either choose to rent a golf buggy or jump on the free shuttle buses to make your way around the island. Golf buggies can be hired from just outside the resort centre or straight from the airport when you arrive, with rentals for 2 hours, 4 hours or 24 hours. The shuttle bus runs every 15 minutes (daily 6.50am to 11pm) and runs between Front Street, all the major hotels, the resort centre, Catseye Beach and the marina.

Most of the island is within walking distance though so, no matter where you are, you're never far away from where you need to go.

When to go
Hamilton Island has some pretty great weather all year round so there's really no bad time to visit, but try to avoid travelling during the school holiday periods and public holiday long weekends to avoid the extra crowds.

Where to stay
There are plenty of great accommodation options, with **Whitsunday Apartments**, **Reef View Hotel**, **Palm Bungalows** and the **Beach Club** all found along the main strip, overlooking the palm tree-lined Catseye Beach.

Hamilton Island Holiday Homes offers holiday houses all over the island, and often come with a golf buggy to use - great for groups and families.

And then of course there's **Qualia**, the ultra-exclusive resort, that takes island luxury to a whole new level, with restaurants and experiences that are only for Qualia guests. If you can splurge, this is the place for you!

Need to know
When you arrive on Hamilton Island, make sure you download the Hamilton Island App, which is available for both iPhone and Android devices. It includes live weather updates; an events guide for everything that's happening on the island including locations and start times; a bus timetable and map to all the bus stops; guides and listings for the bars, restaurants, services and points of interest around the island; ferry timetables and even live flight information for all the flights arriving and departing from Hamilton Island Airport.

Also, as friendly as they seem, don't make friends with the local cockatoos. While they look super cute most of the time, they will steal anything you leave out and try to destroy your hotel room if they get inside. They are used to people being around and have no problem getting up close and personal, so always keep an eye out for them on your balcony.

Get planning
For everything you need to plan your visit to Hamilton Island, head to hamiltonisland.com.au and download the app, or check out @hamiltonisland on social media for all the inspo.

TORRES STRAIT ISLANDS

Part of Australia, but a world of its own

OFF-THE-BEATEN TRACK | CULTURE BUFFS

For the ultimate off-the-beaten track destination, head to the beautiful Torres Strait Islands, between the top of Queensland and Papua New Guinea. You don't often hear much about the Torres Strait Islands as a destination to visit but, wow, were we blown away by how charming this little island paradise is.

If you don't know very much about the Torres Strait, let me quickly get you up to speed. A collection of around 275 islands sitting in some of the most beautiful water in the world, the Torres Strait Islands are technically the most northern part of Australia. Only about 14 of the islands are inhabited today, with 4500 people living across all 14 islands, and 3000 of them living on Thursday Island.

Torres Strait Islanders are the Indigenous people of the Torres Strait Islands, as well as being First Nations Australians, however they are of Melanesian descent meaning they are ethnically and linguistically quite different from the Aboriginal people of Australia. There are two Torres Strait Islander communities on the mainland of Cape York at Bamaga and Seisia. Torres Strait Islanders sometimes refer to themselves as Zenadth Kes, a term that is made from the Torres Strait language names for the four winds of the region. It's all smiles in the Torres Strait, with friendly locals that make you feel like part of the family as soon as you step off the boat and begin your weekend.

PLAN YOUR TRIP FOR

Every second September (odd years) the **Winds of Zenadth Cultural Festival** comes to Thursday Island, where the communities of the Torres Strait flock to showcase their individual customs and cultures in an exciting and vibrant celebration. It's thought to be one of the best First Nations events in Queensland, so a great one to plan your trip around.

Bright blue water surrounds Thursday Island
Opposite top Hamilton Island Main Pool
Opposite bottom Cheeky cockys love to hang around the balconies

CAN'T MISS

To make the most of your weekend in the Torres Strait you can either choose to hop between the islands, or base yourself on Thursday Island and visit some of the surrounding islands on short trips. Getting between the islands is quick and easy with a ferry transfer or water taxi.

Thursday Island:

The main island and hub of the Torres Strait, it's affectionately called T.I or Waibene by the locals. Thursday Island has the most to see and do of any of the islands and is the perfect place to base yourself. The main street on T.I is Douglas Street, where you can find the grocery store, boutique clothing stores, souvenir shops and a few cafes. **Uncle Frankies Cafe** is a favourite for locals and visitors, and a great place to head for breakfast or lunch.

Get your bearings and learn more about the island with local guides on the **Peddells bus tour**. It's a great way to find out more about T.I and hear about some of its history, as well as see all the highlights, including the **Green Fort Lookout** (*see* opposite), **Thursday Island cemetery**, and the **Gab Titui Cultural Centre** (*see* opposite).

The **beaches** around Thursday Island are home to some of the bluest, most inviting water we have ever seen. You're not going to be able to resist jumping in for a swim. Despite being so far north, there are no crocodiles here, so there's nothing stopping you!

Have a beer at the 'top pub', technically the most northern pub in all of Australia. Also known as the **Torres Hotel**, it's a great spot for a beer or a meal (order small, as portion sizes are absolutely huge), and it's open for lunch and dinner.

Learn more about the region and the culture of the Torres Strait Islanders at the **Gab Titui Cultural Centre**. Throughout the art gallery here you can find all kinds of artwork, historical artefacts, masks and headdresses, as well as learn more about the land of the Kaurareg Nation, the Traditional Custodians of the Kaiwalagal region, which includes the inner islands of the Torres Strait. You can really immerse yourself in the spirit of the Torres Strait here, with incredible dances and performances sharing stories, myths and legends about the land and the sea.

Head to **Green Fort Lookout** at either sunrise or sunset, for the best views across the islands, where you can see all the way out to Narupai (Horn Island), Prince of Wales Island, Hammond Island and Friday Island, and even out to the mainland of Australia on a clear day. Green Fort was built as a response to a Russian war scare and is one of the most well-preserved 19th-century forts still standing in Australia. It was manned during both World War I and World War II.

Friday Island:

Friday Island is actually home to a working pearl farm called **Kazu Pearls**. It is owned by Kazuyoshi Takami and he gives you a presentation about pearl farming, how they extract the pearls and shows you exactly where all the magic happens. You can even buy pearls harvested straight from the farm in their little gift shop. The lunch served at Kazu Pearls is a highlight of your visit, with lots of different Japanese dishes and cuisines. The Kazu Pearls tour goes for about three hours, normally at either 11.30am or 2.30pm. You will need to book at least one day in advance (minimum six people required for the tour to go ahead) by calling Kazuyoshi on (07) 4069 1268.

Narupai (Horn Island):

Just across the harbour from Thursday Island, Narupai (Horn Island) is another busy island in the Torres Strait. Narupai has a population of about 700 people, and was an important air base during World War II. You can jump on a tour of the island, which takes you on a guided bus tour of significant World War II sites around it, as well as a visit to the famous **Torres Strait Heritage Museum and Art Gallery**.

Prince of Wales Island:

Kind of where the locals have their holiday houses, Prince of Wales Island is remote and quiet and completely off-the-grid. There are lots of waterfalls to explore and **Bluefish Point** is said to be one of the best fishing spots in the region. The island used to be a cattle station, and there's still a small number of wild cows wandering around it.

The Torres Hotel, Australia's northernmost pub
Opposite Sunset in northern Queensland

Where

The Torres Strait Islands are in between the northern tip of Queensland and Papua New Guinea.

Getting here

Narupai (Horn Island) Airport (HID) is the only airport in the Torres Strait Islands. Qantas has regular flights between Cairns and Narupai (Horn Island), which is the easiest way to get there for a weekend getaway. There are a number of different ferry services that then connect the islands together. Keep an eye out for **McDonald Charter Boats** to get you over to Thursday Island.

If you're road tripping along the Pacific Coast Highway to Cape York, you can catch a ferry transfer with Peddells from Seisia, which takes about an hour and 10 minutes each way.

When to go

During the winter months (May to Sept) is the best time to visit Cape York and the Torres Strait Islands. The weather is hot and dry during winter, with clear skies and sunny days. Being in such a tropical location, the summer months are part of the wet season, which can be particularly brutal up there. Depending on the rainfall, many of the roads and water crossings on the way up to Cape York can be closed, which often means you can't even get up to Seisia or the tip if it has been raining. Roads can be closed for days, or sometimes even weeks at a time, only reopening when it's safe to do so.

Main island

Thursday Island is described by the locals as the heart of the Torres Strait Islands. In fact, it is considered the big city to anyone living on the neighbouring islands.

Where to stay

Base yourself on Thursday Island to be right in the heart of the action, with a small number of motels, holiday homes and guest houses available.

Need to know

The main language spoken here is Torres Strait Creole (also known as Brokan and Yumplatok), which is used across all the islands, as well as in the West Papuan border area, Cape York and many island communities around mainland Australia. There are also two other languages spoken on the islands - Western-Central Torres Strait and Eastern Torres. However most of the island also speaks English, so you won't have any issues if you don't know the native languages.

Get planning

There's not many resources to plan a trip to the Torres Strait Islands. We found peddellsferry.com.au the most helpful, and if you want to give them a call or send them an email to help you plan, they're always super fast to get back to you.

OUTBACK QUEENSLAND

Experience the glittering towns of the outback

ADVENTURERS | NATURE LOVERS

The barren Queensland outback absolutely blew our minds. We didn't know what to expect before we arrived, which made our experience out there even better. A weekend here takes you to a completely different world. From dinosaurs to opals, and landscapes that will make your jaw drop, we haven't been able to stop raving about the unique towns we found in outback Queensland since we left.

Outback Queensland is actually a huge region, which is unsurprising really, given that it is part of the second-biggest state in the country. It's broken up into five regions, the Central West, Far West, South West, Eastern and North West. If it's your first time visiting the outback, head straight for the heart, where you'll find Longreach and Winton. Both are incredibly unique Aussie towns, and it's only a short two-hour drive between them, so you can definitely explore both in one weekend. We've added a few other highlights in too, in case you want to extend your trip.

Longreach and Winton are also the birthplace of Qantas, which celebrated its 100th birthday in 2020. Winton won't let anyone forget their part in this iconic history though, with the first ever Qantas board meeting taking place at the Winton Club.

There's something so special about these outback towns, which you can instantly see and feel by how affectionately the locals tell their stories. They are all so proud of their home, happy you've come to experience it and ready for you to fall in love with their towns too.

PLAN YOUR TRIP FOR

For the ultimate outback weekend, plan your visit during the iconic **Winton Way Out West Fest**. Generally in April each year, it's a huge festival of Australian artists and musicians, providing entertainment and celebrations for six days. You can't beat the location of this one, with the outback scenery making the festival that much better.

Outback landscapes in Winton
Opposite Way Out West in Winton

CAN'T MISS
Top highlight:
If there's only one thing you do in outback Queensland, make sure it's the **Rangelands Rifts and Sunset Tour** with Vicki from **Red Dirt Tours**. The tour takes you about 15 minutes from Winton to a private property, where erosion has created an incredibly epic landscape. It might just be the best secret we uncovered on our travels. You jump through a small crack in the earth to find these crazy huge rift formations that you would never have expected to be there. The tour then takes you to the perfect sunset spot, where you watch the sun slowly drop below the horizon as the outback glows around you.

Longreach
The official home of Qantas, Longreach is the largest town in outback Queensland. Start your visit by snapping a photo with the iconic 'Welcome to Longreach sign' right at the entrance to town. Qantas was born in the outback, and originally known as Q.A.N.T.A.S (Queensland and Northern Territory Aerial Services). Visit the **Qantas Founders Museum** where you can walk on the wing of a plane, sit in a cockpit and get an iconic photo inside a jet engine. For an extra special experience, come back in the evening for their **Luminescent Longreach** light and sound show, surrounded by Qantas aircrafts.

Take a tour of **Camden Park Station**, a working sheep and cattle station that was visited twice by Queen Elizabeth and Prince Phillip. Tours are run by Outback Dan, and include a guided tour, followed by dinner and drinks at their favourite sunset spot on the station.

Make sure you shop up a storm at **The Station Store** in the heart of town. This is an incredible outback emporium, with everything from clothing, hats and boots, to leatherwork, homewares, books and more.

Take a **sunset cruise** along the Thomson River with **Outback Aussie Tours** to learn more about how it's even possible for such a big river to be found in the middle of the barren outback, and then have dinner at **Smithy's Outback Dinner & Show** right along the bank of the river, with a delicious spread, great wine, live entertainment and good company under the starry night sky.

Winton
Winton's claim to fame is that the iconic Australian song, *Waltzing Matilda* was written by Andrew Barton ('Banjo') Paterson in 1895 when he was visiting Winton from Sydney. They're super proud of this legacy, with the museum at the visitor centre having a section dedicated just to this story.

Winton also seems to be Australia's dinosaur capital. Home to the **Australian Age of Dinosaurs**, where you can view the largest collection of dinosaur fossils in the world. We definitely weren't expecting that! Because of all the black soil around Winton, fossils are often found well preserved and close to the top of the earth. There's a real-life lab here too, where volunteers are working to recover actual fossils that have been found in the surrounding farms. About 110 kilometres south-west of Winton you can also go to the **Dinosaur Stampede National Monument** at Lark Quarry. More than 3300 tracks and footprints were immortalised in stone, estimated to be 95 million years old.

Have dinner at a couple of the pubs on the main street to meet the real locals and characters of the town. The food here is excellent - we especially loved the **North Gregory Hotel** and the **Tattersalls Hotel**. Before you leave, make sure you grab a photo with the **'Winton Way Out West'** sign next to the football field at the end of town. And of course, don't forget to jump on the **Rangelands Rifts and Sunset Tour** mentioned earlier - definitely a highlight of our whole visit to outback Queensland.

Outback Queensland

Opalton

About an hour and 10-minute drive south-west of Winton is the tiny opal mining town of Opalton. You might have seen it before on the Discovery Channel show *Opal Hunters*, where some of the characters from the mines spend their day searching for the beautiful and elusive boulder opals. You're able to try your luck fossicking for an opal out here - just make sure you're not too close to anyone else's claim or any of the huge mines - you don't want to fall into a pit you can't get out of. You can stay at the **Opalton Bush Camp** that has been built by some of the local miners. They can often be found in the camp kitchen having a smoko together. They're very friendly and love a chat, so make sure you say hi.

Julia Creek

A tiny town sitting on the Flinders Highway, Julia Creek is often a rest stop for people driving between Queensland and the Northern Territory. But it has become even more popular lately due to the **Julia Creek Caravan Park's artesian bathhouses**. Each bathhouse is made from a rain tank and includes two huge comfy baths, with an open view across the scrub. After a long day of travel there's nothing better than soaking in the bath with a cheese platter and a wine, watching the sunset over the vast outback. It is extremely popular, so book in advance so you don't miss out - especially if you're hoping for a specific time of the afternoon.

BEST PHOTO SPOTS

All of the best photo spots can be found on the **Rangelands Rifts and Sunset Tour** (*see* p.215). Walking through landscapes that you have never seen before, it feels like it's completely out of this world. And of course, the 'Winton Way Out West' sign is an iconic photo.

Where

Right in the centre of Queensland, in the middle of the outback is where you'll find Longreach and Winton.

Getting here

For a weekend away, there are direct flights to Longreach Airport (LRE) from both Brisbane and Townsville on QantasLink, of course. If you're visiting as part of a bigger road trip, Longreach is 1200 kilometres from Brisbane or about 700 kilometres from Rockhampton, Townsville or Mount Isa. The roads are fairly flat and easy, but can be very popular with wildlife, especially at dawn and dusk, so make sure you drive carefully. For a unique way to travel, you can also jump on the *Spirit of the Outback* train from Brisbane.

Getting around

To make the most of your time in outback Queensland you can rent a car from the airport in Longreach, giving you the freedom to explore between towns and maximise every minute of your weekend.

When to go

Visit in the winter months (April to Oct), which are a little bit cooler during the day, making conditions better for exploring and walking around, while still offering lovely sunny days. In the summertime (Nov to March) a lot of the different tour companies and businesses shut down, as they are not viable during the extremely hot months, so you'll also be limited as to what experiences you can check out.

Need to know

There's no fuel between towns out here, so make sure you have a full tank before you leave each town along the way.

Get planning

Head to outbackqueensland.com.au to start planning your trip to this golden outback, or check out @outbackqueensland on socials for all the best spots.

Sunset cruise on the Thomson River
Opposite Julia Creek Caravan Park's artesian bathhouse

Can't-miss place
Binalong Bay, larapuna (Bay of Fires, *see* p.227)

Top experience
Spotting wild wombats at Cradle Mountain (*see* p.236)

National Parks Pass
A National Parks Pass is required to visit any of the national parks around Tasmania. Depending on how long you're planning to be in Tassie, you can choose between a daily pass for $40 per vehicle for up to 24 hours, or maximise your visit with a holiday pass for $80 per vehicle (up to eight people) for up to 2 months. Annual, two-year and a one-park pass for Cradle Mountain only are also available. A National Parks Pass allows you access to all national parks in Tassie, including the use of the shuttle bus at Cradle Mountain. You can purchase your pass online at passes.parks.tas.gov.au, at any of the National Park visitor centres or onboard the *Spirit of Tasmania*.

Important dates
- Taste of Tasmania (Jan)
- MONA FOMA (Jan)
- Royal Hobart Show (Oct)
- Table Cape Tulip Festival (Oct)
- Sydney to Hobart Yacht Race (Dec)

Time zone
Tasmania follows the Eastern Standard Australian Time Zone (GMT +10), with daylight savings time (GMT +11) from September until March.

Stay connected & get featured
Follow @tasmania for all the inspiration and best places to visit, and have your Tassie photos featured by using hashtags #discovertasmania or #tassiestyle.

Helpful websites:
- Caravanning caravanningtas.com.au
- National Parks parks.tas.gov.au
- Fishing ifs.tas.gov.au/ols

Tasmania

Sitting off the mainland of Australia, separated by Bass Strait, the island of Tasmania is an untouched paradise full of natural beauty, and plenty of hidden hot spots that are still very much off-the-beaten track. From the unexpected white sand beaches along the East Coast (*see* p.226), to the rugged mountain landscapes of the West Coast (*see* p.236), and Hobart (*see* p.220) and Launceston's charms (*see* p.230) in between, there's always a new pocket of Tasmania waiting to be uncovered.

For a weekend escape filled with food and wine, it seems like everything in Tassie is locally produced, with farm-to-table restaurants, seafood caught alongside restaurants, and renowned wineries, breweries and distilleries.

There are famous art galleries and museums, and markets offering locally made goods, as well as the biggest lavender farm in the Southern Hemisphere (*see* p.232), and more wild wombats on Maria Island (*see* p.228) than you will find anywhere else.

Get the full Tassie experience by travelling across Bass Strait with your car on the *Spirit of Tasmania*. It's an experience all of its own, with the added bonus of being able to head off on your weekend adventure the minute you're off the ferry.

HOBART

The Traditional Owners of nipaluna (Hobart) are the Muwinina people

CULTURE BUFFS | FOODIES

Whilst it might be the smallest capital city in Australia, Hobart certainly doesn't let its size hold it back – packing so much into such a small area. The city is charming and sweet to walk around with an abundance of convict-era architecture, making it look like a preserved moment in time. Hobart sits right on the Derwent River, with the beautiful mountain backdrop of kunanyi (Mt Wellington).

Hobart has quickly become a place that you don't want to miss. From controversial art galleries designed to shock, to award-winning restaurants, delicious local wines and some of the freshest seafood going round, there's really so much to experience in and around this pretty little city.

Make sure you plan enough time on your weekend visit to explore beyond Hobart to its surrounds, like the convict-built town of Richmond or infamous Port Arthur.

PLAN YOUR TRIP FOR
Visit Hobart over the week of the New Year in January for **Taste of Tasmania**, Australia's biggest and longest-running food and wine festival, set alongside the stunning docks in the heart of Hobart. There are incredible performances, live music and mouthwatering gourmet food to be tried, showcasing the very best that Tasmanian producers have to offer. A few of the other festivals that Hobart is famous for include MONA FOMA (mid-Jan), the Royal Hobart Show (Oct) and Falls Festival (Dec).

CAN'T MISS
Start your Saturday morning with a visit to the iconic **Salamanca Market** (8.30am to 3pm). It's without a doubt one of the best markets we've been to around Australia, with more than 300 stalls.

Take a step back in time with a walk around the suburb of **Battery Point**, just up the hill from Salamanca. One of the earliest areas to be developed in Hobart in the early 1800s, the charming streets and sandstone buildings make you feel like it has been pretty much untouched for well over a hundred years. Take a self-guided walk through the winding laneways and past the old seafarers' cottages.

Pick the clearest part of the day to visit **kunanyi (Mt Wellington)**. Standing 1271 metres above sea level, the summit feels worlds away from the city, with expansive views across all of Hobart and beyond on a clear day. It's important to note that driving conditions can change suddenly, with fog, ice and snow, and sometimes the Pinnacle Road is closed due to snow.

After your trip up the mountain, head to the historic **Cascade Brewery**, the oldest brewery in Australia, operating since 1824. To learn more about this iconic brand, you can also jump on the **Cascade History and Brewery Experience**, for a behind-the-scenes tour.

Jump on a **Hobart Historic Cruise** along the Derwent River. There are two one-hour cruise options, with the north route taking you past the Botanic Gardens, Government House and under the Tasman Bridge, and the south route passing by Battery Point, Sandy Bay, the Casino and towards Bellerive Bluff.

Get up close and personal with some of Australia's most-loved native wildlife, and see the elusive Tassie Devil in real life at **Bonorong Wildlife Sanctuary**. Rehabilitating as many healthy animals as they can back into the wild. Bonorong also runs a Tasmanian-wide wildlife volunteer rescue service.

Take a trip out to **Richmond**, a heritage town full of Georgian buildings. Its iconic attraction is the Richmond Bridge, the oldest bridge still in use in Australia, built in 1823.

Hobart is home to **MONA**, the Museum of Old and New Art, one of Australia's most controversial museums, with exhibits that are designed to be thought-provoking and confronting.

Eat and drink your way across Hobart, with award-winning restaurants and incredible fine-dining options popping up all over the place, most using the very best local Tassie produce. Head to the Salamanca area and the wharves and piers for dinner. Some of our favourites are **Pancho Villa**, **The Wharf Hotel** and **Ti Ama**.

DAYTRIPS

Learn about Tasmania's dark convict history with a visit to **Port Arthur Historic Site**, Australia's most intact and evocative convict site which operated from 1830 to 1877. It's a UNESCO World Heritage Site, with many of the buildings being restored to what they used to be. Start your visit by jumping on an introductory guided walking tour.

BEST PHOTO SPOTS

You can't go past the views at **kunanyi (Mt Wellington)** on a clear day, particularly at sunrise to watch the sun rising over the city, or sunset to watch the sky turn into a fairy floss mixture of pinks and oranges. It's just beautiful.

Where
Hobart is located in south-east Tasmania.

Getting here
Hobart Airport (HBA) is the main airport servicing Tasmania, with direct flights to Hobart from all major cities around Australia and regular services from every state. If you're catching the *Spirit of Tasmania* from Melbourne to Devonport, Hobart is a 3-hour drive from Devonport.

Getting around
From the airport it's about a 20-minute drive into the main city of Hobart, over the Tasman Bridge. Pick up a rental car right from the airport or jump on the SkyBus that will take you into the heart of the city.

Hobart city is an easy place to walk around, but if you're wanting to explore a little further a hire car is a good idea.

When to go
Being the most southern state in the country you can expect many crisp, windy days, and summer lasting for a very short period each year. Visit in January or February if you're hoping for some sunshine and warmer weather, however November and December or March and April are great months if you're planning on doing a lot of hiking. Pack a warm jacket no matter what time of the year you travel!

Where to stay
Hobart is quite a small city, so no matter where you decide to stay you're probably not going to be very far from the action. One of the best places to base yourself is in the Salamanca Place and Battery Point area. Positioning yourself here puts you within walking distance of the main city, the waterfront, heaps of restaurants, bars and cafes and the Salamanca Market on Saturdays. It's a great area to take the time to explore and soak in during your visit.

Get planning
You can find the Tasmanian Travel and Information Centre right in the middle of town, only a short walk away from Salamanca Place at 20 Davey Street, Hobart. For everything you need to know, head to discovertasmania.com.au and hobartandbeyond.com.au or check out @tasmania and @hobartandbeyond on social media.

Majestic views over Hobart
Previous Bridestowe Lavender Estate

BRUNY ISLAND

Tassie's own natural island paradise

FOODIES | NATURE LOVERS

Close enough to Hobart for a daytrip, but far enough for a whole weekend, is the beautiful rugged landscape of Bruny Island. Made up of a north and south island, held together by the iconic and narrow isthmus called The Neck, Bruny Island feels like a country dream, with long dry grass, tall gumtrees and an abundance of wildlife everywhere you turn. It's a place for hikers, nature lovers and those wanting to immerse themselves for a weekend in the great outdoors, with white sandy beaches and dramatic cliff faces, as well as the beautiful South Bruny National Park.

Known as Lunawanna-alonnah to the local Nuenonne people, Bruny Island has a rich Aboriginal history, as well as being a stop for some of the earliest European explorers, with the first visit to the island as early as 1642. These days, Bruny Island is home to around 620 people and deceptively large as it stretches approximately 100 kilometres in length.

Bruny is simply the perfect place to experience the Tasmanian countryside, while also allowing yourself plenty of time to sample all the different delicacies the island has to offer, with wineries, cheese makers, oyster farmers, berry growers and chocolatiers all over the island. You're never far away from a delicious snack or Tassie drop.

BEST PHOTO SPOTS

Of course, you can't go past the views at The Neck, with sweeping views over the top of the southern part of Bruny Island, as well as the isthmus and the two seas coming together, often in different colours. Visit during the golden hour on a clear day for some of the most beautiful photo opportunities.

The view from The Neck

CAN'T MISS

In the morning:
Explore **South Bruny National Park** at the bottom of South Bruny, brimming with towering cliffs overlooking long sandy beaches and the beautiful surrounding ocean. The park is also home to **Cape Bruny Lighthouse**, Australia's second-oldest lighthouse that can be found at the very tip of Bruny Island. Standing tall at 13 metres high since 1835, you can go inside and climb it on a tour with **Bruny Island Safaris**.

Embark on some of the hiking trails around Bruny Island, which offer spectacular landscapes and views that can't be found by car. **The Cape Queen Elizabeth Walk** is a 2-hour return (12km) moderate hike and a favourite for North Bruny - it follows the trail between Big Lagoon and Little Lagoon and climbs up Mars Bluff. On South Bruny, the **Labillardiere Peninsula Walk** generally takes about 5 to 7 hours (18km return) taking you around the whole peninsula, including to beaches, dry forests, Mt Bleak and coastal headlands. There are lots of steep sections and rocky trails on this walk, so always be careful and come prepared.

In the afternoon:
Experience the best of Bruny Island from the water on a cruise with **Pennicott Wilderness Journeys**, an award-winning 3-hour cruise to explore some of the rugged coastline of Bruny Island. Taking you alongside some of Australia's highest sea cliffs and to the powerful spot where the Tasman Sea meets the Southern Ocean, you're likely to spot seals, dolphins, migrating whales and a plethora of birds.

Overflowing with wineries and organic local produce, Bruny Island is home to so many delicious food and drink options to keep you taste testing your way across the island for a whole weekend. Some of the best stops include:

- **Bruny Island Premium Wines** has alfresco dining looking right over the vineyards and tumbling yellow hills. It has an extensive menu of tapas, gourmet burgers, platters and tacos all made with local Bruny Island produce, as well as their signature wines - our favourite is the pinot noir.
- At **Bruny Island Berry Farm** (closed during winter), it's great fun to pick your own strawberries, raspberries, blackberries and blueberries, try some berry flavoured ice-cream or pancakes and pick up some berry jam for later.
- **Bruny Island Cheese & Beer Co.** is where you can immerse yourself in the eucalyptus forest with a cheese platter and a Bruny beer. There are all kinds of cheeses to try that are made right here, as well as homemade relishes and wood-fired sourdough bread. Yum!
- **Get Shucked Oyster Farm** has some of the freshest oysters that are sustainably farmed in the waters right off Bruny Island. Their *fuel for love* slogan will be what sucks you in - you won't be able to resist.
- At **Bruny's House of Whisky**, you can taste test your way through their award-winning menu of single malts, or head to the restaurant to experience their whisky and fine food matching, with some of the best Tasmanian gourmet foods.
- **Bruny Island Chocolate** is a little roadside stop, full of tasty chocolate and fudge treats made right on the premises.

In the evening:
Climb the 279 steps to reach the top of **The Neck** for the most spectacular views across Bruny Island. This is the spot halfway across the isthmus, where the Neck connects North Bruny and South Bruny together. During the golden hour and at sunset the sky really puts on a show for the prettiest views.

At the top, you'll see the **Truganini Memorial**. Take some time to reflect on the life of Truganini who endured horrendous crimes against her family, was forced to live on missions at different times in her life, and worked tirelessly to protect her people. The memorial celebrates Truganini's life and resilience.

Make your way back down the stairs to the beach where you can sometimes spot fairy penguins emerging from the sea and returning to their burrows after a hard day in the ocean.

Head to the **Bruny Hotel** for dinner for a great menu of fresh seafood and pub classics. It's a favourite for locals and visitors alike, with great views over the channel, and it also offers accommodation. It's thought to be the southernmost pub in Australia.

DAYTRIPS

Make the most out of your foodie weekend with a quick daytrip to the **Huon Valley**, an area of Southern Tassie that is full of small farms and orchards, breweries and distilleries. Cherries, peaches, strawberries and nectarines (just to name a few) grow wild, while grapes are grown for some incredible cool-climate wines. **Willie Smith's Apple Shed** is a favourite stop, as is **Longley Organic Farm's** roadside stall, **Grandvewe** sheep cheesery and **Hartshorn Distillery**.

Where

Bruny Island is located off the coast of Kettering, in southern Tasmania.

Getting here

From Hobart, drive 40 minutes to Kettering to catch the SeaLink Bruny Island ferry service. The ferry runs every half hour during the summer months and peak holiday periods, with more than 20 services a day and operates on a first-come, first-served basis. You can't book a particular departure time - simply head to the wharf and join the line. It takes just 15 to 20 minutes to get to Bruny Island from the mainland of Tassie, and tickets cost just $38 for a return vehicle, while passengers travel free of charge. They often have deals for taking caravans and trailers over to the island as well, so look online at sealinkbrunyisland.com.au before you go.

Getting around

It's best to have your own wheels on Bruny to take you to all the different beaches, foodie stops and more remote locations like the lighthouse and beaches along South Bruny.

When to go

Visit Bruny Island during the summer months from December to March to take advantage of the warmer weather and getting out into nature. There are more ferries during the summer months and everything on the island is open, while a much smaller selection stays open for winter.

Main towns

Adventure Bay and Alonnah are two of the larger towns on the island, with lots of places to stay close by. There are different types of accommodation, with holiday houses, cottages and luxury lodges scattered across the island, as well as basic hotel accommodation and plenty of camping and caravanning options. Check the accommodation availability in advance, as there's only so many places and the island can book out during the warmer months.

Where to stay

For the ultimate Bruny Island weekend experience, book a stay at the **Hundred Acre Hideaway Hot Tub Retreat**, where you can soak in your very own wood-fire hot tub on a private deck while taking in the views of South Bruny National Park and the Southern Ocean. It's the ultimate wilderness retreat, completely off the grid and powered by solar, wind and gas, giving you a truly immersive experience.

Need to know

You will need a National Parks Pass to visit South Bruny National Park. It's a good idea to purchase this in advance at passes.parks.tas.gov.au, as there is nowhere to purchase it once you arrive at the park. More info can be found on p.218.

Get planning

Start planning your trip by visiting brunyisland.com and brunyisland.org.au, and check out @tourismbrunyisland and @brunyislandaustralia for all the best spots to visit.

Countryside charm
Opposite Make sure to sample the local food and wine during your stay

EAST COAST

Explore the Great Eastern Drive

NATURE LOVERS | FOODIES

For the ultimate East Coast Tasmanian itinerary, combine a visit to Freycinet National Park with larapuna (Bay of Fires) on the Great Eastern Drive, with plenty of stops along the coastline in one whirlwind weekend. Two of Tassie's most spectacular sites and not-to-be missed destinations, it's just a short hour and 40-minute drive between the two.

Home to the iconic Wineglass Bay, Freycinet National Park is a can't-miss spot on any visit to Tasmania, with its white sandy beaches, secluded bays, dramatic granite peaks and abundant wildlife. The national park occupies the majority of the Freycinet Peninsula, looking out to the Tasman Sea from the eastern side and back towards the Tasmanian coastline in the west. There is no shortage of natural beauty here, with incredible views everywhere you turn, some of the most picturesque hikes around Australia and, of course, incredible food and wine to keep you going during your visit.

The beaches at larapuna are just spectacular, with some of the clearest turquoise water and bright white sand, seeming even more contrasting mixed with the orange boulders that are found along the beach. The area received its settler name, Bay of Fires, when Captain Tobias Furneaux sailed past in 1773, and from the water he could see the flames from the palawa people's fires around the beaches. It has been said that this name also comes from the bright orange lichen that grows on the granite boulders that line the beaches and tumble into the water.

To make the most of your visit to the East Coast of Tasmania, plan your trip in a loop from Launceston, to give you more time to explore all the incredible spots this unique coastline has to offer.

BEST PHOTO SPOTS
There's no bad view of Wineglass Bay. Whether you choose to check it out from the lookout platform, the top of Mt Amos, from the ground on the beach or from a scenic flight over Freycinet National Park, you'll never get a bad angle at Wineglass Bay.

East Coast

CAN'T MISS

In the morning:

Start your morning super early with a hike to the top of **Mt Amos** for the very best sunrise views over Wineglass Bay and Freycinet National Park. The hike only takes around 3-hours return (4km) from the base carpark, but it's a tough one, with incredibly steep and rocky parts of the trail taking you high above the ground level. If you're not up for it, you can opt instead for the hike to the Wineglass Bay Lookout, which begins in the same carpark and takes about an hour and a half and still gives you some great views about halfway up, or continue on for a half-day trek where you can walk right down to the beautiful, perfectly curved Wineglass Bay to actually set foot on the beach.

Pop into **East Coast Natureworld**, a wildlife sanctuary about 30 minutes out of Freycinet National Park to get up close and personal with Tasmanian devils, hand feed kangaroos and wallabies and walk through the open emu pen. It's also a great place to come and meet some of their wombats if you haven't been able to spot a wild one yet! You can also make a booking for a special night tour during peak times to see their nocturnal residents.

Take a scenic flight above all of Freycinet National Park on a short flight with **Air Freycinet**. Giving you stunning aerial views over Wineglass Bay, the Hazards and the whole Freycinet Peninsula, it allows you to appreciate more of the rugged coastline and grab a photo of Wineglass Bay in all its curvy glory. Flights start from just 30 minutes, and run all day long, so it's easy to choose a flight time when the weather is clearest during your visit.

Pack a picnic and head down to **Honeymoon Bay**, a secluded spot for a recovery swim and a picnic lunch after your hike up Mt Amos or to the Wineglass Bay lookout. Fringed with a eucalyptus forest and located between two rocky headlands, Honeymoon Bay offers stunning views over the dramatic Hazards Mountains. It's just a short walk from the visitor centre, but feels like miles away from everyone else.

In the afternoon:

Head to **Devil's Corner Cellar Door and Lookout** to try their award-winning local wines (some of the most delicious in Tasmania in my opinion), signature wood-fired pizza, seafood caught right from the local bays and an outstanding view over Great Oyster Bay. They have live music on Sunday afternoons and you can book in advance to secure a taste testing platter. All their wines are incredible but make sure you try a glass of their new Pinot Noir Rose, it's delicious.

Pop into **Freycinet Marine Farm** to try some of the freshest Tassie oysters and seafood. With an onsite restaurant, as well as a small shop so you can grab your seafood and take it with you to cook up yourself, it doesn't get much fresher than this. You can also jump on a tour with **Oyster Bay Tours** where you get the chance to wade out into the water, harvest oysters straight off the rack and enjoy your super fresh oysters plucked straight from the ocean.

Spend an afternoon exploring the coastline of **larapuna (Bay of Fires)**, and its many crystal-clear rockpools that are dotted along the shoreline. The water is just spectacularly blue and clear, and the huge orange lichen boulders that line the beach just make it even more impressive. For some of the best views follow the signs that lead to **The Gardens** - you won't be disappointed stopping anywhere along **Binalong Bay**, or head to **Skeleton Bay Reserve** for some of the larger rockpools and a great place to swim.

A little further north, **wukalina (Mt William National Park)** also has beautiful beaches and the brightest white sand along the shore. Honestly, it's hard to believe these beaches are even in Tassie, they're so tropical looking. You can often spot native wildlife roaming around the park too, with kangaroos, wombats, echidnas and Tassie devils.

In the evening:

One of our favourite fine-dining experiences in Australia is at **The Bay Restaurant** in Freycinet Lodge. With intimate tables for two facing full-length windows overlooking the bay and the Hazards in the distance, there is no better dinner view on the East Coast. The seasonal menu offers regional produce, the best Tassie seafood and award-winning wine.

Devil's Corner Cellar Door
Opposite The Gardens at larapuna (Bay of Fires)

DAYTRIPS

To get your wombat fix, take a half- or full-day trip across to **Maria Island**. The island, wukaluwikiwayna in the language of the palawa people, is a paradise for wombats, with these cute little guys running all over the island, never shying away from a photo opportunity, and plenty of babies to be spotted trailing behind their mums. You can get to Maria Island from Triabunna on the **Encounter Maria Island ferry**, which has multiple sailings each day. A return ticket will cost $45, you will need to carry a National Park Pass with you, and you can reserve a bike for your visit to make it easier to explore a little further. The only cars on the island belong to the park rangers.

Aerial view over Freycinet National Park
Opposite top Main street of Coles Bay
Opposite bottom Feeding kangaroos at East Coast Natureworld

Where
Stretching along the whole East Coast of Tasmania, Freycinet National Park and Coles Bay can be found around the middle of the state, with larapuna (Bay of Fires) sitting a little more on the north-east corner.

Getting here
Launceston Airport (LST) in northern Tasmania is the closest airport to many of the best spots along the East Coast. There are direct flights to Launceston from Melbourne, Sydney or Brisbane, and then it's about a 2-hour drive to the town of St Helens and Binalong Bay at larapuna (Bay of Fires), or Coles Bay and Freycinet National Park.

Getting around
Pick up a rental car from the airport to have the freedom to explore as many spots along the East Coast as you can fit into your weekend.

When to go
To make the most of the beautiful white sand beaches along the East Coast, visit during summer (Dec to Feb) for the best weather. The sun is often shining, and the days are long and warm. However, it's always good to throw a jacket and a jumper into your luggage, because you never really know exactly what you're going to get with the weather in Tassie. If you're coming for the hiking, visit during autumn (March to May) or spring (Sept to Nov) for cooler conditions without the real icy chill of winter.

Main towns
Most of the towns along the East Coast are quite small, however you can still find everything you need for a great weekend. Coles Bay is the main town around the Freycinet National Park area, while St Helens is the main holiday town about a 20-minute drive from larapuna (Bay of Fires).

Where to stay
Check in to **Freycinet Lodge** for one of our favourite places to stay along the East Coast. Secluded, on the waterfront, and within Freycinet National Park, the lodge has accommodation options for all budgets, with ultra-luxurious chalets, as well as family cabins, each with a private balcony making you feel like you're right in the middle of the forest. The lodge is so peaceful, with a private beach nearby offering some of the best sunrises for your stay.

At larapuna (Bay of Fires), you can't go past free camping in Binalong Bay, where you can camp right alongside the beach overlooking that beautiful blue water. You can find camping grounds at Grants Lagoon, Swimcart Beach, Cosy Corner and Sloop Reef, or there are plenty of holiday rentals around the bay.

There is also lots of accommodation options in the holiday towns of Orford, Bicheno and St Helens.

Need to know
Along the East Coast, you'll find Freycinet National Park, Maria Island National Park, Douglas-Apsley National Park, Bay of Fires Conservation Area, St Columba Falls State Reserve and wukalina (Mt William National Park) which all require a National Parks Pass (*see* p.218) to enter. There are individual park passes or a holiday pass to choose from, which gives you the freedom to explore as many parks as you want for up to eight weeks.

Get planning
Start planning your road trip at eastcoasttasmania.com or check out @eastcoasttasmania on socials for all the best spots.

LAUNCESTON

One of Australia's oldest cities

FOODIES | NATURE LOVERS

Often overlooked by its sister city in the south, and seemingly a big country town in the middle of the Tasmanian countryside, Launceston is a destination all of its own. With an ever-changing seasonal line-up of things to do and see, this little city boasts the largest lavender field in the Southern Hemisphere (for perfect photo opportunities), beautiful historical buildings and architecture, a thriving arts scene, as well as being within a short drive to some of the state's best beaches and wilderness regions.

Just like the rest of Tasmania, Launceston has an impressive foodie scene, with cute cafes, restaurants and fine dining popping up all over the city; wineries, breweries and distilleries all within a short drive, and no shortage of pretty places to visit along the way. Slow down and unwind on a visit to Launceston, come for the air, the slower pace of life, and a very chilled weekend away with farm stays in the heart of the city and dessert houses serving late night sugary treats.

Launceston has its own airport, with direct flights from cities along the East Coast of Australia, making it an easy choice for a quick weekend getaway.

PLAN YOUR TRIP FOR

Head to Launceston in January for **MONA FOMA**, Tasmania's favourite summer festival full of light, colour and sound, with a music line-up that boasts 90 per cent Tassie-based talent, art exhibits, video installations, themed cocktail menus, free exhibitions and performances, and plenty of food and drinks. The dates and schedule of events change every year, with new and exciting additions all the time.

Golden hour views of the Tamar Valley

CAN'T MISS

In the morning:

Head out to **Bridestowe Lavender Estate**, the largest lavender farm in the Southern Hemisphere, with an estimated 650,000 plants stretching over 200 kilometres. The plants are in bloom from December to January, when the farm bursts to life and all you can see is purple for miles. Grab yourself a morning tea snack and try some of their lavender scones, lavender cookies, or a scoop of lavender ice-cream on a warm afternoon.

Pop into the **Harvest Launceston Community Farmers' Market** held every Saturday (8.30am to 12.30pm), where you can stock up on goodies from the local area with 40 producers selling all kinds of fresh produce, including cheese, bread, seafood, fruit and veggies, nuts, honey, flowers, wines, beers, spirits and more. The vendors are often changing, so there's a new spread to check out each week.

Visit the **Queen Victoria Museum & Art Gallery** for some of northern Tassie's best art, history and natural science exhibits. It also has a great permanent exhibition called 'The First Tasmanians: Our Story' that pays respect to the local Tyerrenotepanner, Leterremairrener and Panninher clans, and shares a bit about their customs and culture. It's a great place to find out more about the history of Tassie and its ancestors.

In the afternoon:

Jump on a **Taste Walk Talk Tour**, where local couple Brock and Fiona share their favourite foodie spots with you. You can choose from a day, afternoon, pre-dinner or Sunday brunch tour, where you'll be taken to some of Launceston's best bars, cafes and restaurants and learn about the food and drinks straight from the producers.

Spend an afternoon exploring **Cataract Gorge Reserve**, which is surprisingly found right in the heart of the city. It's a lovely spot for a dip or a picnic on a warm afternoon, with a large swimming pool set strikingly against the bright green grass, overlooking the gorge. Take a chairlift ride over the gorge to the top for some of the best views, where you can often find peacocks and wallabies roaming around, stroll through the fern-filled Victorian garden or take a hike along the clifftop following the Zig Zag track.

Explore the **Tamar Valley Wine Route** in the **Tamar Valley**, which begins only 20 minutes out of the city. It's known for its exceptional chardonnay, riesling and pinot noir, with more than 32 wineries that sit along the route. Some great stops include **Brady's Lookout** for beautiful views over the Tamar River and the **Tamar Valley Wine Centre**, where you can taste test wines from many of the different vineyards in the region.

In the evening:

Test out some of the best restaurants across the city, which all offer different specialities and quirky unique features. Some of the best include **Stillwater** at the historic Ritchie's Flour Mill, **Bread & Butter** at the Tasmanian Butter Co. factory, **Black Cow Bistro** for the ultimate Australian meat menu and **Rupert & Hound** for fresh seafood over the water.

End your day on a sweet note with a visit to **Charlie's Dessert House** on Charles Street with more desserts, macaroons, cupcakes and sweet treats than you can choose from. Everything on the menu is just OMG mouth-wateringly delicious. The perfect spot for any occasion.

DAYTRIPS

Explore a little further along Tassie's northern coast by checking out the **Northern Forage** road trip, taking you from Derby in the east, a small town that kind of looks like a ski resort except for all the mountain bikers, across to Stanley in the west, a very pretty coastal town with historical houses set into The Nut - an ancient volcanic plug surrounded by the ocean. Choose a couple of spots to road trip out to and experience some of northern Tassie's dramatic coastline along the way.

BEST PHOTO SPOTS

You can't go past **Bridestowe Lavender Estate** for some of the best Insta photos around Launceston. With the stunning back drop of Mt Arthur and endless rows of purple lavender, you can always find a place away from any other people to take the perfect shot.

Where

Launceston is in northern Tasmania.

Getting here

With its own airport, you can fly directly into Launceston Airport (LST) from Melbourne, Sydney and Brisbane.

Getting around

Pick up a rental car at the airport to explore Launceston at your own pace, or you can get into the city via shuttle bus which costs about $15 per adult one way, or jump in a taxi from about $35 each way.

Alternatively, if you decide to bring your car over on the *Spirit of Tasmania*, it's just over an hour's drive from Devonport to Launceston.

When to go

As with most of Tasmania, visit Launceston during the summer months (Dec to Feb) for the best experience, when the weather is warmer, the days are longer, and there is plenty to do outdoors. This is also the best time to visit if you're coming to see the lavender, as it's the only time of the year when you'll find the purple blooms.

Where to stay

There are plenty of great places to stay in Launceston, with boutique hotels and cute accommodation choices popping up around the city all the time.

A great choice is **Change Overnight** - Australia's only social enterprise hotel (and only one of two in the whole world), where you get to choose a cause to give back to with the profits from your booking. Choose from causes such as Beyond Blue, Act For Kids and Victory School of Hope in Vanuatu. The self-contained apartments are sleek, modern and comfy, with self-check-in, and free wi-fi and undercover parking.

If you're travelling in a self-contained caravan or motorhome, check out **Old Mac's Farm** right in the heart of Launceston. For only $15 per night, you can't get a caravan park closer to the city, where no bookings are required and you can just turn up and choose a spot.

Get planning

To start planning your visit to Launceston, head online to tasmania.com/points-of-interest/launceston and to discovertasmania.com.au/about/regions-of-tasmania/launceston-and-north for all the best places.

Fields of purple at Bridestowe Lavender Estate
Opposite Main street of Launceston

Captain's Rest

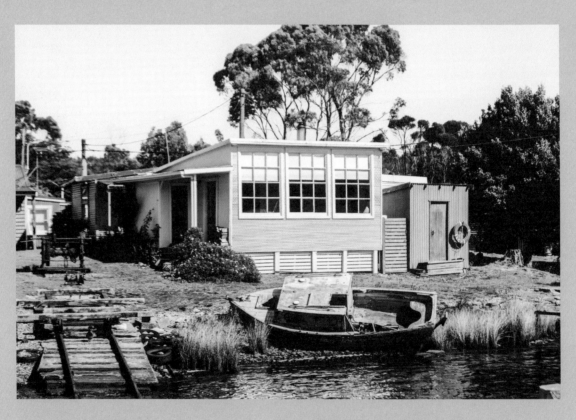

Get completely off-the-beaten track for a romantic weekend and immerse yourself in a tiny historical fishing village just five minutes from the coastal town of Strahan. Captain's Rest is a tiny little shack that has a wall full of spectacular antique windows that overlook the waters of Lettes Bay, where you can watch the sunrise over the mountains or the clouds roll in, depending on the time of year that you visit.

Every detail of Captain's Rest has been meticulously thought out and designed to give you the complete experience. There's a small porch, timber-lined walls, a jetty out the front, row boats floating in the water, and a family of ducks that wander between the cottages, happily quacking you a hello as they pass. Choosing every decoration and accessory for its unique characteristics and Tassie charm, you can find paddles in the bedroom, ropes, buoys and trunks scattered around, and the innate feeling of stepping into the home of a fisher.

During our stay, we enjoyed roasting marshmallows by the roaring fire in the evening, cheese plates and wine on the jetty, reading a book in the warmth of the afternoon sunshine under the stunning antique windows, slowly rowing around the bay, rest, sleep and plenty of fresh air. If you spot a fisher coming in with a catch, they're often more than happy to sell you a fresh fish for dinner. It was our favourite place in Tassie to completely relax, unwind, disconnect from screens and enjoy the experience of staying somewhere completely different and quite simply, magical.

After falling in love with Captain's Rest and understandably wanting to create your very own oasis by the sea, check out **The Hosting Masterclass** by the Captain's Rest owner Sarah Andrews. The masterclass is the perfect introduction to creating your own dream Airbnb space, with an online program and face-to-face events that teach you everything you need to know about getting started, advice and pricing, creating a house name and story, styling, practicalities and management, social media and marketing and heaps more. With a lifetime of incredible experiences, from being a scientist in London to sailing the world and being shipwrecked in Mexico, Sarah is a treasure trove of stories and insightful information, helping her students pop up unique and Insta-worthy Airbnbs all over the world.

IMPORTANT INFO

Captain's Rest is super popular, so it's usually booked out months in advance. It's a good idea to get in early if there's a particular date that you want to visit, or plan your visit around their next available check in. For more information and to book your visit, head online to Airbnb. Before you arrive make sure to read all the details under 'about this space' in the listing, so you know what to expect. Due to the remote location of Strahan and Captain's Rest, it's a good idea to bring everything you might need or want with you.

The Hosting Masterclass is held at different times throughout the year, with classes in Tasmania, Victoria and South Australia, as well as their online courses which are available all throughout the year. To find out more and book your spot, head to thehostingmasterclass.com.

WESTERN TASMANIA

Tasmania's wild, untamed jungle

NATURE LOVERS | ADVENTURERS

The western half of Tasmania is, quite simply, a wild wilderness. It's home to winding roads, tiny little harbourside towns, expansive rivers, ancient rainforests, giant sand dunes and one of the biggest populations of wild wombats in Australia. It's untamed, wild and rugged, and the kind of place where you can drive for hours without passing another car.

Best known for the spectacular Cradle Mountain, there is so much more to explore as you venture further west. There's the historical mining town of Queenstown, the stunning harbourside town of Strahan, the Wilderness World Heritage Area of the Gordon River, and Australia's steepest golf course in Rosebury, as well as peculiar places like Gordon Dam that reflect the state's hydroelectricity history.

A weekend in West Tassie will require a little more planning than other places around the state. There are many places with little-to-no phone reception, towns and fuel stops can often be quite far apart, and if you don't have a plan you could feel like you've just found yourself lost in the wilderness. To make the most of your time here, plan out an itinerary to give yourself more time exploring and less time driving back and forth between locations. The roads are windy, with plenty of corners that you'll need to take slowly, not many places to overtake, and rapidly changing driving conditions due to mountain weather patterns, so make sure to factor that into your travel times.

BEST PHOTO SPOTS

You can't beat the view over Strahan Village at sunset from **View 42° Restaurant & Bar**, which overlooks Macquarie Harbour and the main street of town. Come for a glass of wine and the sunset or stay to enjoy the seafood buffet. It's a great little spot in the west.

Opposite Sunset over Strahan Village

CAN'T MISS

In the morning:

Start your morning by beating the crowds with an early visit to **Cradle Mountain**. One of Tasmania's most iconic locations, Cradle Mountain is home to glacial lakes, snow-covered mountains, ancient rainforests, spectacular views and plenty of different hiking trails to explore it all. The main attraction here is **Dove Lake**, which is extra special during sunrise, with incredible views of the mountain from every angle and stunning reflections on the lake early in the morning. When you get to the Dove Lake track head straight to the right to find the famous boatshed, featured heavily in Cradle Mountain photos.

Still within Cradle Mountain National Park, jump off the included park shuttle bus at **Ronny Creek** and take a walk along the boardwalk to spot wild wombats grazing on grass amongst the hilly mountain side. If you've been trying to spot a wombat for ages with no luck, this is the place to go. We saw several wombats both times we visited Ronny Creek, including a couple of cute little babies following behind their mamas.

Jump on a cruise of the Gordon River onboard the *Spirit of the Wild* with **Gordon River Cruises** from Strahan, to explore some of the beautiful Tasmanian Wilderness World Heritage Area. See the famous reflections and learn more about the history of this stunning place with your knowledgeable onboard guides. The cruise goes for about 6 hours and includes a buffet lunch and walking tours of Heritage Landing and Sarah Island, which has a very interesting convict history.

You've never been on a railway like this before! Throw yourself completely into the wilderness on an epic train journey with **West Coast Wilderness Railway**. With half-day and full-day journeys that take you through ancient rainforests and historical towns and back again, it's the kind of scenery that you simply can't drive to. This railway is the only way to explore this deep into the Tassie wilderness, while also taking you to great towns in the west such as Strahan and Queenstown.

In the afternoon:

Take a drive out to the **Gordon River Dam**, the tallest dam in Australia (standing at 140 metres), impressively built in the largest lake in Tasmania. Sitting in Strathgordon, it's

definitely a bit of a drive out but the scenery of the Franklin-Gordon Wild Rivers National Park along the way is well worth it. You can even walk along the top of the dam to admire the impressiveness of this curved wall. Not for people who suffer from vertigo!

While you're in **Franklin-Gordon Wild Rivers National Park**, explore a little of the Tasmanian rainforest, with walking trails to suit all levels of fitness through the diverse landscapes of the west. With walks from as short as one kilometre, to multi-day return hikes, you can do as little or as much as you want.

Drive out to **The Edge of the World** at Gardiners Point, south of Arthur River. It might sound a little dramatic, but from this spot the ocean sweeps halfway around the world, in the longest uninterrupted expanse of ocean on the globe. There is nothing for ages and ages, and the wild landscapes definitely make you feel like you're standing on the edge of the world.

Explore the **ghost town of Linda** just out of the town of Queenstown with its moon-like landscape. Like Queenstown, Linda was once one of the world's richest mining towns and surrounded by picturesque mountains and dramatic landscapes, where you can still find the skeleton of the Royal Hotel that once used to be the hub of the town. While it was a rough, but busy town in the mining days, it's been abandoned since the 1950s, and is now really just for those who like to explore spooky spots.

In the evening:
Spend the golden hour wandering around Strahan village, one of the cutest little towns in Tasmania sitting alongside the Gordon River. With boats coming in and out of the harbour as the sun sets, it's just such a peaceful town to experience. Head to **Hamer's Bar & Bistro** for delicious steaks right on the waterfront, or head up to **View 42° Restaurant & Bar** for a delicious seafood buffet and views over the whole village.

Where
Along the whole western side of Tasmania.

Getting here
Plan ahead to decide on the itinerary for your route and to ensure you choose the most efficient way to arrive. Choose between flying into either Hobart Airport (HBA), which has daily direct flights from every capital city (except Darwin), or Launceston Airport (LST), with daily direct flights from Melbourne, Sydney and Brisbane. Pick up a rental car at the airport; or you can bring your own car and travel to Tasmania on the *Spirit of Tasmania* and start your West Tassie adventure from Devonport.

Getting around
Rent a car to explore Western Tasmania, but be prepared before you hit the road. With winding roads, few fuel stops, little-to-no phone reception outside the towns, and not many other cars on the road, it's a good idea to plan ahead when driving in the west. Load your directions before you head off (and carry a paper map), and always know where the next town and fuel stop is so you don't find yourself stuck on the side of the road.

Glamping at Truffle Lodge
Opposite Wombats at Cradle Mountain

When to go

The Western half of Tasmania experiences every type of weather pattern throughout the year. Summers are mostly warm and sunny, with temperatures consistently around the mid-20°C, while winters can see regular snow fall in some of the highest parts of the region. The west is also the wettest region in Tasmania, where the rainforest meets the sea. Whether you like the warm or the cold weather you always get a little bit of everything in this part of Tassie, so bring a beanie, jacket and sunscreen no matter what time of the year you visit.

Main towns

Queenstown is the largest town in Western Tasmania, a historic mining town that lies in a valley between Mount Lyell and Mount Owen. Queenstown is about a 3-hour, 40-minute drive from Hobart or a 3-hour, 10-minute drive from Launceston. You can also find the historic and pretty town of Strahan sitting on a harbour, one of our favourite places to stay in the region.

Where to stay

With towns that are super spread out and an expansive coastline to explore, there are an endless number of choices when it comes to where to stay in Western Tasmania. For the ultimate romantic getaway and an ultra-luxurious experience you can't go past **Eagles Nest** in West Kentish, which offers several unique houses surrounded by spectacular views, outdoor baths, open fireplaces, spa experiences, and plenty of space all to yourself. It's a stunning spot to immerse yourself in nature, breathe in that fresh air and spend a weekend recharging.

Another great place to stay to immerse yourself in the wilderness of Western Tasmania is **Corinna Wilderness Experience**, one of the most remote places in Tasmania, sitting along the Pieman River and only accessible by barge. With unique cottages and cabins that are wedged into the takayna (Tarkine) rainforest, you'll feel like you've entered another world. Corinna also offers some great experiences to their guests, including kayaking, river cruises, hikes, fishing and nature experiences.

Need to know

Around Western Tasmania you will find Southwest National Park, Cradle Mountain - Lake St Clair National Park, Franklin-Gordon Wild Rivers National Park, Walls of Jerusalem National Park, and Savage River National Park, as well as several others, which will all require a National Parks Pass (see p.218) to enter. There are individual park passes or a holiday pass to choose from, which gives you the freedom to explore as many parks as you want for eight weeks.

Get planning

Head to westcoasttas.com.au and northwesttasmania.com.au for everything you need to know on your adventure to the west, and check out @westcoasttas and @visitnorthwesttasmania for all the best spots to stop at along the way.

INDEX

12 Apostles, Port Campbell Vic. 44
18 Degrees, Broome WA 137
1770 Qld 191, 193

A

Aboriginal Art and Culture sites, Gariwerd (Grampians) Vic. 48
Aboriginal Cultural Tour, Bookyanna (Point Pearce) SA 94
Aboriginal Cultural Ways, Ballina NSW 14
Abrolhos Islands WA 124
Adder Rock, Minjerribah (North Stradbroke Island) Qld 180
Adelaide SA 72-3, 89
Adelaide Arcade, Adelaida SA 72
Adelaide Central Markets, Adelaide SA 72
Adelaide Fringe Festival, Adelaida SA 72
Adelaide Hills SA 73, 74
Adelaide Oval, Adelaide SA 72
Adelaide River NT 144, 159
Adelaide Zoo, Adelaide SA 72
Admirals Arch, Flinders Chase National Park SA 82
Adventure Bay, Bruny Island Tas. 225
Adventure Bay Charters, Port Lincoln SA 84
Aggies Fresh Fruit Stall, Glossop SA 102
Agnes Water Qld 191, 192, 193
Air Freycinet Tas. 227
Aireys Inlet Vic. 44
Aireys Inlet Pub, Aireys Inlet Vic. 44
Airlie Beach Qld 198, 201, 202, 204, 205, 207, 209, 210
Alamonta Beach SA 86
Albany WA 132, 134
Albany Whale Museum, Albany WA 134
Albury NSW 51
Aldinga SA 79
Alfred Nicholas Gardens, Sherbrooke Vic. 38
Algebuckina SA 106
Alice Springs NT 89, 150-3, 154
Alice Springs Desert Park, Alice Springs NT 152

Alice Springs Telegraph Station Historical Reserve, Alice Springs NT 89, 152
Allansford Vic. 42
Alonnah, Bruny Island Tas. 225
Alowyn Gardens, Yarra Glen Vic. 38, 40
Alpine Nature Experience, Mount Hotham Vic. 55, 58-9
Amaze'n Margaret River, Margaret River WA 130
A Maze'N Things, Cowes Vic. 66
Amity Point, Minjerribah (North Stradbroke Island) Qld 179, 180
Androssan SA 93
Angaston SA 76
Angkerle Atwatye (Standley Chasm), Western MacDonnell Ranges NT 152, 154
Anglesea Vic. 45
Anglesea Golf Club, Anglesea Vic. 43
Anglesea Riverbank Market, Anglesea Vic. 43
Anna Bay NSW 14
Anzac Hill, Alice Springs NT 152
Apex Bakery, Tanunda SA 74
Apollo Bay Vic. 44, 45
Appellation Restaurant, Marananga SA 75
Arajilla Retreat, Lord Howe Island NSW 19
Arcadia, Yunbenun (Magnetic Island) Qld 190
Arkaroo Rock, Flinders Ranges SA 90
Arkaroola SA 91
art galleries
    Broken Hill NSW 24
    Minjerribah (North Stradbroke Island) Qld 179
art murals, Tumby Bay SA 84
Arthur Bay Lookout, Yunbenun (Magnetic Island) Qld 188
Arthur River Tas. 237
Arthurs Seat Eagle, Arthurs Seat Vic. 62
Arts Factory Lodge, Byron Bay NSW 11
astronomical observatory, Arkaroola SA 91
Atherton Tablelands Qld 196, 197
Atlantic, The, Byron Bay NSW 11
Australia Zoo, Beerwah Qld 176

Australian Age of Dinosaurs, Winton Qld 215
Australian War Memorial, Canberra ACT 30
Australian Wildlife Centre, Healesville Sanctuary, Healesville Vic. 40
Aviation Museum, Darwin NT 144
Ayers Rock Resort, Yulara NT 147, 148

B

Babinda Boulders, Babinda Qld 196
Balconies, The, Gariwerd (Grampians) Vic. 48, 49
Baldwin Distilling Co., Canberra ACT 32
Baleen Rockpool, Whalers Way SA 84
Ballina NSW 10, 14
Balloon Adventures, Barossa Valley SA 74
Bamaga Qld 211
bareboating, Whitsundays Qld 206-7
Bargara Qld 193
Barinura (Little Bondi Beach), East Arnhem Land NT 170
Barista, Brewer, Wine Cycle Tour, Barossa Valley SA 74
Barmera SA 102
Barossa Bike Hire, Nuriootpa SA 74
Barossa Farmers Market, Angaston SA 74
Barossa Valley SA 73, 74-6
Barossa Valley Apartments, Tanunda SA 76
Barossa Valley Cheese Company, Angaston SA 74
Barossa Valley Chocolate Company, Tanunda SA 74
Barossa Vintage Festival, Barossa Valley SA 74
Barrack Street, Perth WA 110
Barramundi Gorge, Kakadu National Park NT 164
Barrkmalam (Jim Jim Falls), Kakadu National Park NT 164, 165
Basin, The, Rottnest Island WA 113
Batemans Bay NSW 26, 29
Bathers Way, Newcastle NSW 14
Bathurst Island, Tiwi Islands, NT 166, 168
Battery Point Tas. 220
Bawaka, East Arnhem Land NT 170
Bay Club, The, Broome WA 137
Bay of Fires (larapuna) Tas. 226, 227, 229

Bay of Fires Conservation Area Tas. 229
BBQ Father, The, Exmouth WA 116
Beach Club, Hamilton Island Qld 210
Beach Hotel, Byron Bay NSW 10
Beachcomber Lodge, Lord Howe Island
　NSW 19
beaches
　　Byron Bay NSW 9
　　Cape Le Grand National Park
　　　WA 122
　　Thursday Island Qld 212
Beaches and Cream, Byron Bay NSW 10
Beachport SA 99, 100
BEANd Roastery, San Remo Vic. 66
Beaten Track Brewery, Kalgoorlie
　WA 140
Beehive Falls, Gariwerd (Grampians)
　Vic. 48
Bega NSW 27
Bega Cheese Heritage Centre,
　Bega NSW 27
Bell Gorge WA 138
Bells Beach Vic. 43
Bell's Milk Bar, Broken Hill NSW 22
Ben Boyd National Park NSW 27
BentSpoke Brewing Company,
　Canberra ACT 32
Bermagui NSW 27
Berri Estate Winery & Cellar Door,
　Glossop SA 104
Berri SA 102
Berry Springs NT 144
Bert's Restaurant, Bundaberg Qld 193
Betka Beach Vic. 68
Betty's Beach, Whitsunday Island
　Qld 204
Big Strawberry, Tocumwal NSW 50
Big Winch, Coober Pedy SA 97
Big4 MacDonnell Range Holiday Park,
　Alice Springs NT 153
Binalong Bay Tas. 227
Binydjarrna (Daliwuy Bay), East
　Arnhem Land NT 170
Birds Eye View, Exmouth WA 116
Bitter Springs, Mataranka NT 157
Black Cow Bistro, Launceston Tas. 233
Black Diamond Lake, Collie WA 130
Blinky Beach, Lord Howe Island
　NSW 18
Block Arcade, Melbourne Vic. 36

Blowhole, Whalers Way SA 84
Blue Hills Berries & Cherries, Silvan
　Vic. 38
Blue Lagoon, The, Lord Howe Island
　NSW 19
Blue Lake, Mount Gambier SA 100
Blue Monkey Restaurant, Kalgoorlie
　WA 140
Blue Mountains NSW 4–7
Blue Mountains Explorer Bus,
　Katoomba NSW 7
Blue Pearl Bay, Hayman Island Qld 205
Blue Pool, Bermagui NSW 27
Blue Pool, Blue Mountains NSW 4
Bluefish Point, Prince of Wales Island
　Qld 212
Bluff Knoll, Stirling Range National
　Park WA 133
Bond Store, Wallaroo SA 94
Bondi NSW 3
Bondi Beach NSW 2
Bondi Beach pool, Bondi Beach NSW 2
Bondi to Coogee Coastal Walk, Sydney
　NSW 2
Bondi to Manly track, Sydney NSW 2
Bonorong Wildlife Sanctuary, Hobart
　Tas. 220
Booderee National Park NSW 27
Bookyanna (Point Pearce) SA 94
Boranup Karri Forest, Boranup
　WA 130
Boroka Lookout, Gariwerd (Grampians)
　Vic. 46, 49
Botanic Gardens, Perth WA 110
Boughshed Restaurant, Monkey Mia
　WA 126
Boulder Historical Street, Boulder
　WA 140
Boundary Hotel, The, Brisbane Qld 176
Bourke Street Mall, Melbourne Vic. 37
Boutique Cruises, Rottnest Island
　WA 113
Bowali Visitors Centre, Jabiru NT 164
Brachina Gorge, Flinders Ranges
　National Park SA 91
Brady's Lookout, Rosevears Tas. 232
Brambuk Aboriginal Cultural Centre
　and Visitors Information Centre,
　Halls Gap Vic. 48
Bread & Butter, Launceston Tas. 233

Breakaways, The, Kanku-Breakaways
　Conservation Park SA 98
Bremer Bay WA 134
Bremer Island NT 172
Bridestowe Lavender Estate,
　Bridestowe Tas. 232, 233
Bright Vic. 57
Brighton Beach Vic. 36
Brisbane Qld 176–7
Brisbane Festival, Brisbane Qld 176
Brisbane River, Brisbane Qld 176
Broad Arrow Tavern, Kalgoorlie
　WA 140
Broken Hill NSW 22–5
Broken Hill Regional Art Gallery,
　Broken Hill NSW 24
Bronte Beach ocean pool NSW 2
Broome WA 136–8
Broome Whale Watching, Broome
　WA 136
Brown Lake, Minjerribah (North
　Stradbroke Island) Qld 179
Bruny Hotel, Bruny Island Tas. 224
Bruny Island Tas. 222–5
Bruny Island Berry Farm, Bruny Island
　Tas. 224
Bruny Island Cheese & Beer Co.,
　Bruny Island Tas. 224
Bruny Island Chocolate, Bruny Island
　Tas. 224
Bruny Island Premium Wines, Bruny
　Island Tas. 224
Bruny Island Safaris, Bruny Island
　Tas. 224
Bruny's House of Whisky, Bruny Island
　Tas. 224
Buccaneer Archipelago WA 137
Buku-Larrnggay Mulka Arts Centre,
　Yirrkala NT 170
Bunbury WA 128, 131
Bundaberg Qld 191, 192, 193, 200, 201
Bundaberg Barrel, Bundaberg Qld 192
Bundaberg Botanic Gardens, Bundaberg
　Qld 192
Bundaberg Region Qld 191–3
Bundaberg Rum Distillery, Bundaberg
　Qld 192
Bundy Belle, Bundaberg Qld 192
Bungalow Bay Koala Village, Yunbenun
　(Magnetic Island) Qld 189, 190

Bunjil's Shelter, Gariwerd (Grampians) Vic. 48
Bunyeroo Gorge, Flinders Ranges National Park SA 91
Burleigh Heads Qld 181
Burrungkuy (Nourlangie) Rock, Kakadu National Park NT 164
Busselton WA 128, 129, 131
Busselton Jetty, Busselton WA 129
Butcher, Baker Winemaker Trail, Barossa Valley SA 74
Butterfly Sanctuary, Kuranda Qld 195
Butterfly walk, Yunbenun (Magnetic Island) Qld 189
Byron Bay NSW 8–11, 12, 15
Byron Bay Dive Centre, Byron Bay NSW 9
Byron Bay Luxury Homes, Byron Bay NSW 11
Byron Bay Surf and Bike Hire, Byron Bay NSW 11
Byron Community Market, Byron Bay NSW 9
Byron Wellbeing Retreats, Byron Bay NSW 9

C
Cable Bay Beach, Inneston SA 95
Cable Beach, Broome WA 136, 137
Cactus Country, Strathmerton Vic. 50
cage diving with great white sharks, Port Lincoln SA 84
Cage of Death at Crocosaurus Cove, Darwin NT 144
Cahills Crossing, Kakadu National Park NT 164, 165
Cairns Qld 197, 198, 200, 201
Camden Park Station, Longreach Qld 215
Cameron Corner Qld 24
Canberra ACT 30–3
Canoe the Riverland, Renmark SA 102
Canungra Valley Vineyards, Canungra Qld 181
Cape Arnhem, East Arnhem Land NT 170
Cape Banks Lighthouse, Carpenter Rocks SA 100
Cape Bruny Lighthouse, Bruny Island Tas. 224

Cape Byron Lighthouse, Byron Bay NSW 9
Cape Byron Marine Park NSW 9
Cape Jaffa Wines, Mount Benson SA 100
Cape Jervis SA 83
Cape Kitchen, The, Newhaven Vic. 66
Cape Le Grand National Park WA 120, 122, 123
Cape Leeuwin WA 130
Cape Leveque WA 137
Cape Naturaliste WA 130
Cape Queen Elizabeth Walk, The, Bruny Island Tas. 224
Cape Range National Park WA 116, 118–19, 127
Cape Schanck Lighthouse, Cape Schanck Vic. 62
Cape Spencer Lighthouse SA 94
Cape to Cape Trail, Margaret River Region WA 130
Cape Tribulation Qld 197, 198
Cape Wiles, Whalers Way SA 84
Cape Willoughby SA 83
Cape Woolamai Vic. 64
Cape York Qld 194, 201, 211, 213
Capital Brewing Co., Canberra ACT 32
Cappella Lodge, Lord Howe Island NSW 19
Captain Cook Cruises, Perth WA 110
Captain Cook Highway Qld 196
Captain's Rest, Strahan Tas. 234–5
Carnarvon WA 127
Carpenter Rocks SA 100
Carrara Markets, Carrara Qld 182
Carrickalinga Beach SA 78
Cascade Brewery, Hobart Tas. 220
Cascade History and Brewery Experience, Hobart Tas. 220
Castle Hill, Townsville Qld 189
Casuarina Campground, Inneston SA 95
Cat Bay National Surfing Reserve, Phillip Island Vic. 66
Cataract Gorge Reserve, Launceston Tas. 232
Catseye Beach, Hamilton Island Qld 209
Cecilia's On Hay, Kalgoorlie WA 140
Centre Place, Melbourne Vic. 36
Champagne Pools, K'gari (Fraser Island) Qld 186
Change Overnight, Launceston Tas. 233

Chapel Street, South Yarra Vic. 36
Charles Knife Canyon, Cape Range National Park WA 116
Charlie's Dessert House, Launceston Tas. 233
Chase 'n' Thyme Island Tours, Lord Howe Island NSW 18
Cherryhill Orchard, Wandin East Vic. 38
Chinaman's Beach, Agnes water Qld 192
Chinaman's Island Walking Track, Yarrawonga Vic. 50
Chinatown, Adelaida SA 72
Chinatown, Melbourne Vic. 37
chocolate factory, Broken Hill NSW 22
Churchill Island Heritage Farm, Churchill Island Vic. 64
Circular Quay, Sydney NSW 2
City Circle Tram, Melbourne Vic. 36
Clare Valley SA 73, 74
Clarkes Beach Holiday Park, Byron Bay NSW 11
Cleland Wildlife Park, Cleland SA 73
Cleveland Qld 180
Clubhouse Restaurant, Dent Island Qld 209
coastal walks
    Croajingolong National Park Vic. 68
    Kiama NSW 27
    North Coast NSW 14
Coffin Bay SA 86
Coffin Bay National Park SA 84, 86
Coffin Bay Oysters, Coffin Bay SA 86
Coffs Harbour NSW 15
Cohuna Vic. 51
Coldstream Brewery, Coldstream Vic. 40
Coles Bay Tas. 229
Collective Markets, The, Brisbane Qld 176
Collie WA 131
Collins Street, Melbourne Vic. 36
Commonfolk Coffee, Mornington Vic. 62
Condigup Tavern, Esperance WA 122
Coober Pedy SA 89, 96–9, 106, 107
Cooinda Lodge, Kakadu NT 165
Cooktown Qld 197
Coonawarra SA 100
Coopers Alehouse Restaurant, Wallaroo SA 94

Coorong National Park SA 100
Coral Bay WA 126
Coral Coast WA 124–7
Corinna Wilderness Experience, Corinna Tas. 239
Cottesloe Beach WA 110
Cowards Springs SA 106
Cowes Vic. 66
Cradle Mountain Tas. 236
Cradle Mountain - Lake St Clair National Park Tas. 236, 239
Crawley Edge Boatshed, Perth WA 111
Crayfish Pool, Blue Mountains NSW 4
Croajingolong National Park Vic. 68
Crooked Post, The, Lord Howe Island NSW 18
Cruise Whitsundays, Airlie Beach Qld 205, 209, 210
Crystal Castle & Shambhala Gardens, Montecollum NSW 10
Cullen Wines, Margaret River WA 130
cultural tours/activities
        Bookyanna (Point Pearce) SA 94
        Cairns Qld 200
        Coral Coast, WA 126
        East Arnhem Land NT 170
        Esperance, WA 122
        Flinders Ranges, SA 90
        Gaagal Wanggaan National Park NSW 14
        Gariwerd (Grampians) Vic. 48
        Gold Coast Qld 181
        Katherine NT 158
        Monkey Mia WA 126
        North Coast NSW 14
        Rottnest Island, WA 113
        South-West, WA 133
        Tiwi Islands NT 166, 168
        Torres Strait Islands Qld 211, 214
        Uluru NT 147
        Wilpena Pound SA 90
        Yorke Peninsula, SA 94
Cumberland River Walk, Lorne Vic. 44
Currumbin Beach Qld 181
Currumbin Wildlife Sanctuary, Currumbin Qld 182
Curtain Springs Inn NT 156
Cygnet Bay Pearl Farm, Broome WA 137
Cylinder Beach, Minjerribah (North Stradbroke Island) Qld 179

D
Daintree Rainforest Qld 195, 197, 198
Daliwuy Bay, East Arnhem Land NT 170
Dalmanyi WA 138
Dampier Peninsula WA 137
Dandenong Ranges Vic. 38–41
D'Arenberg, McLaren Vale SA 78
Darling Harbour, Sydney NSW 2
Darwin NT 89, 144–5, 166, 168
Darwin Military Museum, Darwin NT 144
Daydream Island Qld 202, 205
Deadmans Beach, Minjerribah (North Stradbroke Island) Qld 179
Deck Chair Cinema, Darwin NT 144
Deep Creek Conservation Park SA 77, 78
Denmark WA 132, 133
Dent Island Qld 209
Derby Tas. 233
Derby WA 138
Desert Palms, Alice Springs NT 153
Devils Corner Cellar Door and Lookout, Apslawn Tas. 227
Devil's Marbles (Karlu Karlu) NT 152
Devonport Tas. 238
Diamond Bay, Sorrento Vic. 62
Didgeridoo Dreaming Night Tour, Monkey Mia WA 126
dingoes, K'gari (Fraser Island) Qld 186
Dinner Plain, Vic. 54, 57
Dinosaur Stampede National Monument, Lark Quarry Qld 215
Discovery Bus Tour, Rottnest Island WA 113
Discovery Rottnest Island, Rottnest Island WA 114
distilleries and breweries
        Broome WA 137
        Bundaberg Qld 192
        Canberra ACT 32
        Coldstream Vic. 40
        Cowes Vic. 66
        Exmouth WA 116
        Healesville Vic. 40
        Hobart Tas. 220
        Huon Valley Tas. 225
        Kalgoorlie WA 140
        Kingscote SA 80
        Loch Vic. 68
        Renmark SA 102
        Wilkadena SA 102

DOC Pizza and Mozzarella Bar, Mornington Vic. 62
dog fence, Coober Pedy SA 97
Dolphin Swim Australia, Port Stephens NSW 14
dolphins (snubfin), Broome WA 136
Domaine Chandon, Coldstream Vic. 40
Dorringo National Park NSW 14
DoubleTree by Hilton, Alice Springs NT 153
Douglas-Apsley National Park Tas. 229
Dove Lake Tas. 236
Down The Rabbit Hole, McLaren Vale SA 78
Dreamtime Dive & Snorkel, Cairns Qld 200
Dreamworld, Gold Coast Qld 183
Dromana Vic. 63
Dudley Wines, Cuttlefish Bay SA 82
Dundee's @ Cairns Aquarium, Port Douglas Qld 196
Dunsborough WA 131
Dunwich, Minjerribah (North Stradbroke Island) Qld 180

E
Eagles Nest, Brisbane Qld 176
Eagles Nest, West Kentish Tas. 239
East Arnhem Land NT 170–3
East Coast Tas. 226–9
East Coast Natureworld Tas. 227
Echo Point, Blue Mountains NSW 4
Echuca Vic. 50, 51
Echuca Farmer's Market, Echuca Vic. 50
EcoBoat Adventure Tour, Cowes Vic. 66
Eden NSW 26, 27, 29
Edge of the World, The, Gardiners Point Tas. 237
Elephant Rocks, Williams Bay National Park WA 134
Elinjaa Falls, Millaa Millaa Qld 196
Ell Creek, K'gari (Fraser Island) Qld 186
Ellery Creek Big Hole, Western MacDonnell Ranges NT 152, 154
Elsey National Park NT 157
Emporium, Melbourne Vic. 37
Emu Bay SA 82
Emu Bay Lavender Farm, Wisanger SA 80
Encounter Maria Island ferry Tas. 228

Enlighten Festival, Canberra ACT 30
Erlunda Roadhouse NT 155
Erskine Falls, Lorne Vic. 44
Esperance Chalet Village, Esperance WA 123
Esperance Stonehenge, Esperance WA 122
Esplanade Resort & Spa, The, Lakes Entrance Vic. 69
Ethel (shipwreck), Innes National Park SA 94
Eureka Skydeck, Melbourne Vic. 37
Eurong Beach Resort, K'gari (Fraser Island) Qld 187
Evening Experience, The (at) Spirits of the Red Sand, Gold Coast Qld 182
Exmouth WA 115–17, 119, 127
Experance WA 120–3
Eyre Peninsula SA 84–7

F
Fairhaven Vic. 43
Falls Creek Vic. 55
Farm @ Byron Bay, The, Ewingsdale NSW 10
Festival of the Sun, Port Macquarie NSW 12
Field of Light, Uluru NT 147
Fingal Bay NSW 14
First Drop Wines, Nuriootpa SA 75
Fish Hook Bay, Rottnest Island WA 113
fishing
    Bermagui NSW 27
    Darwin NT 144
    K'gari (Fraser Island) Qld 186
    Murray River, Vic & SA 50, 104
    Yorke Peninsula SA 94
Fitzroy Island Qld 197, 200
Fiume at the Fantauzzo, Brisbane Qld 176
Flavours of the Riverland, Barmera SA 102
Fleurieu Peninsula SA 73, 77–9
Flinders Vic. 62
Flinders Beach, Minjerribah (North Stradbroke Island) Qld 180
Flinders Chase National Park SA 80, 82
Flinders Ranges SA 90–2, 107
Florence Bay, Yunbenun (Magnetic Island) Qld 190

food trucks, Cylinder Beach, Minjerribah (North Stradbroke Island) Qld 179
For The Love of Grape, Echuca Vic. 50
Fort Nepean, Portsea Vic. 62
Fortitude Valley Qld 176
Forts Walk, Yunbenun (Magnetic Island) Qld 188
fossicking, Coober Pedy SA 96
Four Mile Beach, Port Douglas Qld 196
Four Pillars Distillery, Healesville Vic. 40
Foxy's Bar, Fitzroy Island Qld 197
Francois Peron National Park WA 126, 127
Franklin-Gordon Wild Rivers National Park Tas. 237, 239
Fraser Explorer Tours, K'gari (Fraser Island) Qld 186, 187
Fraser Island Qld 184–7
Fremantle WA 110, 111, 114
Frenchman Peak, Cape Le Grand National Park WA 122
Freycinet Lodge, Coles Bay Tas. 227, 229
Freycinet Marine Farm, Coles Bay Tas. 227
Freycinet National Park Tas. 226, 227, 229
Friday Island Qld 212
Froth Craft Breweries, Exmouth WA 116

G
Gaagal Wanggaan National Park NSW 12
Gab Titui Cultural Centre, Thursday Island Qld 212
Gabo Island Lighthouse, Gabo Island Vic. 68
Gaia Retreat and Spa, Brooklet NSW 9
Gallery of Modern Art (GOMA), Brisbane Qld 176
Gan Gan Hill Lookout, Nelson Bay NSW 14
Gantheaume Point, Broome WA 137
Gap, The, Torndirrup National Park WA 133
Garanhan (Macassan Beach), East Arnhem Land NT 170
Gardens, The, Bay of Fires Tas. 227
Gariwerd (Grampians) Vic. 46–9
Geoffrey Bay, Yunbenun (Magnetic Island) Qld 188

Geordie Bay, Rottnest Island WA 113
Georgie Bass Café & Cookery, Flinders Vic. 62
Geraldton WA 124, 127
Get Shucked Oyster Farm, Bruny Island Tas. 224
Giant Stairway, Blue Mountains NSW 4
Giant Tingle Tree, Walpole WA 134
Gibson Steps, Port Campbell Vic. 44
Gippsland Vic. 67–9
Gippsland Food & Wine Trail, Gippsland Vic. 68
Gippsland Lakes Vic. 68
Gipsy Point Vic. 68
Glen Helen Gorge, Western MacDonnell Ranges NT 152, 154, 156
Glenbrook Gorge, Glenbrook NSW 4
Glenelg SA 72, 73
Glossop SA 102, 104
glow worms, Blue Mountains NSW 5
Go Ride A Wave Surf School, Torquay Vic. 43
Go Sea Kayaking, Byron Bay NSW 9
Gold Coast, The Qld 181–3
Golden Outback, The WA 139–41
Golden Quest Discovery Trail, outback WA 141
golf
    Anglesea Golf Club, Anglesea Vic. 43
    Dent Island Qld 209
    Lord Howe Island NSW 18
    Nullarbor Links WA 140
golf buggy hire, Hamilton Island Qld 209
Goodwill Bridge, Brisbane Qld 176
Goolwa SA 50, 77
Goompi Trail, Minjerribah (North Stradbroke Island) Qld 179
Gordon River Tas. 236
Gordon River Cruises, Strahan Tas. 236
Gordon River Dam, Strathgordon Tas. 236–7
Gorge Walk, The, Minjerribah (North Stradbroke Island) Qld 179
Govetts Leap Lookout, Blue Mountains NSW 4
Gove Boat Club, Nhulunbuy NT 170, 173
Grampians Grape Escape, Halls Gap Vic. 46

Grampians National Park Vic. 46–9
Grampians Wine Tour, Stawell Vic. 48
Grandvewe, Huon Valley Tas. 225
Granite Skywalk, Porongurup National Park WA 134
Great Alpine Road Vic. 54–5
Great Barrier Reef, The Qld 197, 198–201
Great Barrier Reef Festival, Airlie Beach Qld 202
Great Barrier Reef Marine Park Qld 188
Great Ocean Road Vic. 42–5
Great Ocean Road Chocolaterie and Ice Creamery, Bellbrae Vic. 43
Great Otway National Park Vic. 44
Great Sandy National Park Qld 187
Great Southern Distilling Company, Robinson WA 134
Green Fort Lookout, Thursday Island Qld 212
Greenly Beach SA 84, 87
Greens Pool, Williams Bay National Park WA 134
Groote Eylandt NT 172
Grunske's By The River Seafood Market and Restaurant, Bundaberg Qld 193
Guided Kangaroo Tour, Anglesea Golf Club, Anglesea Vic. 43
Gungkurdul (Twin Falls), Kakadu National Park NT 165
Gunlom Falls, Kakadu National Park NT 164, 165
Gunlom Infinity Pool, Kakadu National Park NT 162
Gwalia WA 141
Gym Beach, Marion Bay SA 94, 95

H
Hahndorf SA 72
Hahndorf Inn, Hahndorf SA 72
Haigh's Chocolate Factory, Parkside SA 72
Halls Gap Vic. 46, 49
Hamelin Bay WA 129
Hamer's Bar & Bistro, Strahan Tas. 237
Hamilton Island Air's Journey to the Heart Tour, Hamilton Island Qld 209
Hamilton Island Beach Sports Hut, Hamilton Island Qld 209

Hamilton Island Qld 202, 204, 205, 208–10
Hanging Rock, Blue Mountains NSW 5
Hanson Bay Wildlife Sanctuary, Karatta SA 80
Hardware Lane, Melbourne Vic. 36
Harrietville Vic. 57
Hartleys Crocodile Adventures, Wangetti Qld 196
Hartshorn Distillery, Huon Valley Tas. 225
Harvest Kitchen, Vine Vale SA 75
Harvest Launceston Community Farmers' Market, Launceston Tas. 232
Hattah-Kulkyne National Park Vic. 50
Hawker SA 90
Hawkings Point, Yunbenun (Magnetic Island) Qld 189
Hayman Island Qld 202, 205
Healesville Sanctuary, Healesville Vic. 40
Heart Reef, Great Barrier Reef Qld 200, 208
Heartbeat of the Murray, Swan Hill Vic. 50
helicopter rides, Heart Reef, Great Barrier Reef Qld 209
Hellfire Bay, Cape Le Grand National Park WA 122
Hello Koalas Sculpture Trail, Port Macquarie NSW 14
Hells Hole, Caveton SA 100
Heritage Landing, Gordon River Tas. 236
Hermannsburg NT 156
Heron Island Qld 201
Hervey Bay Qld 187
Hill Inlet, Whitsunday Island Qld 204
Hill Inlet Lookout, Whitehaven Beach, Whitsunday Island Qld 202
Hobart Tas. 220–1
Hobart Historic Cruise, Hobart Tas. 220
Honeymoon Bay Tas. 227
Hook Island Qld 205
Horizontal Falls, Kimberley Region WA 137
Horizontal Falls Seaplane Adventures, Broome WA 137
Horn Island Qld 212, 213
Horseshoe Bay, Port Elliot SA 78

Horseshoe Bay, Yunbenun (Magnetic Island) 190
Hosting Masterclass, The, Strahan Tas. 235
hot-air ballooning
    Barossa Valley SA 74
    Canberra ACT 30
    Melbourne Vic. 36
    Yarra Valley Vic. 38
Hotel Sorrento, Sorrento Vic. 62
Hotham Alpine Resort Vic. 57
Hotham Alpine Village Vic. 54, 57
Hotham Heights Vic. 54
Howling Husky, Mount Hotham Vic. 54
Hugh Hamilton Wine, McLaren Vale SA 78
Hundred Acre Hideaway Hot Tub Retreat, Bruny Island Tas. 225
Hunter Valley NSW 3
Huon Valley Tas. 225
Hutt Lagoon WA 124

I
Ikara (Wilpena Pound) 90, 92
Ikara-Flinders Ranges National Park SA 90–2
Ikoymarrwa, Kakadu National Park NT 164
In2thewild NSW 20–1
Indigenous Sea Rangers, Cairns Qld 200
Indijup Beach, Yallingup WA 130
Injidup Nature Spa, Yallingup WA 130
Innes National Park SA 93, 94, 95
Innestown SA 94
Intercontinental Hayman Island, Hayman Island Qld 205
Iron Bar, Port Douglas Qld 196
Island Arts Creative, Minjerribah (North Stradbroke Island) Qld 179
Island Explorer, Rottnest Island WA 113
Island Explorer Bus, Rottnest Island WA 114

J
Jabiru NT 164, 165
Jackalope, Merricks North Vic. 52
Jacob's Creek Wines, Roland Flat SA 75
Jamala Wildlife Lodge, Canberra ACT 30
James Price Point, Broome WA 136
Jan Juc Vic. 43

Jellurgal Aboriginal Cultural Centre, Gold Coast Qld 181
Jellybean Pool, Blue Mountains NSW 4
Jenolan Caves, Jenolan NSW 5
Jervis Bay JBT 32
Jervis Bay Marine Park NSW 27
Jervis Bay Wild, Huskisson NSW 27
Jim Jim Falls (Barrkmalam), Kakadu National Park NT 164, 165
John Simons Flora & Fauna Sanctuary, Broken Hill NSW 24
Josephine's Gallery & Kangaroo Orphanage, Coober Pedy SA 97
Julia Creek Qld 216
Julia Creek Caravan Park's artesian bathhouses, Julia Creek Qld 216
Julian Rocks Nguthungulli Nature Reserve, Byron Bay NSW 9
jumping crocodiles
    Adelaide River NT 144
    Wangetti Qld 196
Jurabi Turtle Centre, Exmouth WA 116
Jurien Bay WA 124

K
Kakadu National Park NT 144, 162–5
Kalbarri National Park WA 126, 127
Kalbarri Skywalk, Kalbarri National Park WA 126
Kalgoorlie WA 139–41
Kalgoorlie Super Pit, Kalgoorlie WA 140
Kangaroo Island SA 80–3
Kangaroo Island Brewery, Kingscote SA 80
Kangaroo Island Spirits, Cygnet River SA 80
Kangaroo Island Wildlife Park, Duncan SA 82
Kangaroo Point Lookout, Brisbane Qld 176
Kangaroo Sanctuary, Alice Springs NT 152
Kanku-Breakaways Conservation Park SA 98
Karijini National Park WA 116
Karlu Karlu (Devil's Marbles) NT 152
Kata Tjuta NT 146, 147, 148
Katanning WA 132
Katherine NT 89, 144, 157–9

Katherine Gorge, Nitmiluk National Park NT 157
Katherine Hot Springs, Katherine NT 158
Katherine Outback Experience, Katherine NT 158
Katnook Coonawarra Cellar Door, Coonawarra SA 100
Katoomba Night Walk, Katoomba NSW 5
kayaking
    Minjerribah (North Stradbroke Island) Qld 179
    Rabbit Island NSW 18
Kazu Pearls, Friday Island Qld 212
Kennedy Range National Park WA 116
Kennett River Koala Walk, Kennett River Vic. 44
Kepa Kurl Eco Discovery Tour, Esperance WA 122
Kettering Tas. 225
K'gari (Fraser Island) Qld 184–7
Kiama NSW 26, 29
Kiama Coast Walk, Kiama NSW 27
Killen Falls, Tintenbar NSW 10
Killer Whale Museum, Eden NSW 27
Kilsby Sinkhole, Moorak SA 100
Kimberley WA 138
King Island Wilderness Retreat, Grassy SA 83
Kingfisher Bay Resort, K'gari (Fraser Island) Qld 187
Kings Canyon NT 154, 155
Kings Canyon Resort NT 156
Kings Canyon Rim Walk, Kings Canyon NT 155
Kings Creek Station NT 155, 156
Kings Cross, Sydney NSW 3
Kings Park, Perth WA 110
Kingscote SA 83
Kingsford Homestead, Kingsford SA 76
Kingston SE SA 100
Koala Conservation Centre, Rhyll Vic. 64
Koala Gardens, Kuranda Qld 195
Koala Hospital, Port Macquarie NSW 14
Kojonup WA 132
Kookynie WA 141
kunanyi (Mount Wellington), Hobart Tas. 220, 221
Kuranda Qld 195, 197

Kuranda Original Markets, Kuranda Qld 195
Kwartatuma (Ormiston Gorge), Western MacDonnell Ranges NT 152, 154

L
Labillardiere Peninsula Walk, Bruny Island Tas. 224
Lady Elliot Island Qld 193
Lady Musgrave Island Experience, Lady Musgrave Island Qld 193, 200
Lagoon Beach, Lord Howe Island NSW 18
Lake Alexandrina SA 77, 99, 100
Lake Ballard WA 140, 141
Lake Burley Griffin, Canberra ACT 32
Lake Cave, Boranup WA 129
Lake Hillier Scenic Flight, Esperance WA 120
Lake McKenzie, K'gari (Fraser Island) Qld 184, 187
Lake Mulwala, Yarrawonga Vic. 50
Lake Wabby, K'gari (Fraser Island) Qld 184
Lakes Entrance Vic. 68
Lamington National Park Qld 181
Larapinta Walking Trail, Tjoritja NT 152
larapuna (Bay of Fires) Tas. 226, 227, 229
LARC! Tour, Bundaberg Qld 193
Larry the Lobster, Kingston SE SA 100
Lasseters, Alice Springs NT 153
Launceston Tas. 226, 230–3
Leura NSW 4
Lightfood & Sons, Calula Vic. 68
Limestone Coast SA 99–101
Linda (ghost town) Tas. 237
Line of Lode Lookout, Broken Hill NSW 24
Lirrwi Tourism, Yirrkala NT 170
Litchfield National Park NT 144, 145
Little Blue Lake SA 100
Little Bondi Beach, East Arnhem Land NT 170
Little Creatures, Fremantle WA 110
Little Dip Conservation Park SA 100
Little Parakeet Bay, Rottnest Island WA 113
Little Sahara, Vivonne Bay SA 82
Little Salmon Bay, Rottnest Island WA 113

Living Desert Sculpture Park, Broken Hill NSW 24
Loch Ard Gorge, Port Campbell Vic. 44
Loch Brewery & Distillery, Loch Vic. 68
Locks Well Beach SA 86
Lone Pine Koala Sanctuary, Brisbane Qld 176
Lonely Beach, East Arnhem Land NT 170
Longley Organic Farm, Huon Valley Tas. 225
Longreach Qld 214, 215, 216
Lord Howe Environmental Tours, Lord Howe Island NSW 18
Lord Howe Island NSW 16–19
Lorne Vic. 44, 45
Love Cabins, Wollemi NSW 7
Loveday 4x4 Adventure Park, Loveday SA 104
Lucky Bay, Cape Le Grand National Park WA 122, 123
Lucky Bay Brewing, Esperance WA 122
Lucky Bay Campground, Cape Le Grand National Park WA 123
Luminescent Longreach, Longreach Qld 215
Luna Park, St Kilda Vic. 36
Lyndoch SA 76

M
Macassan Beach, East Arnhem Land NT 170
McCrae Vic. 62
MacDonnell Ranges NT 152, 154
MacKenzie Falls, Gariwerd (Grampians) Vic. 48
McLaren Vale SA 73, 74, 77–9
Macquarie Harbour Tas. 236
Macquarie Pass National Park NSW 27
Mad Max Museum, Silverton NSW 22
Made on Minjerribah, Minjerribah (North Stradbroke Island) Qld 179
Maggie Discovery Tour with Aquascene, Yunbenun (Magnetic Island) Qld 188
Magnetic Island Qld 188–90
MAGNT Darwin, Darwin NT 144
Maguk Waterhole, Kakadu National Park NT 164
Maheno (shipwreck), K'gari (Fraser Island) Qld 186

Main Beach, Minjerribah (North Stradbroke Island) Qld 179, 180
Mainoru Outback Store NT 173
Malappar Traveller, Nitmiluk Gorge NT 158
Mallacoota Vic. 68, 69
Manjimup WA 131
Manly Beach NSW 2
Manta Bommie, Minjerribah (North Stradbroke Island) Qld 179
Manta Ray Fraser Island Barge, K'gari (Fraser Island) Qld 187
Mantarays, Exmouth WA 116
Margaret River WA 128, 130, 131
Margaret River region WA 128–31
Margaret River Surf School, Margaret River WA 129
Maria Island Tas. 228
Maria Island National Park Tas. 229
Marina Tavern, Hamilton Island Qld 209
Marksie's Stockman's Camp, Lansdowne NT 158
Marla SA 105, 107
Marree SA 105, 107
Mataranka NT 157, 159
Mataranka Thermal Pool, Mataranka NT 157
Matso's Broome Brewery, Broome WA 137
Mecure Kakadu Crocodile Hotel, Jabiru NT 165
Melbourne Vic. 36–7
Melbourne Central, Melbourne Vic. 36
Melbourne Cricket Ground (MCG), Melbourne Vic. 37
Melbourne Star, Docklands Vic. 36
Melbourne Street Art, Melbourne Vic. 36
Melville Island, Tiwi Islands, NT 166
Memory Cove, Port Lincoln National Park SA 86, 87
Menindee NSW 24
Merchant & Maker, McCrae Vic. 62
Mereenie Loop NT 154, 155, 156
Merimbula NSW 26, 29
Merry Beach, Kioloa NSW 27
Metung Vic. 68
Miami Marketta, Broadbeach Qld 182
microlight flight, Exmouth WA 116
Mildura Vic. 50, 51

Millaa Millaa Falls, Millaa Millaa Qld 196
Mimosa Rocks National Park NSW 27
Mindil Sunset Markets, Darwin NT 144
Miners Memorial, Broken Hill NSW 24
Minjerribah (North Stradbroke Island) Qld 178–80
Minnehaha Falls, Blue Mountains NSW 4
Mission Beach Qld 194, 197
Moline (Ikoymarrwa) Rock Hole, Kakadu National Park NT 164
Mon Repos Turtle Encounter, Bundaberg Qld 193
MONA (Museum of Old and New Art), Hobart Tas. 220–1
MONA FOMA, Launceston Tas. 230
Monkey Mia WA 126
Montalto Vineyard and Olive Grove, Red Hill South Vic. 62
Moonlight Cinema, Melbourne Vic. 37
Moonta Bay SA 95
Moreton Island Qld 177
Morgan's Beach Shack, Sorrento Vic. 62
Mornington Vic. 62, 63
Mornington Peninsula Vic. 60–3
Mornington Peninsula National Park Vic. 62
Morris Point Lookout, Mereenie NT 155
Mosely Beach Club, The, Glenelg SA 72
Mossman Gorge Qld 195
Mount Amos Tas. 227
Mount Barker WA 132
Mount Baw Baw Vic. 55
Mount Buller Vic. 55
Mount Charlie Reservoir, Kalgoorlie WA 140
Mount Coot-tha Qld 176
Mount Eliza Vic. 60, 63
Mount Gambier SA 99, 100, 101
Mount Gower, Lord Howe Island NSW 18
Mount Hotham & the snowfields Vic. 54–9
Mount Kosciuszko NSW 50
Mount Lofty SA 73
Mount Lyell Tas. 239
Mount Martha Pillars, Mount Martha Vic. 62
Mount Martha Vic. 62, 63

Mount Ohlssen Bagge, Wilpena Pound
  SA 90
Mount Owen Tas. 239
Mount Schank SA 100
Mount Sonder, Townsville Qld 189
Mount Tamborine Qld 183
Mount Wellington, Hobart Tas. 220, 221
Mount William, Gariwerd (Grampians)
  Vic. 48
Mount William National Park
  Tas. 227, 229
Mountain Culture Beer Company,
  Katoomba NSW 5
Mulgumpin (Moreton Island) Qld 177
Mundi Mundi Lookout, Silverton
  NSW 22, 24
Murphy's Haystacks, Calca SA 87
Murramarang National Park NSW 27
Murray River, Vic & SA 50–3, 99, 100,
  101, 102, 104
Murray River Queen, Renmark SA 104
Murray Sunset National Park Vic. 50
Museum of the Goldfields, Kalgoorlie
  WA 140
Myall Lakes NSW 14
Myrtleford Vic. 57

N

Nambung National Park WA 126, 127
Naracoorte Caves National Park
  SA 99, 100
Narkoojee Winery, Glengarry North
  Vic. 68
Narupai (Horn Island) Qld 212, 213
National Anzac Centre, Albany WA 134
National Circuit, Canberra ACT 32
National Dinosaur Museum, Canberra
  ACT 30
National Gallery of Australia, Canberra
  ACT 30
National Gallery of Victoria, Melbourne
  Vic. 37
National Museum of Australia,
  Canberra ACT 30
National Zoo and Aquarium, Canberra
  ACT 30
Natural Bridge, Torndirrup National
  Park WA 133
Nature's Window, Kalbarri National
  Park WA 126

Nawurlandja Rock, Kakadu National
  Park NT 164
Neck, The, Bruny Island Tas. 222, 224
Ned's Beach, Lord Howe Island NSW 18
Nelly Bay, Yunbenun (Magnetic
  Island) 190
Newcastle NSW 14, 15
Newcastle City Farmers Market,
  Newcastle NSW 14
Newcastle Ocean Baths, Newcastle
  NSW 14
Ngamadjidj's Shelter, Gariwerd
  (Grampians) Vic. 48
Ngaut Ngaut Conservation Park SA 102
Nhulunbuy NT 170, 173
Night Noodle Market, Melbourne Vic. 36
night skiing and snowboarding, Mount
  Hotham 55
Ninety Mile Beach Vic. 68
Ningaloo Coast WA 115–17
Ningaloo Reef WA 115–19
Ningaloo Whale Shark Festival,
  Exmouth WA 115
Nitmiluk Gorge, Nitmiluk National
  Park NT 157, 158
Nitmiluk National Park NT 157, 158, 159
Nitmiluk Visitors Centre, Nitmiluk
  Gorge NT 158
Noarlunga SA 77
Nobbies Ocean Discovery, Summerlands
  Vic. 64
Nobbies sea-cave, Phillip Island Vic. 66
noodling, Coober Pedy SA 96
Noosa Qld 177
Noosa Chocolate Factory, Noosaville
  Qld 177
North Coast NSW 12–15
North Gregory Hotel, Winton Qld 215
North Stradbroke Island Qld 178–80
Northern Forage road trip Tas. 233
Notel, Melbourne Vic. 37
Nourlangie Rock, Kakadu National
  Park NT 164
Nullarbor Links (golf course), Kalgoorlie
  WA 140
Numuy (Turtle Beach), East Arnhem
  Land NT 170
Nuriootpa SA 76
Nut, The, Stanley Tas. 233
Nyungar Tours, Perth WA 110

O

ocean pools, Sydney NSW 2
Ocean Reach Brewing, Cowes Vic. 66
Ochre Pits, Western MacDonnell
  Ranges NT 152, 154
oil storage tunnels, Darwin NT 144
Old Bus Depot Markets, Canberra
  ACT 30
Old Mac's Farm, Launceston Tas. 233
Old Settlement Beach, Lord Howe
  Island NSW 8
Old Timers Mine, Coober Pedy SA 96
Old Whalemans Grotto, Whalers Way
  SA 84
Olympic Pool, Sydney NSW 2
Omeo Vic. 57
One Tree Hill, Hamilton Island Qld 209
Onkaparinga Gorge National Park SA 78
Oodnadatta SA 105, 106
Oodnadatta Track SA 105–7
Opal Festival, Coober Pedy SA 96
opal stores, Coober Pedy SA 96
Opalton Bush Camp, Opalton Qld 216
Opalton Qld 216
open-roof 'Barbie' car, Yunbenun
  (Magnetic Island) Qld 188
O'Reilly's Rainforest Retreat, Canungra
  Qld 181
Ormiston Gorge, Western MacDpnnell
  Ranges NT 152, 154
Otway Fly, Weeaproinah Vic. 44
Outback Aussie Tours, Longreach
  Qld 215
Outback Cycling, Alice Springs NT 152
Outback NSW 22–5
Outback Queensland 214–17
outdoor drive-in cinema, Coober Pedy
  SA 97
Ovolo Nishi, Canberra ACT 33
Oyster Bay Tours, Coles Bay Tas. 227
Oyster HQ, Coffin Bay SA 86

P

Pacific Estate Oysters, Stansbury SA 94
Paddle Hub, The, Canberra ACT 32
Padre White Lookout, Albany WA 134
Palace Hotel, Broken Hill NSW 24
Palm Bungalows, Hamilton Island
  Qld 210
Palm Cove Qld 195

Pancho Villa, Hobart Tas. 221
Panny's Amazing World of Chocolate, Newhaven Vic. 66
Paperbark Forest Boardwalk, Agnes Water Qld 192
Parachilna SA 90
Parachilna Prairie Hotel, Parachilna SA 91
Paringa Estate, Red Hill South Vic. 62
Parliament House, Canberra ACT 32
Parndana SA 83
Parrtjima – A Festival In Light, Alice Springs NT 150
Passage Peak Lookout, Hamilton Island Qld 209
Patakijiyali Museum, Bathurst Island NT 166
Paxton Wines, McLaren Vale SA 78
Paynesville Vic. 68
Pearl Farm Discovery Tour, Broome WA 137
Pebbly Beach, Shoalhaven NSW 27
Pedal & Flipper, Rottnest Island WA 113, 114
Peddells bus tour, Thursday Island Qld 212
Penfolds Stonewall vineyards, Barossa Valley SA 74
Penguin Discovery Centre, Phillip Island Vic. 66
Penguin Island WA 110
Penguin Parade, Phillip Island Vic. 66
Peninsula Hot Springs, Fingal Vic 62
Penneshaw SA 83
Pennicott Wilderness Journeys, Bruny Island Tas. 224
Pepina Falls, Middlebrook Qld 196
Perth WA 110-11, 127
Perth Cultural Centre, Perth WA 110
Perth Festival, Perth WA 110
Phillip Island Vic. 64-6
Phillip Island Grand Prix Circuit, Ventnor Vic. 66
Phillip Island Winery, Ventnor Vic. 64
Piaf Day Spa, Healesville Vic. 40
Piccaninnie Ponds, Wye SA 100
Picnic Bay, Yunbenun (Magnetic Island) Qld 189, 190
Piggery, The, Sherbrooke Vic. 38
Pine Creek NT 159

Pine Trees, Lord Howe Island NSW 19
Pink Roadhouse, Oodnadatta SA 105, 106
Pinky's Beach, Rottnest Island WA 113
Pinky's Beach Club, Rottnest Island WA 113
Pinnacle Cliffs, K'gari (Fraser Island) Qld 186
Pinnacle Walk, The, Gariwerd (Grampians) Vic. 48
Pinnacles, The, Ben Boyd National Park NSW 27
Pinnacles, The, Cape Woolamai Vic. 64
Pinnacles Desert, Nambung National Park WA 126
Pioneer Settlement, Swan Hill Vic 50
Point Hicks Lighthouse, Tamboon Vic. 68
Point Lookout, Minjerribah (North Stradbroke Island) Qld 178, 180
Point Nepean Vic. 62
Point Pearce SA 94
Pondalowie Surf Break SA 94
Pony Fish Island, Melbourne Vic. 37
Poornarti Aboriginal Tours, Denmark WA 133
Porongurup National Park WA 134
Port Albert Vic. 68
Port Arthur Historic Site, Port Arthur Tas. 221
Port Augusta SA 84, 92
Port Campbell Vic. 45
Port Douglas Qld 195, 198, 201
Port Douglas Sunday Markets, Port Douglas Qld 195
Port of Echuca, Echuca Vic. 50
Port Elliot SA 78
Port Fairy Vic. 45
Port Lincoln 84, 87
Port Lincoln National Park SA 84, 86
Port Macquarie NSW 12, 14, 15
Port Macquarie Coastal Walk, Port Macquarie NSW 14
Port Noarlunga South SA 79
Port Noarlunga South Beach SA 78
Port Stephens NSW 14, 15
Port Willunga SA 78
Portland Vic. 45
Portsea Polo, Portsea Vic. 60
Portsea Vic. 60, 63
Pretty Beach, Shoalhaven NSW 27

Pride of the Murray, Echuca Vic. 50
Prime West Grill, Kalgoorlie WA 140
Prince Henry Clifftop Walk, Blue Mountains NSW 4
Prince of Wales Island Qld 212
Princetown Vic. 44
Pro Hart Gallery, Broken Hill NSW 24
Prom Country Cheese, Moyarra Vic. 68
Proserpine Qld 201, 205
PS Canberr, Echuca Vic. 50
PS Emmylou, Echuca Vic. 50
PS Industry, Renmark SA 102
PS Pyap, Swan Hill Vic. 50
Pt Leo Estate, Merricks Vic. 62
Puffing Billy steam train, Belgrave Vic. 38
Purple Hens Wines, Rhyll Vic. 64-6

Q
Qantas Founders Museum, Longreach Qld 215
QT Canberra, Canberra ACT 33
Qualia, Hamilton Island Qld 210
Quarterdeck Restaurant, The Ville Resort, Townsville Qld 189
Queen Victoria Market, Melbourne Vic. 36
Queen Victoria Museum & Art Gallery, Launceston Tas. 232
Queensland Museum, Brisbane Qld 176
Queenstown Tas. 236, 239
Questacon, Canberra ACT 30

R
Rabbit Island NSW 18
Radical Bay, Yunbenun (Magnetic Island) Qld 188
Rainbow Bay, Gold Coast Qld 181
Rainbow Beach Qld 187
Rangelands Rifts and Sunset Tour, Winton Qld 215, 216
Rapid Bay SA 79
Raymond Island Vic. 68
Razorback Lookout, Flinders Ranges National Park SA 91
Recherche Archipelago WA 120
Red Banks, Whalers Way SA 84
Red Centre Way NT 154-6
Red Dirt Tours, Winton Qld 215
Red Gum BBQ, Red Hill Vic. 62

Red Hill Cherry Farm, Red Hill Vic. 62
Redbank Gorge, Western MacDonnell Ranges NT 152, 154
Reed Lookout, Gariwerd (Grampians) Vic. 48
Reef HQ, Townsville Qld 189
Reef View Hotel, Hamilton Island Qld 210
Reef World (pontoon), Great Barrier Reef Qld 200
Remarkable Rocks, Flinders Chase National Park SA 82
Renmark SA 51, 102, 104
Restaurant 259, Kalgoorlie WA 140
Rex Smeal Park, Port Douglas Qld 196
Richmond Tas. 220
Riverland SA 102–4
Riverland Bar, Melbourne Vic. 37
Robe SA 99, 101
Roebuck Bay, Broome WA 136
Ronny Creek, Cradle Mountain Tas. 236
Rooftop Cinema, Melbourne Vic. 37
Rosebud Vic. 63
Rosebury Tas. 236
Rotamah Island Vic. 68
Rotary Lookout, Esperance WA 122
Rottnest Island WA 112–14
Rottnest Voluntary Guides, Rottnest Island WA 113
Royal Flying Doctor's Visitors Centre, Broken Hill NSW 22
Royal Mail Hotel, Dunkeld Vic. 48
Royal National Park NSW 3
RSL, Coober Pedy SA 97
Rundle Mall, Adelaida SA 72
Rupert & Hound, Launceston Tas. 233
Rye Vic. 63

S
Sacred Canyon & Adnyamathanha Engravings, Wilpena Pound SA 90
Sails, Hamilton Island Qld 209
St Columba Falls State Reserve Tas. 229
St Helens Tas. 229
St Mary Peak, Wilpena Pound SA 90
Sal Salis Ningaloo Reef, Cape Range National Park WA 118–19
Salamanca Market, Hobart Tas. 220
Salt Water Murris, Minjerribah (North Stradbroke Island) Qld 179

Saltwater Phillip Island, Newhaven Vic. 66
Samuel's Gorge, McLaren Vale SA 78
San Remo Pier, San Remo Vic. 64
Sand & Wood Restaurant, Kingfisher Bay Resort, K'gari (Fraser Island) Qld 186
Sandalford Estate, Swan Valley WA 110
Sarah Island, Macquarie Harbour Tas. 236
Savage River National Park Tas. 239
scenic flights
    Exmouth WA 116
    Heart Reef, Great Barrier Reef Qld 200, 209
    Ikara (Wilpena Pound) 90
    Shark Bay WA 126
    Uluru NT 147
Scenic Heritage Railway, Kuranda Qld 195
Scenic Railway, Katoomba NSW 4
Scenic World, Katoomba NSW 4
Schulz Butchers, Angaston SA 74
Sea Cliff Bridge, Wollongong NSW 27
Sea Explorer Sunset Cruise, K'gari (Fraser Island) Qld 186
sea lions swim
    Jurien Bay WA 124
    Port Lincoln SA 84
Sea Safari Tour, Broome WA 137
Sea World, Gold Coast Qld 183
Seal Bay Conservation Park SA 80
SeaLink Rottnest Island, Rottnest Island WA 114
Seaspray Vic. 68
Seisia Qld 211, 213
Sellicks Beach SA 78
Seppeltsfield (winery), Seppeltsfield SA 74–5
Seventy-Five Mile Beach, K'gari (Fraser Island) Qld 184
Shark Bay WA 124
Shark Bay Aviation, Denham WA 126
Shark Island NSW 14
Shaw Island Qld 205
Shell Beach, Inneston SA 94, 96
Shell Beach Conservation Park WA 126, 127
Sheoak Falls, Lorne Vic. 44
Shinju Matsuri – the Festival of the Pearl, Broome WA 136

Shoalhaven's 100 Beach Challenge, South Coast NSW 27
Shrine of Remembrance, Melbourne Vic. 36
Signal Point, Lord Howe Island NSW 16
Silly Goat Cafe, Broken Hill NSW 22
Silo Art Trail, Grampians Vic. 46
Silver City Art Centre & Mint, Broken Hill NSW 22, 24
Silverband Falls, Gariwerd (Grampians) Vic. 48
Silverton NSW 22
Silverton Gaol, Silverton NSW 22
Silverton Hotel, Silverton NSW 22
Simpsons Gap, Western MacDonnell Ranges NT 152, 154
sinkhole diving, Limestone Coast SA 100
Skeleton Bay Reserve, Binalong Bay Tas. 227
Ski and Ride School, Mount Hotham Vic. 54
skiing, Vic. 54–7
skydiving, Gold Coast Qld 181
SkyPoint Observation Tower, Gold Coast Qld 182
Skyrail Rainforest Cableway Qld 195
snorkelling
    Dreamtime Dive & Snorkel, Cairns Qld 200
    Lady Musgrave Island Qld 193, 201
    Rottnest Island WA 113
    Yunbenun (Magnetic Island) Qld 189
snowfields, Vic. 54–9
Snowshoe to Fondue, Alpine Nature Experience, Mount Hotham Vic. 55, 59
SnowStuffPark, Mount Hotham Vic. 54
Social Society, The, Exmouth WA 116
Somerset Apartments, Lord Howe Island NSW 19
Sorrento Vic. 62, 63
Sorrento Back Beach Vic. 62
Sounds of Silence dinner, Uluru NT 147
South Bruny National Park Tas. 222, 224, 225
South Coast NSW 26–9
South Coast Food & Wine Festival, South Coast NSW 26
South Gorge, Minjerribah (North Stradbroke Island) Qld 179

South Melbourne Market, Melbourne
Vic. 36
South-West, WA 132–5
Southern Great Barrier Reef Qld 198,
200
Southwest National Park Tas. 239
Spell & The Gypsy Collective, Byron
Bay NSW 9
Spirit Australia Cruises, Goolwa SA 100
Spirits of the Red Sand, Gold Coast
Qld 182
Split Point Lighthouse, Airey's Inlet
Vic. 44
Splitters Falls, Gariwerd (Grampians)
Vic. 48
SS Admella (shipwreck), Carpenter Rocks
SA 100
Standley Chasm, Western MacDonnell
Ranges NT 152, 154
Stanley Tas. 233
Station Store, The, Longreach Qld 215
Stenhouse Bay, Innes National Park
SA 94
Stenhouse Bay Campgrounds,
Inneston SA 95
Stillwater, Launceston Tas. 233
Stirling Range National Park
WA 133, 134
Stockton Bight Sand Dunes, Worimi
Conservation Lands NSW 14
Stokes Bay SA 80, 83
Stokes Hill Lookout, Flinders Ranges
National Park SA 91
Stones of the Yarra Valley, Coldstream
Vic. 40
Straddie Adventures kayaking tour,
Minjerribah (North Stradbroke
Island) Qld 179
Straddie Wood Fire Pizza, Minjerribah
(North Stradbroke Island) Qld 179
Strahan Tas. 234–5, 236, 239
Strathgordon Tas. 237
Strathmerton Vic. 50
street art
Broken Hill NSW 22
Darwin NT 144
Streeter's Jetty, Broome WA 136
Streets Beach, Brisbane Qld 176
Stuarts Well Roadhouse NT 155
Sugarloaf Rock WA 130

sunrise platform, Ulura NT 147
sunset cruises
Darwin Harbour NT 144
Gold Coast Qld 182
Longreach Qld 215
sunset viewing platform, Ulura NT 147
Sunshine Cycles, Byron Bay NSW 11
Sunshine Street Food, Minjerribah
(North Stradbroke Island) Qld 179
Surfers Paradise Beach Qld 181
SWallow Cave, Lorne Vic. 44
Swan Hill Vic 50, 51
Swan Valley WA 110
swimming holes
Blue Mountains NSW 4
Whalers Way SA 84
Sydney NSW 2–3
Sydney Harbour Bridge, Sydney NSW 2
Sydney Opera House, Sydney NSW 2

T

takayna (Tarkine) rainforest Tas. 239
Talla Rock Pools, Port Lincoln National
Park SA 87
Tallebudgera Creek, Gold Coast Qld 181
Tamar Valley Tas. 232
Tamar Valley Wine Centre, Exeter
Tas. 232
Tamar Valley Wine Route, Tamar Valley
Tas. 232
Tangalooma Island Resort, Mulgumpin
(Moreton Island) Qld 177
Tangalooma Shipwrecks, Mulgumpin
(Moreton Island) Qld 177
Tantanoola Caves Conservation Park
SA 100
Tanunda SA 76
TarraWarra Estate, Yarra Glen Vic. 40
Tasmanian Wilderness World Heritage
Area 236
Taste Bundaberg Festival, Bundaberg
Qld 191
Taste Great Southern, South-west
WA 132
Taste of Riverland Day Tours, Renmark
SA 102
Taste Walk Talk Tour, Launceston
Tas. 232
Tattersalls Hotel, Winton Qld 215
Telstra Tower, Canberra ACT 33

Terrace at Emporium Hotel, The,
Brisbane Qld 176
Tesselaar Tulip Festival, Silvan Vic. 38
The Atlantic, Byron Bay NSW 11
The Balconies, Gariwerd (Grampians)
Vic. 48, 49
The Basin, Rottnest Island WA 113
The Bay Club, Broome WA 137
The Bay Restaurant, Freycinet Lodge,
Coles Bay Tas. 227
The BBQ Father, Exmouth WA 116
The Blue Lagoon, Lord Howe Island
NSW 19
The Boundary Hotel, Brisbane Qld 176
The Breakaways, Kanku-Breakaways
Conservation Park SA 98
The Cape Kitchen, Newhaven Vic. 66
The Cape Queen Elizabeth Walk, Bruny
Island Tas. 224
The Collective Markets, Brisbane
Qld 176
The Crooked Post, Lord Howe Island
NSW 18
The Edge of the World, Gardiners Point
Tas. 237
The Esplanade Resort & Spa, Lakes
Entrance Vic. 69
The Evening Experience at Spirits of the
Red Sand, Gold Coast Qld 182
The Farm @ Byron Bay, Ewingsdale
NSW 10
The Fresh Fish Place, Port Lincoln
SA 86
The Gap, Torndirrup National Park
WA 133
The Gardens, Bay of Fires Tas. 227
The Ghan (rail adventure) 88–9
The Gold Coast Qld 181–3
The Golden Outback WA 139–41
The Gorge Walk, Minjerribah (North
Stradbroke Island) Qld 179
The Great Barrier Reef Qld 197,
198–201
The Grounds of Alexandria, Alexandria
NSW 2
The Hosting Masterclass, Strahan
Tas. 235
The Mosely Beach Club, Glenelg SA 72
The Neck, Bruny Island Tas. 222, 224
The Nut, Stanley Tas. 233

The Onsen Retreat and Spa, Dinner Plain Vic. 55
The Paddle Hub, Canberra ACT 32
The Piggery, Sherbrooke Vic. 38
The Pinnacle Walk, Gariwerd (Grampians) Vic. 48
The Pinnacles, Ben Boyd National Park NSW 27
The Pinnacles, Cape Woolamai Vic. 64
The Rocks, Sydney NSW 2
The Social Society, Exmouth WA 116
The Station Store, Longreach Qld 215
The Terrace at Emporium Hotel, Brisbane Qld 176
The Villas - Barossa, Marananga SA 76
The Ville Resort, Townsville Qld 189
The Wharf Hotel, Hobart Tas. 221
The Whitsundays Qld 198, 201, 202–10
Thistle Cove, Cape Le Grand National Park WA 122
Three Blue Ducks, The Farm @ Byron Bay, Ewingsdale NSW 10
Three Sisters, Blue Mountains NSW 4
Thursday Island Qld 211, 212, 213
Thursday Island cemetery, Thursday Island Qld 212
Ti Ama, Hobart Tas. 221
Tidal River Vic. 68
Time Travel & Gorgeous Gorges 4WD tour, Wilpena Pound SA 90
Tinamba Hotel, Tinamba Vic. 68
Tiwi by Design with SeaLink NT tour, Tiwi Islands NT 166
Tiwi Island Retreat, Bathurst Island 168
Tiwi Islands NT 166–9
Tjoritja (West MacDonnell National Park) NT 152, 154, 156
Todd Mall Markets, Alice Springs NT 152
Tomaree Head Summit Walk, Shoal Bay NSW 14
Toms Cap Vineyard Retreat, Willung South Vic. 68
Top Didj Cultural Experience, Katherine NT 158
Top End Safari Camp, Peninsular Way Region NT 160–1
Torndirrup National Park WA 133, 134
Taronga Zoo, Mosman NSW 2
Torquay Vic. 42, 43, 44, 45

Torres Hotel, Thursday Island Qld 212
Torres Strait Heritage Museum and Art Gallery, Narupai (Horn Island) Qld 212
Torres Strait Islands Qld 211–13
Townsville Qld 188, 189, 190
Travellers Autobarn (campervans), Perth WA 127
Triabunna Tas. 228
Tropical North Queensland 194–7
Truganini Memorial, Bruny Island Tas. 224
Turquoise Beach, Exmouth WA 116
Turtle Beach, East Arnhem Land NT 170
Twenty Third Street Distillery, Renmark SA 102
Twin Falls, Kakadu National Park NT 165
Two People's Bay Nature Reserve WA 133, 134
two-up, Kalgoorlie WA 140

U
Ubirr Rock Art Site, Kakadu National Park NT 164
Uluru NT 146–9, 155, 156
Uluru Camel Tours Farm, Yulara NT 147
Uluru Cultural Centre, Yulara NT 147, 148
Uluru Hop On Hop Off Bus, Yulara NT 148
Uluru-Kata Tjuta National Park NT 146, 147, 148, 150, 155
Umoona Museum & Opal Mine, Coober Pedy SA 96
Umpherston Sinkhole, Mount Gambier SA 99, 100
Uncle Frankies Cafe, Thursday Island Qld 212
underground bars, Coober Pedy SA 96
underground church, Coober Pedy SA 96
underground shops, Coober Pedy SA 96
Underground Spirits, Canberra ACT 32
UNESCO World Heritage Sites
    NSW 4, 14, 16
    NT 162
    SA 100
    Qld 189, 195, 197, 198
    WA 115

Unkya LALC Cultural Eco Tours, Gaagal Wanggaan National Park NSW 14
Upper Settlement Beach, Lord Howe Island NSW 18

V
Valley of the Giants Treetop Walk, Walpole-Nornalup National Park WA 133, 134
Vasse Felix, Margaret River WA 130
Victor Harbor SA 78
View 42° Restaurant & Bar, Strahan Tas. 236, 237
Villas, The - Barossa, Marananga SA 76
Ville Resort, The, Townsville Qld 189
Vintners Secret Vineyard Cellar Door, Bundaberg Qld 193
Vivonne Bay SA 80, 83
Vivonne Bay General Store, Vivonne Bay SA 80
Voyager Estate, Margaret River WA 130

W
Wadjemup Lighthouse, Rottnest Island WA 113
walking tour, Bundaberg Qld 192
walking trails
    Lord Howe Island NSW 18
    Wilpena Pound SA 90
Wallaroo SA 94
Walls of Jerusalem National Park Tas. 239
Walpole-Nornalup National Park WA 133
Wangaratta Vic. 54, 57
Wanuwuy (Cape Arnhem), East Arnhem Land NT 170
Warner Bros. Movie World, Gold Coast Qld 183
Warrnambool Vic. 45
West Coast Explorer Tour, K'gari (Fraser Island) Qld 186
West Coast Wilderness Railway Tas. 236
West MacDonnell National Park NT 152, 154, 156
Western Australia Gourmet Escape, Margaret River WA 129
western Tasmania 236–9

WET Deck at W Brisbane, Brisbane Qld 176
Wet Tropics World Heritage Area Qld 194, 198
Wet'n'Wild, Gold Coast Qld 183
whale shark experience, Exmouth WA 116
Whale Watch Western Australia, Bremer Bay WA 134
whale-watching
 Bremer Bay WA 134
 Broome WA 136
 Eden NSW 27
 Exmouth WA 116
 Gold Coast Qld 181
 K'gari (Fraser Island) Qld 186
 Minjerribah (North Stradbroke Island) 178, 180
 North Coast NSW 15
 Perth WA 110
Whalers, Exmouth WA 116
Whalers Way SA 84, 87
Wharf Hotel, The, Hobart Tas. 221
Whistler Wines, Stone Well SA 75
White Cliffs NSW 24
White Water World, Gold Coast Qld 183
Whitehaven Beach, Whitsunday Island Qld 202, 204, 208, 209
Whitehaven Beach & Hill Inlet Chill and Grill tour, Whitsunday Island Qld 209
Whitsunday Apartments, Hamilton Island Qld 210
Whitsunday Island Qld 202, 204
Whitsundays, The Qld 198, 201, 202–10
Wilderness Coastal Walk, Croajingolong National Park Vic. 68
wildflowers, Coral Coast WA 126
Wilkadene Woolshed Brewery, Wilkadena SA 102
William Creek SA 106
William Ricketts Sanctuary, Mount Dandenong Vic. 40
Williams Bay National Park WA 134
Williamstown SA 76
Willie Smith's Apple Shed, Huon Valley Tas. 225
Willunga Farmers Market, Willunga SA 78
Willunga SA 78, 79

Wilpena Pound Resort, Wilpena Pound SA 90, 92
Wilpena Pound Resort Visitors Centre, Wilpena Pound SA 90, 92
Wilson's Hire Service, Lord Howe Island NSW 19
Wilsons Promontory Vic. 67, 69
Wilsons Promontory National Park Vic. 69
Windin Falls in Wooroonooran National Park Qld 195
Windjana Gorge National Park WA 138
Windmill at Bargara, Bargara Qld 193
Winds of Zenadth Cultural Festival, Thursday Island Qld 211
Wineglass Bay, Freycinet National Park Tas. 226, 227
Winter Night Market, Melbourne Vic. 36
Winton Qld 214, 215, 216
Winton Way Out West (sign), Winton Qld 215
Winton Way Out West Fest, Winton Qld 214
Wirra Wirra, McLaren Vale SA 78
Wodonga Vic. 51
Wollemi NSW 7
Wollongong NSW 27, 29
Woodside Beach Vic. 68
Woody Island Nature Reserve WA 122
Woolshed Cave, Talla SA 87
Wooroonooran National Park Qld 195
Worimi Conservation Lands NSW 14
wukalina (Mt William National Park) Tas. 227, 229
Wula Gura Nyinda Eco Cultural Tours, Monkey Mia WA 126
Wurrumiyanga, Bathurst Island NT 166
Wye River General Store, Wye River Vic. 44

Y
Yallingup WA 128, 131
Yarra Valley Vic. 38–41
Yarra Valley Chocolaterie & Ice Creamery, Yarra Glen Vic. 40
Yarra Valley Dairy, Yering Vic. 40
Yarrawonga Vic. 50, 51
Yellow Water Cruise, Kakadu National Park NT 164
Yering Farm, Yering Vic. 40

Yirrkala NT 170
Yorke Peninsula SA 93–5
Yubu Napa Gallery, Alice Springs NT 152
Yulara NT 146, 147, 148, 156
Yunbenun (Magnetic Island) Qld 188–90
Yuraygir Coastal Walk, North Coast NSW 14

Z
Zanders, Broome WA 137
Zillie Falls, Millaa Millaa Qld 196
Zonzo Estate, Yarra Glen Vic. 40

ACKNOWLEDGEMENTS

The biggest thank you goes to my husband, Thom Shaw. Without you, this book simply would not exist. Thank you for driving us thousands and thousands of kilometres across and around Australia. Thank you for taking the leap with me, when I suggested we take a whole year off to travel around our great country (and then extending it when the pandemic derailed our plans). Thank you for flying around the country to take photos in every location we didn't make it to on our lap. Thank you for listening to me and supporting me when I make extreme out-of-the-blue statements and decisions. Thank you for coming with me on every adventure, no matter how crazy it might sound in the beginning.

Thank you to my Mum and Dad, for your unconditional love and support always, for coming to visit us on the road, and for always being so excited for us. Thank you for helping our dreams come to life. For storing our belongings, for giving us a place to live and a shoulder to cry on when we had to come home. For reading my drafts and painting our house, and keeping me sane for the 100 straight days we spent together during the first Melbourne lockdown.

Thank you to Laura and Billy, for letting us park our caravan in your driveway for the whole first lockdown, for always being there to hype us up, and for coming along on all kinds of holidays and adventures with us.

Thank you to my Nan and Nannu, who burned countless candles to keep us safe while we were on the road, made all the curtains for our van and kept sending us cookie dough and fagioli during the lockdowns to keep us smiling.

Thank you to my in-laws, Robbie, Chrissy, Josh and Mollie, for always being there for us with excitement, encouragement and endless support. Sharing our adventures with you made the journey even more fun.

Thank you to Marc Lunedai and Vanessa Kemper, and our whole MC Labour family, for your support and understanding as we chased our dreams. We're so grateful to be part of such a supportive workplace.

Thank you to Melissa Kayser for taking a chance on me with this book and believing in my vision of what this book could be. Thank you to my editors, Megan Cuthbert and Alice Barker, for helping me create the book of my dreams and really bringing it to life. It still feels bizarre to see it all come together in real life.

Thank you to our little Explore Shaw community online, everyone who came along for the journey with us, who shared their experiences, sent us tips and places to visit along the way, and encouraged our travels through the most difficult times. We appreciated every message and comment we received, and have been so lucky to connect with so many other travellers who are exploring Australia.

Photography Credits
All images © Emma Shaw & Thom Shaw, with the exception of the following:
pp. 20–1 in2thewild, p. 65 Dean Faulkner, p. 72 Laura Lawler, pp. 118–9 Sal Salis Ningaloo Reef, p. 39 TarraWarra Estate / Tourism Australia, p. 116 Virgin Australia / Tourism Australia, p. 117, p. 136, p. 137, p. 138 Tourism Australia.

ABOUT THE AUTHOR

Emma Shaw is an Australian travel blogger and content creator, who you might spot on the road travelling in a vintage caravan with her husband Thom. Criss crossing their way around Australia, they are committed to discovering the best of their beloved country, having visited and experienced some of the most beautiful, unique and unbelievable destinations that Australia has to offer. Sharing all of their adventures on her travel blog exploreshaw.com, as well as through social media, travel writing, content creation and photography, Emma wants to encourage you to get out and explore your own backyard, and reignite the excitement. Emma is also a member of the Australian Society of Travel Writers.

Published in 2021 by Hardie Grant Explore,
an imprint of Hardie Grant Publishing

Hardie Grant Explore (Melbourne)
Wurundjeri Country
Building 1, 658 Church Street
Richmond, Victoria 3121

Hardie Grant Explore (Sydney)
Gadigal Country
Level 7, 45 Jones Street
Ultimo, NSW 2007

www.hardiegrant.com/au/explore

The maps in this publication incorporate data ©
Commonwealth of Australia (Geoscience Australia), 2006.
Geoscience Australia has not evaluated the data as altered
and incorporated within this publication, and therefore gives
no warranty regarding accuracy, completeness, currency or
suitability for any particular purpose.

 A catalogue record for this
book is available from the
National Library of Australia

Hardie Grant acknowledges the Traditional Owners of
the Country on which we work, the Wurundjeri people of the
Kulin Nation and the Gadigal people of the Eora Nation, and
recognises their continuing connection to the land, waters and
culture. We pay our respects to their Elders past, present
and emerging.

Ultimate Weekends: Australia
ISBN 9781741177503

10 9 8 7 6 5 4 3 2 1

Publisher Melissa Kayser
Project editor Megan Cuthbert
Editor Alice Barker
Proofreader Cassie Holland
Cartographer Emily Maffei
Design Andy Warren
Typesetting Hannah Schubert
Index Max McMaster

Colour reproduction by Hannah Schubert and
Splitting Image Colour Studio

Printed and bound in China by LEO Paper Products LTD.

 The paper this book is printed on is certified
against the Forest Stewardship Council®
Standards and other sources. FSC® promotes
environmentally responsible, socially beneficial
and economically viable management of the
world's forests.

Publisher's Note: Every effort has been made to ensure that
the information in this book is accurate at the time of going to
press. The publisher welcomes information and suggestions for
correction or improvement.